GW01368440

Samuel Ferguson and the culture of nineteenth-century Ireland

Samuel Ferguson
and the culture of nineteenth-century Ireland

Eve Patten

FOUR COURTS PRESS

Set in 11.5 on 13.5 point Centaur for
FOUR COURTS PRESS LTD
7 Malpas Street, Dublin 8, Ireland
e-mail: info@four-courts-press.ie
http://www.four-courts-press.ie
and in North America for
FOUR COURTS PRESS
c/o ISBS, 920 N.E. 58th Avenue, Suite 300, Portland, OR 97213.

© Eve Patten 2004

A catalogue record for this title
is available from the British Library.

ISBN 1–85182–851–6

All rights reserved. No part of this publication may be
reproduced, stored in or introduced into a retrieval
system, or transmitted, in any form or by any means
(electronic, mechanical, photocopying, recording or
otherwise), without the prior written permission of
both the copyright owner and the publisher of this book.

Printed in Great Britain
by Antony Rowe Ltd, Chippenham, Wilts

Contents

ACKNOWLEDGMENTS	7
LIST OF ABBREVIATIONS	8
INTRODUCTION	9
1 Scotland, Ulster, and the *Hibernian nights' entertainments*	29
2 The *Irish Minstrelsy* review, 1834	52
3 The 'Attractions of Ireland'	77
4 Thomas Davis and the Protestant Repeal Association	99
5 Ireland's architecture	131
6 Culture, antiquarianism and the Royal Irish Academy	155
CONCLUSION	181
BIBLIOGRAPHY	189
INDEX	203

Acknowledgments

The research for this book was conducted over a period of several years, and I must thank numerous individuals who assisted during the course of its long gestation. My thanks are due first and foremost to Terence Brown, for his guidance, encouragement and friendship. Others who offered valuable comments or information along the way include W.J. McCormack, Aodán Mac Poilín, Ciaran Brady and Adrian Rice. I would also like to express my gratitude to those who read the manuscript in its various guises at various times, including Robert Welch, George Watson and Chris Morash, and to acknowledge editors Gerald Dawe and Jack Foster, who published an earlier version of chapter three in *The poet's place: Ulster literature and society* (1991). I am indebted to the staff of the manuscript, archive and general libraries at Trinity College, Dublin; Queen's University, Belfast; the National Library of Scotland; the National Library of Ireland; the British Library; the Royal Irish Academy; the Public Records Office of Northern Ireland and the Linenhall Library, Belfast. My colleagues at the Institute of Irish Studies, Queen's University, Belfast; the Centre for British Cultural Studies, University of Bucharest, and the School of English, Trinity College, Dublin, have been rich sources of intellectual support over the last decade. Thanks finally to my parents, Jim and Pat Patten, and of course, to Kevin, Milo and Esme.

Abbreviations

The following abbreviations appear in the main text or supplementary material:

DUM   *Dublin University Magazine*
NLI   National Library of Ireland
NLS   National Library of Scotland
PRONI Public Record Office of Northern Ireland
SSFID *Sir Samuel Ferguson in the Ireland of his day*
RIA   Royal Irish Academy

Introduction

Three years before his death in 1886, Sir Samuel Ferguson addressed the members of the Royal Irish Academy on what had become, for him, a pressing concern: the building of a sub-aqueous tunnel under Dublin's river Liffey. As an engineering project, he explained, this was by no means straightforward, the sand and gravel bed of the river making it unsuitable for the most common means of tunnel construction in the form of a masonry-built culvert. But would it not be possible to sink an iron-built tubular subway in the river bottom, then to pump it out and connect it to the relevant underground approaches? Furnishing his paper on the topic with diagrams, dimensions, mathematical assessments of water pressure and speculations on construction procedures, he was convinced that this plan was within the range of practical application. Indeed, such a model, he discovered, had already been proposed for a Channel tunnel and implemented at Danzig. But Ferguson's interests in the project related specifically to local needs. His intention was simply to avoid the necessity of a high-level railway bridge over the Liffey, and thereby to preserve for future generations an unimpeded view of 'the architectural beauties bequeathed to us by that splendid race of men who once inhabited Dublin'.[1]

While Ferguson's reputation rests largely on his contributions to Ireland's nineteenth-century literary revivalism, the tunnel project is a reminder of the cultural and intellectual mobility behind the designation, 'man-of-letters', which he tends to attract. His interests across the disparate fields of architecture, music, civil engineering and economic science sit quite comfortably alongside his better-known engagements in poetry and antiquarianism, and mark him out as a quintessentially Victorian polymath. But beyond this his tunnel design – with its ironic combination of nineteenth-century technology and eighteenth-century aesthetics – provides perhaps more accurately than any of his other works, a sense of his determining values in life; values embedded, first, in the urban culture of his adopted home city, and secondly, in a civic sensi-

---

[1] 'On a mode of sub-aqueous tunnelling', *Proceedings of the Royal Irish Academy*, second series, iv, Sciences (1884–8), 78–81. See also Ferguson's designs for a Liffey tunnel, *Irish Builder* 25, no. 576 (15 Dec. 1883), 384. Tara bridge, an elevated railway bridge across the river, opened on 1 May 1891, obscuring central views of the eighteenth-century classical façade of architect James Gandon's Custom House.

bility which repeatedly placed local concerns above the demands of national and imperial ideology.

The aim of this book is to assess the place of Samuel Ferguson within the varied contexts of Irish cultural and political life in the nineteenth century, and to illuminate in particular, the nature and provenance of his enduring civic idealism. But it also pursues a series of necessary adjustments to existing readings of this figure. Ferguson's position in nineteenth-century Irish culture has been complicated not least by the interventions of W.B. Yeats, whose elevation of his predecessor as 'the greatest Irish poet', one of a heroic triumvirate with James Clarence Mangan and Thomas Davis, has proved both seductive and enduring.[2] Subsequent critics have followed Yeats in their tendency to use Ferguson largely for their own ends, and the writer has appeared more often as a convenient ideological marker than as an individual understood in relation to specific historical and cultural conditions. As Peter Denman put it in his 1990 study of the poet, 'although Ferguson's name is readily known to anyone with more than a passing interest in Irish writing of the last century, his name is better known than the substance of his work; he is perceived as a presence rather than as an actual historical component of the tradition'.[3]

It is worth noting how readings of Ferguson have developed since the short studies produced by Malcolm Brown and Robert O'Driscoll in the 1970s, which associated him with the beginnings of a culturally inclusive national literature.[4] During the 1980s, a less complimentary school of thought identified in Ferguson's writing what amounted to the pernicious appropriation of a foreign culture. In a 1985 critique, for example, David Lloyd laid out the essentially Arnoldian premise of Ferguson's critical work, insisting that the writer was concerned chiefly with transforming a Celtic stereotype into the basis of an inclusive Irish identity, thereby developing – through literature – a communal discourse within which a recalcitrant race might be absorbed into the governing imperial context. Matthew Arnold and Samuel Ferguson not only concurred in their socio-cultural objectives, Lloyd argued, but colluded in 'the ethical and political historicism which underwrites the discourse of imperialism'.[5]

---

2 For Yeats, Ferguson was 'the greatest Irish poet, because his poems and legends embody more completely than in any other man's writings, the Irish character, its unflinching devotion to some single aim, its passion'. See 'The poetry of Sir Samuel Ferguson', *Irish Fireside* (9 Oct. 1886), reprinted in J.P. Frayne (ed.), *Uncollected prose of W.B. Yeats* (1970), vol. 1, p. 87. Ferguson is of course grouped with fellow poets Davis and Mangan in Yeats's 'To Ireland in the coming times', from *The Rose* (1895). 3 *Samuel Ferguson: the literary achievement* (1990), p. 8. Denman's book represents the most comprehensive attempt to date to examine Ferguson's poetry, and includes a useful checklist of most of his published writings. 4 See M. Brown, *Sir Samuel Ferguson* (1973), and R. O'Driscoll, *An ascendancy of the heart* (1976). 5 'Arnold, Ferguson, Schiller: aesthetic culture and the politics of aesthetics' (1985), 158–9. See also comments on Lloyd's response to Ferguson in G. Smyth, *Decolonisation and criticism*, p. 221n.

Introduction 11

Reinforcing this view in 1988, David Cairns and Shaun Richards sought to confirm Ferguson's defining role as an Ascendancy agent, whose sequestration of Gaelic texts and artifacts was based entirely on the defensive and hegemonic instincts of his caste, part of a project 'to enter into the study of the Irish past in order to set the rules of its discourse'. This accomplished, 'the identification of the Anglo-Irish and the masses could be underpinned by culture and this would enable the successful proselytization of the Irish and their winning from Popery'.[6] Reliant on the crude assumptions of colonial difference, Ferguson's 'strategic formation' of literary and antiquarian material was thus engineered to provide ballast against the further encroachments of barbarian over civilian, in an accelerating power struggle.

The determined positioning of Ferguson within a linear tradition of imperialist ideology continued in the critical interpretations of the 1990s. Joep Leerssen, for example, suggested that a post-Emancipation panic, brought on by feelings of exclusion and resentment, was 'the main issue in the writings of Samuel Ferguson', while Terry Eagleton depicted the writer as a 'vehement Unionist, [who] set about the task of translating Irish culture into the political needs of the contemporary Protestant junta'.[7] Accordingly, Ferguson's Gaelic ballads were strategically re-written so as to inculcate the idealism of British aristocratic leadership into the mind-set of modern mass Catholic democracy, the act of translation functioning as part of a plan to perpetuate British hegemony through strategic cultural manipulation. And even in Colin Graham's sympathetic treatment of Ferguson's 'negotiated' definitions of Ireland in its imperial harness, an English agenda remained the determining context: it is arguable, he concluded, 'that Ferguson's main aim was to make "Ireland" (as a nation, as a culture) understandable and unthreatening to England'.[8]

Such perspectives have made good use of Ferguson according to the broad brushstrokes of postcolonial theory. But they are, in various ways, limited by historical and ideological hindsight. One of their fundamental problems, moreover, is their underlying assumption that Ferguson stood without reservation for an imperialist and unionist Protestant Ascendancy, a view encouraged to a significant extent by Lady Ferguson's detailed biography of her husband. Published in 1897, *Sir Samuel Ferguson in the Ireland of his day* is a *tour de force*, in many respects, but its priorities are those of the society wife forwarding an inevitably skewed version of her subject several years after his death. Yeats would acidly remark in his review of the book that Lady Ferguson depicts her husband, sur-

6 *Writing Ireland* (1988), p. 31. 7 *Remembrance and imagination* (1996), p. 101; *Heathcliff and the great hunger* (1995), p. 99.
8 *Ideologies of epic* (1998), p. 83. For a similarly sensitive discussion of Ferguson as poet, see R. Welch, 'Constitution, language and tradition in nineteenth-century Irish poetry', in T. Brown and N. Grene (eds), *Tradition and influence in Anglo-Irish poetry* (1992), pp. 7–30.

rounded in later life by various dignitaries of church and state, as a member of a class 'at whose dinner-tables conversation has long perished in the stupor of anecdote and argument'.[9] Attractive in its caricatured diminishment of what was, for Yeats, a problematic social inheritance, this portrait of Ferguson and his contemporaries has tended to prevail.

The identification of Ferguson with the Anglo-Irish Ascendancy however, largely on the basis of his 1848 marriage into a scion of the Guinness family, completely bypasses the co-ordinates of his background, economic position and career path, none of which conformed neatly to any decided social profile. The political heterogeneity of his peer group militates against the idea that he was simply an Ascendancy evangelist ruthlessly engaged in a sustained project of cultural indoctrination. While he frequently had difficulty in defining his own audience, his instinctive feel was for the urban professional activist, and for a civic confederacy which, while it might very well maintain necessary relationships with the landed aristocracy or the Castle, was nonetheless a new and pragmatic voice in Irish political and cultural life.

Recovery of Ferguson is a means of recovering aspects of this social element in nineteenth-century Ireland, and of revealing the complex class dynamics so frequently obscured in popular historical accounts by the sustaining image of an enervated 'Protestant Ascendancy'.[10] Political focus on the Ascendancy within a polarized version of Victorian Dublin has inevitably been at the expense of alternative categories, those existing in discontinuity – to borrow David Lloyd's construction – with a privileged national narrative.[11] In particular, attention has been distracted from the consolidation in the period of a Protestant urban middle class, an oversight compounded by the traditional profiling of the Protestant population as a monolithic landed élite and the identification of a rising, urban middle class exclusively with Catholicism. Yet, as Jacqueline Hill has demonstrated, with reference to the backdrop of 1830s municipal reform and a shifting demographic landscape in the early to middle decades of the nineteenth century, 'Irish Protestantism was as much an urban as a landed phenomenon, and the implications for Irish history are only beginning to be explored'.[12]

---

9 Review of M.C. Ferguson, *Sir Samuel Ferguson in the Ireland of his day*, in *The Bookman* 10 (1906); reprinted in J.P. Frayne (ed.), *Uncollected prose*, vol. 1, p. 405. 10 W.J. McCormack's determined unravelling of the term 'Protestant Ascendancy' has challenged its claim to refer to any clear constituency: by the time of the Revival, he suggests, the 'Protestant Ascendancy' had become bound up in the dedicated process of back-dating, myth-making and nostalgia which laid the groundwork for a Yeatsian sleight-of-hand, and in the pre-Famine decades was more likely to appear in the lowly politicking of metropolitan and corporation debate: *Ascendancy and tradition in Anglo-Irish literary history* (1985), pp. 61–96. See also the revised version of this study, *From Burke to Beckett* (1994), pp. 7–8. 11 See Lloyd's discussion of new historical priorities: *Ireland after history* (1999), pp. 83–4. 12 *From patriots to unionists* (1997), p. 3. Hill also notes the long-term tendency of Irish historians to neglect the Dublin citizen – of whatever denomination – in favour of a supposedly more authentic rural counterpart.

Introduction

In several recent departures, commentators have indeed begun to attend to an urban landscape and the significance of Dublin's nineteenth-century Protestant middle class. They have confronted, in particular, the unpredictable strand of the *professional* middle class; the doctors, clerics and lawyers of a Victorian 'service' culture, who were gradually but steadily usurping the former aristocracy townhouses of Dublin's great eighteenth-century squares – Merrion, Mountjoy and Fitzwilliam.[13] Within this stratum, the dynamics of intellectual, scientific and cultural activity have become visible in studies which, though still subject to the polemics of the 'national question', have nonetheless galvanized interest in the local profile of Ireland's urban Victorians, and in the intellectual aspirations and proclivities they shared with their British regional counterparts.[14] While the chimera of 'Protestant Ascendancy' still looms in the background, the foreground has begun to shift therefore to what W.J. McCormack demarcates as 'the Protestant gentry and professional middle-class' of nineteenth-century Dublin, a small but active, self-regulating group who provided the essence of a 'public sphere' at the heart of Irish intellectual life.[15]

If such a group is distinguishable in this way, both from a landowning élite and a merchant bourgeoisie, then what were the ideological terms in which it was defined? Historical perspectives which configure the Act of Union as a clear watershed between a declining eighteenth-century liberal patriotism and an emergent nineteenth-century nationalist/unionist dialectic inevitably discount, in the process, the possibility of alternative discourses bearing on the complex development of Dublin society.[16] But at grassroots level, various other incentives were available to those who found common interest in professional or cultural engagement, just as various social forces drove the widespread middle-class pursuits of amateur astronomy, history, archaeology and philology. Beyond the perceived hobby-horsing and *divertissements* of the aristocracy, Irish society engaged itself purposefully across a broad spectrum of the arts and sciences.[17]

---

13 See F.O.C. Meenan, 'The Georgian squares of Dublin and the professions', 405–14. 14 Several studies might be included in this category. J.T. Leerssen has examined Irish archaeological and antiquarian pursuits as part of the evolution of self-defining professionalizing structures in Irish Victorian life, in *Remembrance and imagination*. Interest in Irish Victorian scientific communities is registered by J.W. Foster and H. Chesney (eds), *Nature in Ireland* (1997), and N. Whyte, *Science, Ireland and colonialism* (1999), while the ambiguous role played by Irish scholars and intellectuals in the advancement of 'mental cultivation' is considered in L. O'Dowd (ed.), *On intellectuals and intellectual life in Ireland* (1995), and by T. Eagleton, *Scholars and rebels in nineteenth-century Ireland* (1999). 15 *Ascendancy and tradition*, pp. 229–30. J. Habermas suggests that the liberal and bourgeois public sphere was at its height between 1830 and 1880, when the inheritance of an eighteenth-century, 'rational-critical' practice of coffee-house debate, conversational exchange and journalism was transformed into the systematic extra-parliamentary and voluntary political discourse of urban literary culture and 'polite society'. See *The structural transformation of the public sphere* (1989), and also W.J. McCormack's comments on Habermas and the 'bourgeois social sphere' of Victorian Dublin, *From Burke to Beckett*, p. 116. 16 See, for example, Leerssen's identification of a 'gap of liberalism' which opened up between the end of pre-Union patriotism and the rise of nationalist/unionist alignments: *Remembrance and imagination*, pp. 20–4. 17 The question of 'pursuits' is of particular relevance here in view of the impact of post-

And through such engagements, it promoted a discernible if subtle culture of civic sensibility, operating alongside the more familiar ideological trajectories of nineteenth-century Ireland.

Nineteenth-century civic sensibility can be identified first, as a predominantly middle-class phenomenon, bound up with resistance to the claims of metropolitan pre-eminence and centralization. It implied too, a degree of urban self-promotion and assertion. Returning from his visit to Famine-stricken Ireland in the summer of 1849, Thomas Carlyle reported his disappointment on seeing Dublin, a city shabby and decrepit 'like a ragged coat', caught in a spiral of miserable social decline. 'Not now the "Capital" of Ireland', he wrote. 'Here are no longer lords of any kind; not even the sham-lords with their land-revenues come hither now.'[18] But the citizens of Dublin were not bound by such a perspective, and far from seeing themselves as the idiosyncratic and damaged by-product of a colonial adventure, were free to align themselves with the more positive civic images projected by regional cities and towns throughout the British Isles and continental Europe. Manchester, Birmingham, Edinburgh and Bordeaux all created distinctive and enabling civic narratives, looking back, on one hand, to their antecedence in the great cities of the classical and renaissance eras, to the exemplars of Athens, Carthage, Alexandria and Venice, but laying claim at the same time to all the benefits and impulses of modernity, science and progress. Liverpool, which offers perhaps the best parallel for Dublin, thus balanced its industrial and commercial profile on Europe's western seaboard with a flurry of cultural investment in the Victorian period, establishing under the auspices of private patronage and municipal sponsorship, its Athenaeum, Academy of Art and Royal Institution, and styling itself accordingly the 'Florence of the North'.[19] Edinburgh and Manchester followed similar patterns of cultural self-fashioning in the light of their metropolitan juxtaposition, determinedly resisting the label of 'second-rate' and the stigma of provincialism.

Secondly, civic idealism – a Ciceronian precept inflected by a modern urban sensibility – prioritized cultural, literary and scholarly engagements as virtuous *per se*. Derived from a legacy of classical and European social philosophy, and

---

structuralism on the social sciences generally, and a resultant change of emphasis in historical and cultural studies away from the static categories of apparent social class towards the defining, if often provisional, affiliations of cultural practice. Previously, as social historians John Seed and Janet Woolff argue, the relegation of cultural activities to a secondary or superstructural position behind social and economic formations offered misleading pictures of nineteenth-century bourgeois urban society. Now, rather than being viewed as peripheral or dependent aspects of social structure, 'ideological and cultural forms and practices are recognized as crucial elements in the production and maintenance of that social structure itself': *The culture of capital* (1988), p. 9. **18** *Reminiscences of my Irish journey in 1849* (1882), p. 55. **19** See A. Wilson, 'Liverpool as "The Florence of the North"' (1999), and K. Hill, 'Thoroughly imbued with the spirit of ancient Greece: symbolism and space in Victorian civic culture' (1999), for detailed accounts of the civic philosophy behind nineteenth-century urban development in Britain.

Introduction 15

mediated by the moral and economic discourse of the Scottish Enlightenment, civic virtue emphasized the implicit benefits to society of social and cultural interaction.[20] In Scottish Enlightenment tradition, civic virtue was seen as a central tenet of social philosophy: sociability was not a casual indulgence but a moral responsibility and fundamental cultural conviction. As such, it offered an attractive *via media* for a dichotomous society, and arguably, provided the Protestant professionals of nineteenth-century Dublin with fixed co-ordinates amidst the flux of national politics. If it failed to displace the drive of political metanarratives in the period, then an Irish civic idealism was at least an alternative rationale, investing the cultured middle-class professionals of the capital with a sense of place and purpose. And it laid the groundwork for the perception of Dublin as a European city, in which literature and politics, science and industry, tourism, architecture, medicine and antiquarianism each formed essential strands in a self-conscious project towards stability, overlooking when necessary the maelstrom of domestic and imperial relations.

This ideological presence in the cultural *habitus* of nineteenth-century Ireland remains intriguing, and raises a number of related questions concerning the workings of a professional middle-class sensibility in the Irish capital. How, for example, might we distinguish a culture of civic virtue, self-consciously rooted in communal scholarship and engagement, from the more familiar dynamics of nineteenth-century cultural nationalism – typically seen as Protestant compensation for political loss and a Catholic foothold for Repeal? How might the civic impulse, derived from classical and Scottish models, both reinforce and, when necessary, counter, the pull of an imperial hegemony? And through what kind of rhetoric was a civic incentive attached to the pursuit of literary, antiquarian or scientific engagement amongst the membership of Ireland's scholarly societies and academies? Answering these questions brings into play a social profile of the Irish capital as an archetypal Victorian city, and, simultaneously, as a highly volatile environment in which political and cultural identities were part of a fluid system of brokerage.

20 On the Ciceronian sources of civic virtue see the editors' introduction in R. Corbey and J.T. Leerssen (eds), *Alterity, identity and image* (1991). A philosophical tradition of civic idealism is inevitably wide-ranging, but its classical origins may be traced to Aristotelian civic republicanism and *The politics*. Aristotle's emphasis on the necessary interaction of the individual in civic life – the means of his becoming a citizen – was modified by Machievelli and Rousseau, and in the eighteenth century by Locke and Molyneux, who adopted a civic idealism in the context of enlightenment rationalism. Berkeley, in his *Maxims concerning patriotism* (1750), stressed the importance of civic responsibility and the distrust of aristocratic corruption, while Burke endorsed the concept of a virtuous 'natural aristocracy' which would stand above a diverse society. Hegel and Coleridge sought in turn to ally the civic impetus with the interests of the state, and by the latter part of the nineteenth century, the French historian Ernest Renan's conception of *civilité* found its way into Matthew Arnold's thesis of the 'best self', and the cultural redemption of society which might be provided by a middle-class social leadership. See A. McIntyre, *After virtue: a study in moral theory* (1981), and A. Oldfield, *Citizenship and community: civic republicanism and the modern world* (1993).

Samuel Ferguson may be re-located at the heart of an Irish Victorian civic ethos and the culture it helped sustain. A civic incentive is the most plausible common denominator behind his inter-disciplinary, cross-caste and professional interests; the ideological hinterland to his diverse social alliances and political views. His place within a narrative of Irish cultural development framed only by the parameters of a hegemonic imperialism is repeatedly undercut by local, civic incentives, and subverted too, by the frequent disaffections and discontinuities of his political outlook over the five decades of his public career. While Ferguson's social philosophy might be aligned retrospectively with that of Coleridge and Arnold, as Lloyd suggests, it can also be rooted in the trickle-down of Scottish Enlightenment civic humanism, which, fused with a broader liberal patriot inheritance, significantly interrupted the purchase of Ascendancy unionism.

This book aims to reconsider Ferguson therefore, and to do so it examines his class affiliations, his engagements in Victorian urban cultural life, and above all, his links to a tradition of civic sensibility. It begins by assessing the influence of his northern origins, and his transition from the Scottish Presbyterian community of lowland Antrim – where he spent his childhood – to the thriving industrial and commercial town of Belfast where he began writing. During the first quarter of the new century, in the wake of the United Irishmen rebellion of 1798, Belfast retained key elements of a liberal dissenting tradition, elements which were channelled into a series of cultural and educational enterprises. The town developed and consolidated a reputation for cultural, industrial and scientific endeavour, motivated by 'that vigorous, industrious, intellectually alert Presbyterian middle class' which dominated its societies and institutions.[21] Despite its underlying political and religious tensions, it maintained an aura of progressive and civil consensus.

Belfast was inextricably linked, of course, to Scotland; part of the so-called Northern-Athenian confederacy extending across to Glasgow and Edinburgh. The Ulster-Scotland relationship, now well documented in studies of the period, is thus a vital component in Ferguson's cultural and philosophical constitution.[22] On a personal level, he maintained a life-long connection with Edinburgh through his friendship with the family of William Blackwood, publishers of *Blackwood's Edinburgh Magazine*, and through his scholarly and antiquarian connections with Edinburgh University. But in more general terms, the environment of Edinburgh, a city deeply concerned with the complex dynamics of a national culture, and still concerned too, with negotiating its relationship to

---

21 B. Ó Buachalla, 'The Gaelic background' (1987), p. 27.   22 See, for example, I.S. Wood (ed.), *Scotland and Ulster* (1994); G. Walker, *Intimate strangers: political and cultural interaction between Scotland and Ulster in modern times* (1995); T. Devine and D. Dickson (eds), *Ireland and Scotland, 1600–1850* (1983), and E. McFarland, *Ireland and Scotland in the age of revolution* (1994).

London, had relevance for his developing sense of nationality, identity and race. Again, this background interrupts the fluid assimilation of Ferguson to an Irish Ascendancy ethos: it was in Edinburgh rather than Dublin that he was first immersed in the politics of national identity, and in Edinburgh that he was introduced to a workable combination of Tory principles with a liberal cultural and historical philosophy.

The connection to Scotland simultaneously highlights the kind of philosophical resources available to Ferguson – and indeed, to a highly influential generation of Ulster-born intellectuals – as part of a formative civic sensibility. Crucially, the Ulster-Scotland corridor provided access to the legacy of a liberal ethos of civic humanism, inherited from classical republicanism and mediated by the leading thinkers of the eighteenth-century Scottish Enlightenment. The key documents of the Enlightenment, including Adam Ferguson's *Essay on the history of civil society* (1767) and Adam Smith's *Theory of moral sentiments* (1759), combined to sustain a distinct moral philosophy. Civic humanism or, in its evolved formulation, civic virtue, was understood to be a working compound of three elements: first, New Light Presbyterianism, which emphasized the authority of individual conscience and promoted religious tolerance; secondly, the so-called 'Real Whiggery' of Locke and Paine, and thirdly, an Enlightenment rationalism heavily influenced by the didactic moralism of Armagh-born philosopher Francis Hutcheson. Hutcheson's *Inquiry into our original ideas of beauty and virtue* (1725) was central to establishing an ethos of social community within Scottish intellectual tradition. In order to make aesthetic or moral judgments, Hutcheson argued, the individual requires a level of cultivation only attainable through interaction in the *polis*. Society as a whole is responsible for, but is also the beneficiary of, the development of individual sensibility: the civic community acts as a conduit for the virtuous and cultivated citizen, and as a barrier to the excesses of private passion.[23]

This version of civic sensibility passed into a general European public discourse through a related body of journalism and fiction, with the novelists Edgeworth, Maturin and the Banim brothers heading a list of Irish writers indebted in some measure to an eighteenth-century Scottish school of moral and social philosophy.[24] But its long-term influence on Irish social and

---

23 See I. Hont and M. Ignatieff (eds), *Wealth and virtue: the shaping of political economy in the Scottish Enlightenment* (1983); J. Dwyer, *Virtuous discourse: sensibility and community in late eighteenth-century Scotland* (1987); J.G.A. Pocock, *Virtue, commerce and history* (1985), chapter 2, and N. Phillopson, 'The Scottish Enlightenment' (1981). For comprehensive background on the Ulster response see I. McBride, 'The school of virtue: Francis Hutcheson, Irish Presbyterians and the Scottish Enlightenment' (1993), and S.M. Purviance, 'Intersubjectivity and sociable relations in the philosophy of Francis Hutcheson' (1993). 24 On the general diffusion of Scottish Enlightenment ideas via a Scottish literati see J. Dwyer, 'Enlightened spectators and classical moralists: sympathetic relations in eighteenth-century

cultural practice in the nineteenth-century has not been extensively explored. Given that Scottish civic idealism significantly coloured the political complexion of the United Irishmen, and given too, the important conduit provided by the Ulster-Scotland corridor well beyond 1798, it is hardly surprising that such a philosophy laid the groundwork for post-rebellion cultural activists including William Drennan, Charles Teeling and Henry Montgomery.[25] But arguably, it was also the most significant part of the intellectual hinterland from which Ferguson and his northern contemporaries emerged in the early nineteenth-century, and on which they would draw even as a latent or unacknowledged liberal influence after their transition to the more reactionary circles of Dublin society.

If Belfast deserves attention because of its particular social ethos, then Dublin also requires consideration not simply as an imperial outpost, but as a self-aware civic centre. Ferguson's Dublin context has been determined almost exclusively in relation to the supposed cultural flagship of Ascendancy Unionism, the *Dublin University Magazine*, and his critics have tended to use his association with the journal as a stable indicator of his political convictions. This reading relies on the assumption that he condoned the particular brand of anti-Catholic vitriol which surfaced in the magazine in the early 1830s, under the editorship of the O'Sullivan brothers and the young lawyer, Isaac Butt. Little of this relationship can be taken at face value however: the magazine itself was in reality a relatively diverse organ, and Ferguson's relationship to its corporate political philosophy must be understood both in the context of the conventions and protocol of nineteenth-century journalism – the pressure to present a public consensus – and also in the light of major ideological discrepancies which emerged between himself and the editorial leadership of the *Dublin University Magazine*.[26] During the tense aftermath of Catholic Emancipation, Ferguson was to express privately his repugnance to the sectarianism fostered in the magazine under the aggressive unionist leadership of Isaac Butt. The adopted editorial tone jarred with his own inclusive instincts, and the relationship was, as shall be seen, one of acrimony and divergence rather than concord.

Scotland'; K. Sutherland, 'Fictional economies: Adam Smith, Walter Scott and the eighteenth-century novel' (1987), 97–127; and also K. Trumpener, 'National character, nationalist plots: national tale and historical novel in the age of Waverley, 1806–1830' (1993), 691–710. **25** One of the best accounts of such connections in the period is N. Vance's discussion of William Drennan in this context; see his *Irish literature: a social history* (1990), chapter 3. See also M. Elliott, *Partners in revolution: the United Irishmen and France* (1982). **26** Henceforth *DUM*. J.P. McBride offers a definitive study of the magazine in 'The *Dublin University Magazine*: cultural nationality and Tory ideology in an Irish literary and political journal, 1833–1852' (1987). See also W.E. Hall, *Dialogues in the margins: a study of the Dublin University Magazine* (2000).

Ferguson's relationship with the *DUM* remained insecure throughout his career, as he periodically clashed with its extremism. It is therefore a less reliable gauge of his political affiliations than has been supposed. Moreover, it tends to obscure other important determinants of his social and political environment and the significance of his affiliation to a Dublin circle of middle-class professionals. His education at Trinity College associates him not with a privileged Dublin élite but with a set of less affluent middle-class students, many of Ulster origin. W.J. Reader explains that unlike Oxford and Cambridge, the university in Dublin catered for students who were expected to earn their own living, and 'for that reason if for no other, Trinity College was even more professionally-minded, if that were possible, than the universities of Scotland'. Ferguson's decision to pursue a legal career reinforces this position: Medicine, the Church and the Bar represented 'the three liberal professions of the eighteenth century [which] were the nucleus about which the professional class of the nineteenth century were to form'. Members of this class were linked by a common classical education, and derived their status from neither heredity nor money, but from an implicit connection with the established order of state. Law in particular was open to those without private financial resources: since patronage was relatively unimportant, 'the Bar offered an opportunity to those who had little to rely on but their wits and energy'.[27]

The significance of the legal fraternity as a social formation cannot be overestimated here. Dublin's lawyers and barristers played a crucial and often unpredictable role in the formation of a genteel professional culture in the capital. And Ferguson's own long affiliation to the legal profession had precise implications for his work as a cultural activist. He was very much aware of the national feeling aroused for the first time in many Irish legal apprentices who were obliged to travel to London to complete a year's terms at the English Bar. In addition, the combination of high social expectation and low income peculiar to the field appears to have rendered trainee barristers susceptible to nationalist ideals. An article on the Irish Bar in the *DUM* in 1834 suggests that the profession comprised a particularly vulnerable group in this respect: the condition of Irish barristers was one of poverty and obscurity, stated the author, but also of intense and ardent love of country.[28] As a bar-

---

[27] *Professional men: the rise of the professional classes in nineteenth-century England* (1966), p. 135; p. 23, p. 2. See also T.W. Heyck, *The transformation of intellectual life in Victorian England* (1982). On the middle-class mentality of Irish Protestant undergraduates at the university see R.B. McDowell and D.A. Webb, *Trinity College Dublin* (1982), p. 85. [28] Ferguson comments on the Irish presence and national feeling at the London Inns of Court in 'Hilloa, our fancy: flight the first', *DUM* 3 (Jan. 1834), 41. See also Anon, 'The Irish Bar, as it was and as it is', *DUM* 1 (Jan. 1834), 47. The sentiments of the latter piece were not without foundation. Six months earlier Ferguson himself had noted the spread of radicalism amongst his Tory friends in the Inns (letter to W. Blackwood, 11 June 1832, NLS MS 4032 f259). And the article is ironically prescient of events in the late 1840s, when the ranks of the Repeal Association were swelled by

rister on the North-Eastern circuit, to which he was appointed in 1838, Ferguson joined a coterie dominated by Ulster-born liberals steeped in the legacies of 1798. The father of the circuit at the time was Robert Holmes, a Belfast-born patriot with close links to the United Irishmen movement, whose defence of John Mitchel against treason charges in 1848 was the backdrop to a landmark speech against Irish subjugation and 'the withering influence of a provincial subjection'. Under the auspices of Holmes, Ferguson was retained as a member of the defence counsel for the Young Ireland rebels, selected, as one of his obituarists later recorded, 'as well in recognition of his professional qualities as of his political sympathies'.[29]

Ferguson's role as a founder-member of the Protestant Repeal Association in 1848 bore a direct relationship to his position in the legal fraternity, while his welcome reception from Charles Gavan Duffy and the Young Irelanders during this decade was primarily based on his usefulness as an exemplary representative of the *professional* Protestant middle classes. Perhaps the most significant aspect of his professional affiliation was the lead the legal confederacy would take during the late 1840s and early 1850s in rejecting the progress of centralization, widely perceived as a direct threat to the existence and independence of Dublin's courts of law. Interestingly, the campaign of resistance which this inspired was instrumental in defining and promoting the role of the professions as a new hegemony within Irish society, and in the self-identification of the legal fraternity, in particular, as the basis of a new aristocracy in Dublin. An article published in 1851 in the profession's house journal, the *Irish Quarterly Review*, denouncing the proposed removal of the Irish law courts, expressed what came to be familiar sentiments on the social function of the legal brotherhood. 'But though our nobility and titled aristocracy have deserted their country', the author proclaimed, 'an aristocracy even still exists – a professional aristocracy; the aristocracy of learning and talent, and worth and integrity'. Of this aristocracy, the author continued, 'composed, for the most part, of the members of the learned professions, the Bar forms no inconsiderable portion, and tends in no small degree to maintain and support the tone of society in Ireland. Remove the Law Courts, and Dublin will sink to the condition of a provincial town.'[30]

---

large numbers of barristers disaffected by government policies threatening the independence and integrity of the Irish legal system. For the history of the Bar in Ireland see D. Hogan, *The legal profession in Ireland* (1986), and C. Kenny, *Tristram Kennedy and the revival of Irish legal training* (1996). Also useful in relation to the political role of the bar is J. Hill, 'The legal profession and the defence of the *ancien régime* in Ireland, 1790–1840' (1990), and 'The intelligentsia and Irish nationalism in the 1840s' (1980), 73–109. 29 See the recollections of Holmes, author of *The case of Ireland stated* (1847), by J.R. O'Flanagan, *The Irish Bar*, p. 281; W. Frazer, 'Death notice – Sir Samuel Ferguson', NLI MS 5253. 30 Anon., 'The removal of the Irish law courts', *Irish Quarterly Review* 1 (1851), 21.

Members of the Irish legal profession during this period were representative then, of an alternative social formation, now negotiating its terms with the order of state as with the public body as a whole. While the legal fraternity might claim on one hand, judicial authority and a civic role rooted in enlightenment models of community, it inherited on the other, traditions of national independence and dissent. In Ireland, these aspects combined with two vital instincts; a resistance to centralization, and a professionalizing sensibility which frequently constructed networks across existing demarcations of economic, political and – particularly in the wake of O'Connell's reforms – religious denomination.

In the same way Ferguson solicited and consolidated a new social context through his pursuit of Irish antiquarianism, topography and archaeology. During the early 1830s he worked briefly with the team of researchers engaged on the preparation of the Ordnance Survey Memoir of Ireland, the purpose of which was to document the geographical, demographic and cultural aspects of the country in tandem with the government's vast cartographical project. This group, which included Thomas Larcom, later head of the Irish civil service, John O'Donovan the Gaelic specialist, and George Petrie, the artist and antiquarian, provided the young Ferguson with a scholarly milieu which would remain an important resource and point of reference for the rest of his career. Once again his involvement with the Survey has left him open to accusations of strategic collusion with a governmental policy of repressive state intervention in Ireland, but this interpretation ignores both the political heterogeneity of the group concerned, and as shall be seen, the fact that its cultural interests met the arc of imperial intervention at a highly ambiguous tangent.

What the Survey group provided, furthermore, was ballast for Ferguson's emerging sense of a scholarly fraternity as a stabilizing influence on the country as a whole, and as the essence of civic virtue in the capital. The impulse towards the establishment of an identifiable intellectual hegemony in Ireland was not limited to Ascendancy interests: confidence in the country's scientific and cultural leadership was expressed in equal measure by a nationalist contingent, as Charles Gavan Duffy confirmed in his recollections of the late 1840s, ironically with reference to a Scottish precedent. Alluding specifically to the leading scientists, mathematicians and philologists of the Royal Irish Academy, he wrote that 'there were now few Irish gentlemen who did not sympathize with the desire of the Young Irelanders that these men would do for the country what Adam Smith, Hume and Robertson, and in later times, Dugald Stewart and Brown had done for Scotland'.[31] For Ferguson, the Scottish

---

31 *My life in two hemispheres* (1969), vol. 1, p. 91n.

example of intellectual leadership, together with the circumscription of a pre-eminent élite within Ireland, proved consistently attractive as means by which to define a coherent and assertive national consciousness. His sense of affiliation to a class defined neither by economic nor hegemonic determinants, but by scholarship, represents an enduring and stable means of gauging his ideological position.

He was to summarize his feelings on this subject on the occasion of the death of the publisher George Smith. The passage is useful as an illustration of Ferguson's characteristically Victorian ability to cross borders between science and culture, but it is chiefly worth quoting for its conviction in the communal dynamics of scholarship, from whatever discipline. 'The death of Mr George Smith reminds me of the gradual disappearance from this scene of an illustrious band of men of mind and action who made the second quarter of this century a memorable period of social progress in Ireland', he wrote:

> About one half of them are now gone, including Hamilton, Petrie, Todd, McCullagh, and Pim. Larcom and Robinson and Stokes survive. No stronger force of scientific and literary ability ever existed together in this country. Hamilton, a pure mathematician, metaphysician, and poet, looked out from his intellectual observatory over all the realm of mind and matter. He stood so high that all who looked up at all saw and recognised his pre-eminence. James Pim, then junior, in introducing our first line of railway, conceived within prudent realisation the largest views of social advancement due to the locomotive and the electric telegraph. He was a man of ardent imagination; not a poet himself, but the associate not only of engineers and accountants, but of poets, and inspired with an enthusiasm as energetic as theirs, but an enthusiasm compounded with sagacity, that exerted itself in the production of works of mechanical and industrial organisation. He was a great diviner of the capacities of men. As Petrie saw and cultivated the power of O'Donovan and Curry, so he developed the latent workmanlike ability of Dargan. Larcom, then Lieutenant Larcom or Captain, with the statistical genius of Petty combined the higher political economy that we now call sociology, in its most human and sympathising applications. Every development of a self-respecting patriotism that could advance and elevate a people had a place in his Economics. In speaking of Petrie educing the literary ability of O'Donovan, it might be questionable whether Larcom should not have been named as the nurturer of Petrie. But the truth is, that where great and congenial minds are brought together, such as Pim's, Stokes's, Larcom's, Petrie's,

it is impossible to say from which intellectual centre the electric energy proceeds. The power – or rather the involuntary capacity – of imparting enthusiasm is one of the greatest gifts of great men.[32]

Ferguson's emphasis here on the benefits of scholarly interaction and communal engagement highlights the extent to which he perceived individual scholars to be motivated by shared civic ideals and assumptions. It reveals too, the confidence which lay behind his own dependence on a sequence of fellowships, the Blackwood circle in Edinburgh giving way to the Young Irelanders in Dublin, or the Survey group of the 1830s gradually evolving into a fraternity sustained on one hand by the Royal Irish Academy and on the other by an extensive Irish and European network of fellow antiquarian enthusiasts.

It was primarily through his antiquarian work that Ferguson established a supportive community of colleagues and fellow devotees, a group featuring prominently in his wife's account of his mature years. Antiquarianism linked him to an external chain of academies and experts, stretching from Brittany to Copenhagen and providing an alternative international hierarchy to that established by an imperial administration. At the same time, it allied Ferguson with the nationalist incentives of Charles Gavan Duffy, Thomas O'Hagan and John Mitchel as much as with the committees of the Royal Irish Academy, a factor which underlined the quintessentially 'chameleonic' nature of antiquarian research in Ireland at the time.[33] And it engaged him, finally, in yet more brinkmanship with the state, as the gentleman amateur began to give way to the professional archivist and submit to a sustained governmental policy of intervention in the creation of a national heritage.[34] During the 1870s, the government's attempts to bring the Royal Irish Academy's antiquities collection under the control of its museum headquarters in South Kensington met with resistance from Ferguson, along with William Wilde and Lord Talbot de Malahide, providing him with another opportunity to stake a claim for an independent and localized civic body, against the encroaching order of a centralizing authority.[35]

Despite his own official role, from 1867, as deputy keeper of the Public Records, Ferguson lobbied for the independence of the Academy collection

---

32 Cited M.C. Ferguson, *Sir Samuel Ferguson in the Ireland of his day* (1896), vol. 1, p. 70; hereafter, *SSFID*. 33 See E. Crooke, *Politics, archaeology and the creation of a national museum* (2000), p. 98. 34 In Britain, the Victorian impulse to classify and commodify the past was systematically translated into official procedure in a series of administrative measures which included the appointment of six Record Commissions between 1800 and 1831, the passing of the Public Record Act in 1838, the first publication of Calendars of State Papers in 1856 and the establishment of the Historical Manuscript Commission in 1869. See P. Levine, *The amateur and professional* (1986), chapter 5. 35 E. Crooke gives an account of the gradual legislative appropriation of the Academy collection, *Politics, archaeology* pp. 111–14. This will be discussed further in chapter 6.

because of what it represented to him in civic terms. Antiquity was no longer simply a rarefied Ascendancy pursuit, but a significant resource for a modern cultural ideology. The material of a Gaelic heritage provided in the first instance, groundwork for the construction of a contemporary civility. In 1875, writing to Professor John Stuart Blackie in support of the establishment of a Celtic chair at the University of Edinburgh, Ferguson voiced his opinion of the subject in a letter which anticipated much of his presidential address to the Royal Irish Academy seven years later. Listing the many values of Gaelic scholarship he lamented the attitude of 'mingled arrogance and apprehension' shown by the educated classes in Ireland to an inheritance which might, he believed, revitalize the culture of the present day. The primitive appearance of early literature should not be misapprehended:

> It is no answer to say these things are intrinsically ugly, or jejeune, or barbarous. You will probably agree with me that much of the material of the best classic literature is as crude and revolting as anything in Irish or in Welsh story. Raw material, however, to be converted to the uses of cultivated genius, is not all that we might reasonably hope for from such sources. There are ways of looking at things, and even of expressing thought, in these deposits of old experience, not to be lightly rejected by a generation whose minds are restless with unsatisfied speculation, and the very clothing of whose ideas begins to show the polish of threadbareness as much as of culture.[36]

Like the eighteenth-century scholars who, as Leerssen suggests, 'hoped to achieve from the outset with their work a subversion of the image of Gaelic barbarity and its replacement by one of Gaelic antiquity and civilization', Ferguson identified in the primitive artifacts and texts of the past a rich foundation for a civilizing ethos which might somehow temper the volatile, wayward spirit of modern Ireland.[37] From 1848 onwards, his arguments are characterized by a policy which substituted antiquity for authority and culture for politics. 'No longer bound to their country by the ties of national institutions, the heads of society in Ireland have to receive the quickening impulse that will yet make them all they ought to be, from a national literature. What Minerva can no longer do for us, Clio will – Clio has done, for the foundations of that literature are now laid so deeply and substantially that nothing can prevent the ultimate com-

36 Letter to J.S. Blackie, 5 May 1875. Cited M.C. Ferguson, *SSFID*, vol. 2, pp. 220–2. See also Ferguson's 1847 'letter to James MacCullough', in which he endorses the stabilizing effects of national science and literature, and comments by Denman, *Samuel Ferguson*, pp. 140–3. 37 *Mere Irish and Fíor-Ghael* (1986), p. 326.

pletion of the superstructure.'[38] The culture of the past was to be recruited in resistance to the anarchy of the present. Geared to the beneficial effects of educated moral feeling, the cultivated conscience of the 'virtuous few' was no simple act of imperial appropriation, but part rather, of a complex vision of an organic and interdependent civic community.

A further misconception in critiques of Ferguson's career is that he dedicated himself consciously and consistently to a cultural objective formatively expressed in his aggressive review of James Hardiman's *Irish Minstrelsy, or bardic remains of Ireland*, a collection of translations from Gaelic verse, published in 1834. From a literary perspective Ferguson's attack was certainly justified; even Thomas Davis later agreed that such translations from the Irish were 'slavish and despairing'. But the review itself smacks of insecurity – the young critic playing to a hard-line unionist gallery – in its foregrounding of a polarized Irish cultural landscape. In fact the Hardiman review is by no means reliable as an authoritative and definitive manifesto for Ferguson or the *DUM*, in which it was published. The adept translations which Ferguson appended to his four articles of 1834 are prefaced not by a decisive agenda, but by a bombastic collage drawn from a wide currency of eighteenth- and early nineteenth-century political and historical philosophy, exemplifying the writer's susceptibility to trends in contemporary intellectual discourse rather than any great depths of original insight.

Nonetheless, strategic critical interest in the 1834 review, together with a concentration on Ferguson's poetic reputation at the expense of his prose writings, has been a marked deficiency in the evaluation of his career as a whole. If the focus is shifted from his (Yeatsian-driven) reputation as a poet to his achievements in prose, including his literary criticism, historical romance, writings on landscape, antiquities, political economy and architecture, and the texts of public speeches and lectures, what emerges is an archetypal Victorian man-of-letters who functioned neither as an isolated cultural missionary nor as an Ascendancy agent, but as a semi-professional writer obliged to adapt and react to the variegations of contemporary critical and cultural discourse. Static images of Ferguson created by previous studies might thus be replaced by a sense of the writer as a pragmatist, frequently subject to stylistic and political fashion. As Gréagóir O'Dúill suggests, Ferguson's influence derived 'not merely from the capacity to "rhyme and romance", but also from his ability as a propagandist with some pretensions to scholarship, a Victorian ability to popularize academic topics and an instinct to go straight to the sources'.[39] The description recognizes the *work-*

---

38 'The *Annals of the Four Masters*', *DUM* 31 (Mar. 1848), 380. 39 'Sir Samuel Ferguson: administrator and archivist'

ing relationship which existed between Ferguson as a writer and the literary-political journalism which was his platform, and offers a reminder too of the range of material he was obliged to cover, from positions alternating between cultural guru and periodical hack; guises in which he appeared much more frequently than that of the Yeatsian epic poet.

Ferguson's multifarious prose writings also reveal more effectively than his poetry the nature and diversity of his resources. First, he responded to and mediated trends in Ireland's political culture which derived from eighteenth-century sources; the philosophy of the Scottish Enlightenment, the French Revolution, the United Irish rebellion, the ideological residue of Grattan and Burke. Seamus Deane, who identifies some of the long-term precedents for Ferguson's numerous contradictory impulses, highlights the significance of this complex historical legacy:

> A nationalist who was also a unionist, a Protestant preaching intellectual freedom to the Papists whom he held in contempt, a utilitarian who wished to revive a version of romantic Ireland, a believer in the people who defended the supremacy of a caste. But the case is more complex than this array of contradictions would imply. In the first place, cultural nationalism and the defence either of the Union or, before 1800, of the link with Britain, were not all anomalous. The patriot movement of the eighteenth century, of which Ferguson was an inheritor, had given its fidelity to this combination. And the expatriate groups, the absentee intellectuals, led by Burke, had looked to the conciliation of Catholic and Protestant through a policy of voluntary concession to Catholic claims as the only means of preserving the integrity of the British imperial system, with Ireland as a natural and central part of it.[40]

However speculative Deane intends to be in establishing such links, he is right to create a sense of Ferguson's emergence from a conglomerate legacy, a multi-stranded inheritance in which a Victorian imperial Christianity merely provided a veneer over varied – at times even competing – eighteenth-century traditions ranging from Burkean conservatism to libertarian patriotism.

In his extensive prose writings, Ferguson responded to a wide currency of contemporary issues and ideas. Inevitably his writing addresses, often obliquely, the catalytic discourses of nationalism and unionism which he confronted during his flirtation with Repeal in the late 1840s. But more directly, it reflects his

(1986), 118. **40** *A short history of Irish literature* (1986), pp. 67–8.

absorption in the general, even popular trends and formulations of Victorian culture. These include his understanding of history and historical philosophy, particularly as mediated through a Scottish intellectual and literary inheritance, together with his exploitation of Victorian aesthetic practice and landscape painting, intrinsic to his expression of a middle-class urban sensibility. His hesitant approach to religious affiliation also comes into view, partly in terms of the 'Protestant ideal' he developed through his relationship with Thomas Davis, and partly – more problematically – in terms of his impassioned reaction to national apostasy in England, as expressed in his architectural writings and critical attack on John Ruskin. If his enthusiastic cross-bench alliance with Young Ireland suggests the inclusive potential of his civic vision, the bitterness of his response to aspects of Roman Catholic doctrine, filtered metaphorically through his lengthy and abrasive condemnation of the Gothic Revival, reveals the sticking points on which that vision faltered.

In political terms, it would be naïve to suggest that Ferguson's civic idealism was ever significantly out of line with a fundamental Protestant unionism. But in reviewing the considerable body of commentary on literary, political and aesthetic subjects which he produced in response to events – as satirist, propagandist or critic – the political dimensions of his work are expanded rather than reduced. Following current theoretical developments in nineteenth-century studies generally, therefore, this reading of Ferguson attempts to shift emphasis from political teleology to cultural practice, in order to reveal a writer who drew inspiration from varying literary and political contexts and authority from a sequence of ideological and cultural formations. The 'discontinuities' of his life and career become its determining forces, disrupting prevailing versions of his identity which have turned too readily towards reified class categories and hind-sighted metanarratives.

Simultaneously, a re-reading Ferguson is a means of re-reading Victorian Dublin, a means of opening a window on the public sphere which flourished in the nineteenth century, before Yeats began to sew up the joins of Irish cultural tradition. Ferguson's promotion of the city, as a cultural and architectural space in its own right above and beyond the imperial relationship, is inextricable from his affiliations to an urban professional middle class and to a tradition of civic idealism which had as much potential to counter, as to bolster, the Union itself. Dublin, as he imagined it in his 1849 imitation of the third satire of Juvenal, retained an independence regardless of the imperial bond, regardless of pressures towards centralization and rationalization. 'We could teach the British how', he wrote;

[A]ll through life's intricate frame
Social and civic arts are much the same;
How for a quiet life, the proper pride
Of nations also must be gratified;
And teach you, as you live, to govern by
The easy rule of frank civility.[41]

---

[41] '"Dublin", a poem in imitation of the third satire of Juvenal', *DUM* 34 (July 1849), 105.

CHAPTER ONE

Scotland, Ulster and the
Hibernian nights' entertainments

In his *Four years of Irish history*, published in 1883, Charles Gavan Duffy called to mind the face of Samuel Ferguson, and observed how its characteristics bespoke the writer's northern planter roots. With his grave, slow manner of speech, wrote Duffy, Ferguson looked like a solid lawyer, 'a type of the race which gave Drennan and McCracken to Ireland'.[1] The portrait suggests a personality deeply marked by its Ulster origins. Like the 'northern' tag so frequently attached to Ferguson by his Dublin colleagues, it confirms the extent to which his background was seen by his contemporaries as intrinsic to his political and cultural profile.

The Ferguson family originated in Donegore, a district of Antrim described in the Ordnance Survey Memoir as a highly politicized and enlightened parish, particularly active during the 1798 rebellion.[2] Still manifesting strong traits of its Scots planter lineage this rural community, with its traditions of insurgency and dissent, was characteristic of a distinctive social culture in Ulster generally during the early decades of the century. In Belfast, where Ferguson was born in 1810, the energizing legacy of the United Irishmen combined with Scottish and American contacts to fuel a series of pedagogic and intellectual initiatives, and to provide the impetus for a vibrant network of societies, institutions and publications. True, the town's political climate during the early decades of the century was by no means stable. The liberal ideologues who founded the *Northern Whig* newspaper in 1825 met their match and more in an Orangeism awakening again 'like the serpent on the approach of summer', as the *Ulster Magazine* reported.[3] Nonetheless, a free-thinking, modernizing and independent spirit ran through the social and civic environment from which the young Ferguson emerged; a radicalism certainly tempered since 1798, but by no means extinguished.

---

1 *Four years of Irish history* (1883), p. 578. Duffy refers to leading figures in the United Irishmen movement, William Drennan and Henry Joy McCracken. 2 James Boyle, *Ordnance survey memoir for Antrim* (1834), Public Record Office of Northern Ireland (henceforth PRONI), F2 (1838–9), p. 14. According to his wife Ferguson's predecessors were seventeenth-century immigrants to Antrim from south-eastern Scotland. The poet traced his own lineage back to one of the oldest of the Highland clans, Mhic Fhearghuis of Athole, and frequently drew upon Ulster-Scots history and dialect in early writings; *SSFID*, vol. 1, p. 3. Patrick Curley provides details of Ferguson's early life in Antrim and Belfast, and speculates on the family's financial insecurity, in 'William Drennan and the young Samuel Ferguson: liberty, patriotism and the Union in Ulster poetry between 1770 and 1848' (1987). 3 1: 7 (July 1830), 448.

Society in early nineteenth-century Ulster must also be viewed, of course, in the light of its strong relationship with Scotland in the long wake of plantation. There were numerous connective strands to the significance of the Ulster-Scotland axis within the imperial matrix, including the mass enrollment of Ulster's Presbyterian and dissenting students at the universities of Glasgow, Aberdeen and Edinburgh. Elaine McFarland's description of the 'ideological community' of Scotland and Ulster is apt, given the extent to which a mutual investment in the values of civic humanism and New Light Presbyterianism continued to forge bonds between the two societies long after the turn of the century.[4] From an Ulster perspective, moreover, Scotland's comparatively strong domestic culture, enriched by the intellectual legacy of the Scottish Enlightenment, was seen to provide ballast against the social and political pull of the 1707 Union. Scotland in general and Edinburgh, the 'Northern Athens' in particular, provided authoritative points of reference for an Ulster society deeply unsure of its own political and cultural positioning with regard to both Dublin and London.

Samuel Ferguson's introduction to various members of the Edinburgh *literati* in the 1830s was to provide him with a persuasive model of the civic sphere, a model he frequently acknowledged in later years in his pledge to establish a similar community of interest, 'a better Edinburgh', in Dublin.[5] He acclaimed the Scottish capital as a centre of healthy intellectual and scholarly intercourse, but one sustained by a long-term Irish input: in his 1836 articles on the 'Attractions of Ireland', he insisted that a number of eminent Scottish scholars – 'Campbell, Mackenzie, Stuart, Mackintosh, McCulloch' – were originally of Irish stock and that Dublin could boast an equally impressive list in the membership of the Royal Irish Academy.[6] The Scottish parallel enabled him to envisage the workings of civic virtue and cultural engagement without reference to London, and in some respects the visibility of Scotland's internal political fractures merely added to its pertinence for a troubled Irish counterpart. Edinburgh's profile as a literary capital, within which the travesties of Macpherson and the sentimental fabrication of Highland tradition could co-exist with a solid commitment to the brokering of an integral national identity, endorsed a version of cultural nationalism capable of containing diverse paradigms. Scotland's relevance to Ireland, hailed by Ferguson but later too, by Charles Gavan Duffy and Thomas Davis, was no shallow colonial cliché but part of a long-term process of mutual acknowledgement.[7]

---

4 *Ireland and Scotland*, p. 1. 5 Ferguson was to express this wish specifically in a letter to Thomas Davis: '[w]hen I see how we all are working, I hope to see Dublin at least a better Edinburgh'. Cited *SSFID*, vol. 1, p. 139. 6 'Attractions of Ireland, no. 2 – scenery and society', *DUM* 8 (Sept. 1836), 332. 7 Leerssen suggests that Ferguson's references to the Scottish model underline his Ascendancy unionism: '[i]t appears that he would ideally like to

Scotland, Ulster and the Hibernian nights' entertainments

Less visible but deeply important were the philosophical structures and historical paradigms made available to Irish thinkers through a Scottish intellectual inheritance. The question of 'history' dominated professional Enlightenment culture generally, and its specific extrapolation within the parameters of the Scottish Enlightenment, Scotland's eighteenth-century intellectual renaissance in jurisprudence, science and economics, provided the foundation for theories of social development which permeated historical consciousness over ensuing decades. As Scotland became embroiled in the contradictions of progress and modernization, her leading thinkers – Adam Smith, John Millar, William Robertson, Adam Ferguson and Dugald Stewart – responded with a philosophy of society which included, famously, a scale of evolutionary development on which the advance (or retardation) of civilization could be measured. While clearly vulnerable to the colonial apologists of the Victorian period, the idea of distinct social stages, as developed in particular by Adam Smith and Adam Ferguson, dovetailed into immediate Scottish concerns first, with environmental and economic determinism, and secondly, with Scottish concepts of the civic and moral community. The rudiments of their framework quickly gained footholds within the academy as a whole, and even after the eclipse of the Scottish Enlightenment itself, the language of its efforts to determine the progress of civilization continued to trickle down into the Victorian arena of political economy and socio-statistical enquiry.[8]

Critics have occasionally noted the specific bearing of Scottish paradigms of progress on the representation of Ireland in the late eighteenth and early nineteenth centuries. Marilyn Butler reads Maria Edgeworth's fiction, for example, as drawing on Adam Ferguson as much as Montesquieu in order to construct an evolutionary social framework, within which the individual 'grows from irresponsibility into a sense of himself as Civil Man, just as community has advanced from barbarous civility to its modern ordered complexity'.[9] But the sheer proximity of Ulster's intellectual community to the academic fall-out from the Scottish Enlightenment underlines a particularly close point of connection, and an influence readily identifiable in the phraseology of Belfast's more liberal journals and societies. In Ferguson's case, a grasp of Scottish historical philosophy and a familiarity, at the very least, with the work of Adam

---

see Ireland as another Scotland, Dublin as another Edinburgh: both countries led by a British-oriented, loyalist and English-speaking élite centred, next to London, on their own metropolis, loyal to their British status but proud of their non-English heritage, bound in benevolent paternalism to their hinterland of highland peasantry.' *Remembrance and imagination*, p. 185. This rather opportunist treatment of Ferguson diminishes the long-term religious, cultural and political significance of the Scottish connection for an Ulster Presbyterian, post-1798 community.   8 For general surveys of the Scottish Enlightenment see J. Rendall, *The origins of the Scottish Enlightenment* (1978) and A.C. Chitnis, *The Scottish Enlightenment and early Victorian society* (1986).   9 *Maria Edgeworth* (1972), p. 486.

Smith, Adam Ferguson and David Hume can be seen to temper the inflammatory language of the Hardiman review in 1834. More programmatically, the writer's chief prose work of the early 1830s, the sequence of tales which form the *Hibernian nights' entertainments*, may be read as his attempt to standardize, as it were, the progress of Irish history and society according to a Scottish template.

These tales appear on a superficial level as amateur and rather derivative regional romances, but their obvious debt to Walter Scott, together with the increasing narrative complexity of the series, suggest that their author was pursuing a self-conscious agenda through historical fiction. Ferguson's sense of Scott as a philosopher of history and a mediator of Adam Smith, rather than simply as a local colourist, adds conceptual weight to his own shaping of the Irish past into what he termed 'legitimate history'. His chosen format, moreover, belongs to the genre of the national tale, seen by Katie Trumpener to have developed within an Irish-Scottish nexus as a vehicle for the systematic anthropological and historical representation of both countries.[10] Far from simply providing exotic material for an English audience, historical romance of this kind formed a trajectory of domestic self-evaluation, a fictional means to contain and rationalize the incoherent, diverse or recalcitrant social constituents of the nation as a whole. With their artful narration, set-piece historical detail and overt homage to Scott, Ferguson's tales develop from their stilted antiquarian premise into a tentative illustration of Irish social, civic and economic evolution.

Ferguson's background as a writer includes therefore, a dense ideological and philosophical hinterland, reaching back into the radical and dissenting traditions of eighteenth-century Ulster and the dynamic civic centres of Belfast and Edinburgh. What this chapter explores is the nature of the Scots-Ulster 'ideological community' from which he emerged, as a preface to a reading of his *Hibernian nights' entertainments* in the context of Scottish Enlightenment social theory, and ultimately, as a preface to an *oeuvre* which would struggle to retain the remnants of a liberal inheritance within the increasingly polarized arena of Dublin politics.

EDINBURGH, BELFAST, AND THE ENLIGHTENMENT INHERITANCE

The 1707 union between Scotland and England was a major step towards cementing the foundations of a British Anglican empire, but it also exacerbated claims for Scottish cultural separatism. Culture became a primary outlet for the energies of a highly politicized and articulate community, with Edinburgh devel-

---

10 *Bardic nationalism* (1997), chapter 3.

oping a reputation as a modern Athens, 'a true republic of letters in which men sought public reputations by becoming excellent in the arts and sciences'.[11] From the coffee-houses and salons to the learned societies and academies which flourished in the latter half of the eighteenth century, the intellectual ascendancy of the Scottish capital – a city significantly regenerated by the construction of the New Town during the 1780s and 1790s – consolidated on its para-political status in a celebration of the civic ideal. The role of the city as a forum was crucial; the particular pattern of cultural and intellectual engagement in Edinburgh and to a lesser extent in Glasgow and Aberdeen marked these out as cohesive civic units in the flux of the country as a whole. Indeed, the compactness of provincial cities such as Edinburgh and Bordeaux, as opposed to the sprawl of London, encouraged a conformity of viewpoint amidst a comparatively small but dynamic and highly interactive intelligentsia, providing a fertile ground for the proliferation of Enlightenment ideas.[12] A city identity provided a base for collaboration and participation carried out at a certain distance, when necessary, from the scrum of national politics.

Outside the formal structures of politics therefore, but within the distinctly Scottish institutions which survived the Treaty of Union – educational academies, legal system and church – emerged 'an alternative mode of civil and social existence, capable of resisting to some large degree and for some length of time the pressures towards the anglicization of Scottish culture'.[13] Through strong native traditions of philosophy, science, jurisprudence and economic discourse, a Scottish élite found a means of articulating its distinctiveness and maintaining a provincial hegemony, despite its weakened political authority. Numerous individual factors, such as the independent status of Scotland's legal system, and the contact, through emigrant Scottish students, with the liberal Dutch universities of Utrecht and Leyden, increased an overall sense of intellectual and cultural pre-eminence.[14] Through its intelligentsia and *literati* Edinburgh sought to retrieve the self-respect of a capital city, countering the loss of independence with civic assertion, and substituting cultural expression for a political self-definition which had become deeply problematic.

What flourished on the surface as an impulse towards a rich civic sensibility had its roots deep in the social and ethical commentaries of Scotland's leading eighteenth-century philosophers. They, in turn, had built upon classical concepts of the civic forum filtered through Enlightenment rationalism. In the city states of ancient Greece and Rome, and in the philosophy, chiefly, of

---

[11] N. Phillopson, 'The Scottish Enlightenment', p. 32. [12] R. Emerson, 'The Enlightenment and social structures' (1973), p. 101. [13] A. McIntyre, *Whose justice? Which rationality?* (1988), pp. 219–20. [14] See A. Calder, 'The Enlightenment' (1992), on Scotland's intellectual links with European sources of Enlightenment thought.

Aristotle, Polybius, Tacitus and Cicero, the participation of the individual in the *polis* was seen as essential to his development as a citizen, and crucial to the functioning of a communal civic virtue which would guard against corruption. The civic humanist philosophy of the eighteenth century introduced further relevant influences; the legacy of a classical republicanism aimed at curtailing the powers of monarchy and government through the promotion of the civic arena, and the 'Real Whiggery' through which Locke and Paine elevated the role of popular consent as the basis of political authority. Compounded by traditions of 'New Light' Presbyterianism, which emphasized the authority of individual conscience, the result was a philosophy foregrounding civic discourse as authoritative and ultimately, regulatory – a concept which would remain at the core of Scottish philosophical and moral tradition.[15]

In local terms, this tradition was heavily indebted to the didactic moralism of Francis Hutcheson, the Armagh-born moral philosopher who rose to pre-eminence at the university of Glasgow in the 1720s. Hutcheson's *Inquiry into the original of our ideas of beauty and virtue* (1725), a seminal document for the Scottish Enlightenment corpus, sought to establish the rationale behind man's natural disposition towards sociability, and to link this, in turn, to an understanding of values and virtuous conduct. The process of cultivation required the individual 'to partake of a pleasurable community or common sentiment, in which the bonds of community are enhanced by the cultivated sensibility of its members'. The forming of aesthetic judgments was understood to be a collective process, with taste and values forged in the interests of society as a whole. Virtuous behaviour was elicited in the same manner, in the context of community needs and subject to the regulation of the civic body.[16]

Hutcheson's thesis, with its emphasis on the social regulation of the individual will, was echoed in a series of later commentaries. His one-time student Adam Smith, responding to the pressures of fast-paced economic modernization in his 1776 treatise *The wealth of nations*, drew attention to the processes of civic and communal self-regulation operative within a market-led society. More specifically in his earlier work, *The theory of moral sentiments* (1759), Smith focused on the pursuit of virtue in modern life, insisting that the individual find reflections of himself, and thereby a means of self-regulation, in civic engagement. A socially determined civic ethos would guard against the corruption which had befallen the ancient states of Greece and Rome, in encouraging the sacrifice of private interest to the common good. The profile of the citizen as the

---

15 For discussion of the ideological and intellectual make-up of late eighteenth- and early nineteenth-century Scottish society, see J. Dwyer, *Virtuous discourse*, and J.G.A. Pocock, *Virtue, commerce and history*, chapter 2.   16 I. McBride, 'The school of virtue: Francis Hutcheson, Irish Presbyterianism and the Scottish Enlightenment' (1993).

locus for 'right reason' was raised against the spectre of the wayward, selfish individual, and thus the mutual interests of all in collectivity, sociability, civic engagement and communal discourse were guaranteed.

The emphasis placed on concepts of civic virtue helps to explain the extent to which it pervaded a Scottish social ethos in the long term. From its theoretical construction within the academy the civic ideal would spread – at least among an urban intellectual élite – to become a subtle consensus fundamental to patriotic and pedagogic initiatives and strongly influential on a literary and critical agenda. The *literati* of Scotland, suggests John Dwyer, developed a programme which was 'decidedly propagandistic, for they wished to proselytize their polite gospel of virtue and sentiment to a rapidly growing reading public'.[17] Admittedly, this offered little more than an imaginary cohesion: no amount of national self-fashioning could disguise the complex realities of Scotland's semi-colonial condition, nor would a culture of civic responsibility amongst an educated minority obscure the economic and social fissures which divided the country as a whole. From an Irish perspective however, Scotland exhibited a relative stability, manifest in a vibrant social culture and in a tangible civic sensibility which to some degree sheltered its intellectual community from the hazards of constitutional and national affiliation. And the visible manifestations of civic intercourse – the dynamism of Scottish literary and political journals, the range of learned societies and fellowships, the confidence of schools and institutions – suggested a level of social autonomy and cultural self-definition that many in Ireland, including Samuel Ferguson, found attractive.

Ulster's compatibility with Scotland was sustained of course, by numerous parallels and relationships between Belfast, Edinburgh, Aberdeen and Glasgow. Where Scotland looked back to the 1707 union and the Enlightenment, Belfast absorbed the legacy of a United Irishmen rebellion inspired by classical republicanism and civic humanism; an inheritance not only of Molyneux, Swift and Locke but also of Hume, Adam Ferguson and Adam Smith.[18] Like its Scottish counterparts, the town saw the benefits, in the early decades of the nineteenth century, of a transfer of initiative from political into civic activism. Belfast's cultural life represented a confluence of forces, described by Breandán Ó Buachalla as a fortuitous combination of political radicalism and a process of cultural assimilation which had been taking place since the Plantation; 'two complementary and parallel reflexes of an underlying enlightened liberalism.'[19] For different constitutional reasons but with the same underlying ideological premise as its Edinburgh counterpart, a Belfast intelligentsia had begun to define itself through intellectual assertion and civic responsibility.

17 *Sociability and society* p. 6. 18 M. Elliott, *Partners in revolution* (1982), pp. 20 and 27–9. 19 'The Gaelic background', p. 27.

Belfast's strong profile as a centre of intellectual and cultural engagement is evident in the number of societies and associations founded there during the first quarter of the nineteenth century, including the Belfast Literary Society in 1801, the Historical Society in 1811, the Belfast Natural and Philosophical Society in 1825 and the Ulster Gaelic Society in 1830. True, these societies represented the interests of a limited sector of the population and were to a large extent patronized by the same small but mobile group of cultural zealots, but the network they created nonetheless suggests a strong commitment to cultural and scientific discourse within the town. A centenary monograph of the Literary Society, for example, shows the intellectual diversity of the organization, with monthly papers presented on subjects ranging from the capabilities of the harp to the properties of oxygen. Notable lecturers included the classicist, William Bruce, who spoke on the structure of English verse, William Hamilton Drummond, who lectured on topography, the Gaelic scholar William Neilson on Gaelic authors and antiquities, and Henry Joy on the history of the Volunteers in Ireland.[20] With its broad explorative sweep the society was a forum for the kind of deeply committed amateur polymathy that would come to typify the Victorians; prioritizing science, particularly astronomy and mathematics, but fostering in the same spirit of enquiry a strong interest in cultural and historical material, with regular forays into political commentary.

In this, the role of Presbyterianism was crucial. Ian McBride points out that the framework of an eighteenth-century British empire created a context within which Presbyterians 'inhabited a transatlantic subculture stretching from Scotland to Ulster to the American colonies', with particular links forged through education: excluded from Trinity College until 1793, Irish Presbyterians traditionally travelled in large numbers to the main Scottish universities, where they were listed as '*Scoto-Hiberni*' in matriculation records.[21] These sons of Presbyterian ministers, merchants and tenant farmers took with them distinct Ulster traditions of 'New Light' non-subscribing theology and a political activism bequeathed by the rebels of 1798, and returned with a language and outlook energized by Scottish ideas. Almost all the members of the Belfast Literary Society, for example, were educated in Glasgow, an experience which sat comfortably alongside their tendency towards political radicalism. Many had participated in or written about the events of 1798, and several were open supporters of gradual Catholic Emancipation in Ireland. In short, the Presbyter-

---

20 *The Belfast Literary Society, 1801–1901* (1902), pp. 50–60. 21 'The school of virtue', p. 74. E. McFarland calculates that between 1780 and 1809, at least 13% of students matriculating from Glasgow were Irish, and most those from Ulster (*Ireland and Scotland* p. 5). On the role played by students in the diffusion of Enlightenment ideas into Ulster in the period, see I.M. Bishop, 'The education of Ulster students at Glasgow University during the nineteenth century' (1987).

ian element in Ulster society was closely entwined with a political, cultural and intellectual assertiveness sustained well into the nineteenth century by neighbouring Scotland.

Education in Ulster was one of the main beneficiaries of the Scottish link. Several key members of the Belfast Literary Society were closely involved in educational initiatives, and many were affiliated to the new Belfast Academical Institution, at which the young Samuel Ferguson was enrolled in 1823. The school was founded in response to the need for a Presbyterian college in Ireland which would offer a certificate in Arts equivalent to the Scottish M.A. degree, but from its inception in 1810 the Institution was also tied specifically to Ulster's radical dissenting tradition. Its manifesto was outlined in an 1814 opening address given by one of its founders, the poet and former United Irishman William Drennan, who described the academy as a place where 'pupils of all religious denominations should communicate, by frequent and friendly intercourse, in the common business of education, by which means a turn might be given to the national character and habits, and all the children of Ireland should know and love each other'.[22] The Belfast Academical Institution was a statement as much as a school, and very recognizably the product 'of the liberal Belfast business community and intelligentsia, many of whom had been United Irishmen or had United Irish sympathies, and who now found an outlet for their reforming activities in cultural and educational enterprises'.[23]

The school also signalled the translation of political activism into shared investment in the idea of an inclusive national culture. The broad curriculum included the teaching of the Irish language, and attention was persistently drawn to the need for a national literature through the vigorous campaigning rhetoric of the Master of the School of English, Henry Montgomery. Better known as the adversary of Henry Cooke in the series of public theological debates which took place between 1827 and 1829, Montgomery, an advocate of Catholic Emancipation, represented the values of a liberal New Light Presbyterianism which countered the reactionary dogma of Cooke's Old Light Arianism. But within the context of Belfast's academic community, he was a key educational policy maker and a vociferous spokesman for a national literary inheritance. In 1840, he summarized his position in 'An essay towards understanding the causes which have retarded the progress of literature in Ireland and the most efficient means of promoting its advancement'. Read as a public address to the Belfast

---

22 Cited J. Fisher and J.H. Robb, *The book of the Royal Belfast Academical Institution* (1913), p. 205. See also J. Seaton-Reid, *A history of the Presbyterian Church in Ireland* (1853), vol. 3, p. 458. Drennan's role as founder gave the school two tangible links, first to the liberal philosophies of the Scottish Enlightenment, and in particular to the authority of his former mentor and correspondent Dugald Stewart; secondly to the ideological initiatives of 1798. See E. McFarland, *Ireland and Scotland* p. 20.   23 R.G.F. Holmes, *Our Presbyterian heritage* (1985), p. 98.

Rhetorical Society, this essay stressed the need for a literature 'rife with reflections on the distinctive manners, customs, opinions, and peculiar characteristics of the people to whom it belongs'. A genuine native literature would reject servility and imitation, providing a stabilizing force within society, a means of securing a national identity for Ireland outside the vagaries of political change and conflict.[24]

A similar rhetoric was adopted by Ferguson's close friend of his early years, Thomas O'Hagan, who was to become Ireland's first Catholic lord chancellor in 1868. The two men met within a group formed to study the Irish language, and they remained in contact through their training and practice as barristers on the Irish legal circuit. O'Hagan pledged support for O'Connell and Repeal alongside a passionate commitment to Irish culture. In an article of 1830, he acclaimed a long tradition of Irish literary talent, and, invoking the authorities Gibbon, Hume, Adam Smith and Burke, stated that 'a new and blessed time for Ireland' had finally arrived. It had only been through the degeneration caused by political circumstances that Ireland had failed to advance in mental cultivation; the national intellect, which had been restrained in 'sluggish somnolency', would now be revived and restored.[25] These views where reiterated in his 1831 address to the Belfast Historical Society, in which he underlined the importance of an Irish language and literature for the development of national self-respect.

> A peculiar literature is the noblest possession that can belong to a people. It is the out-breathing of their souls, the manifestation of their intellectual power. It affords them a loftier elevation; and a more enduring greatness than any other attainment can bestow. The extension of their territory, the subjugation of their fellow-beings, the increase of their wealth, may occupy the thoughts of the multitude; but to Mind a nation must owe its real grandeur; Thought alone will secure it an immortality and glory.

O'Hagan not only appealed for a regeneration of cultural responsibility in the country, but began to establish a definition of what a national literature should be; 'a literature which has taken its form and impress from the spirit of the people – a literature which is stamped, in clear and lustrous characters, by the genius of our country as her own.' This, together with the noble inheritance of

---

24 Cited L. Lunney, 'Ulster attitudes to Scottishness: the eighteenth century and after' (1994), p. 68. For details of the 'New Light' controversy and resultant schism within the Presbyterian church, see R.G.F. Holmes, *Our Presbyterian heritage*, pp. 100–5. 25 'The past and the future of Ireland, in reference particularly to her national literature', by 'T.H.', *Ulster Magazine* 1:4 (1830), 243–54. O'Hagan initially signed himself simply 'Thomas Hagan': see J. Fisher and J.H. Robb, p. 167.

'national recollection', would provide solid foundations for communality and civic sensibility within Ireland as a whole.[26]

The outlet for O'Hagan's opinions in this period was the *Ulster Magazine*, a short-lived but strikingly professional publication founded by Charles Teeling, formerly one of the Ulster leaders of the United Irishmen rebellion, who had been arrested and charged with treason in 1795. As editor, Teeling pledged his magazine to a policy of tolerance, liberty and enlightenment. He celebrated its participation in the print revolution, invoking one of the magazine's major authority figures, the Scottish philosopher Dugald Stewart, on the need to raise cultivation throughout the whole population in order to create civic stability. Considerable space was devoted to literature, with regular features on icons of national literary endeavour such as Burns, Byron and Moore. In conjunction with its cultural outlook, the magazine aspired towards national self-assertion in its politics, reflecting in its first editorial on the present state of Ulster as a province of missed opportunities in the wake of the glories of the 1780s. The only position to be adopted, it stated, was pro-Repeal. The Union was seen to have failed to meet its promise of equality for Ireland, but the means of its removal must be peaceful and at all times 'dealt with calmly and rationally among the liberal and enlightened people of Ulster'. While drawing inspiration from the legacy of 1798 and the revolutionary political fortunes of France and America, a new campaign for liberty must take a civic rather than a military form. And, as in O'Hagan's address, this radical political spirit was constantly linked to a plea for Irish cultural regeneration: liberty for Ireland might only be achieved in tandem with the restoration of an independent national cultural tradition.[27]

Like the Belfast Literary Society and the Belfast Academical Institution, the *Ulster Magazine* was the product of a particular climate of heightened cultural consciousness and social activism, emerging from the cohesive context of a liberal, educated Belfast community steeped in the vocabulary of Scottish Enlightenment and comfortable with the rhetoric of Irish cultural independence and initiative. Significantly, Ferguson's first known published works, including three verse satires and two 'Ulster Ballads' also appeared here between March 1830 and April 1831. While he later stated that he did not endorse the magazine's political agenda, his affiliation to the publication highlights his early exposure to radical, dissenting and even nationalist tendencies combined with a resurgence of confidence in a national culture.[28] His proximity to a environment within which young firebrands

---

[26] 'Importance of a national literature', by 'T.H.', *Ulster Magazine* 2:18 (1831), 278. [27] *Ulster Magazine* 1:2 (1830), 85; 93. [28] For details of Ferguson's contributions to the *Ulster Magazine* between March 1830 and April 1831 see Denman, *Samuel Ferguson*, p. 203, and Curley, pp. 100–2. Ferguson wrote to Blackwood, 'I have no influence with any paper

such as O'Hagan picked up the loose threads of radicalism and reform from the generation of Drennan, Montgomery and Teeling marks the beginning of a pattern of interest, not in any specific constitutional agenda, but in the will to cultural independence which they expressed, and in the cultural and civic potential which, collectively, they made manifest.

Certainly, the political horizon was far from promising. The public debate between Montgomery and Cooke symbolized for many the increasing divergence between radical tradition and reactionary unionism. Roy Foster has drawn attention to Cooke's ascendancy as evidence that by the 1820s, Ulster had little further use for political and theological liberalism, identifying economic prosperity with the Union.[29] But this view is short on interest in the literary and intellectual machinery of life in Ulster, which was still oiled by the initiatives and values of enlightenment radicalism well into the nineteenth century. The idea that this represented little more than an attenuated spirit of 1798 desperately discharging a redundant political energy is difficult to accept, in view of the freshness of the language and the intensity of motivation which colour the pages of the *Ulster Magazine*. Distinct from political narratives, and endorsed by the relationship with Scotland, the vitality of civic discourse in Belfast and its regions was impressive, and pivotal to Ferguson's developing sense of culturally-defined nationality. The strands which met in him – Scots planter ancestry, lowland Presbyterian radicalism, the philosophy of civic discourse and an admiring familiarity with the Edinburgh literary scene – combined to form an inheritance which undoubtedly shaped his perceptions and sensibility, a latent but undeniable influence on his work as a cultural activist in Dublin.

SCOTT, FERGUSON AND THE NATIONAL TALE

The interests of Scottish Enlightenment philosophy in the nature of civil society and in the relationship between the individual and his civic environment were not abstract concerns; they bore a direct relationship to issues of imperial responsibility and authority, as the progress of colonialism brought 'primitive' societies into direct contact with the 'civilized' imperial centre. In Scotland itself, they emerged in relation to a particular social juxtaposition of rural, feudal clanship and mercantile, urban bourgeoisie. How might the difference and hierarchy between these societies within a national unit be explained? What

---

except a papist repealing radical one started lately by a Roman Catholic friend' (5 Nov. 1833, NLS MS 4035 f213), and later to Charles Gavan Duffy, 'I wrote for poor old Charles Teeling when he had a sort of *Ulster Magazine* afoot about 1830' (1 Aug. 1845, NLI MS 5756, vol. 465).   29 *Modern Ireland* (1989), p. 303.

kinds of responsibility did one society bear towards the other, in terms of encouraging its institutional and civic progress?

In attempting to negotiate such issues, the philosophers and economists of the Scottish Enlightenment turned to the nature of man's social, economic and ultimately civic evolution. Society was understood to be a transitional phenomenon, moving from barbarism towards civilization. Its developmental progress corresponded to a profile common to all nations irrespective of racial differences: in each case society passed through specific and recognizable stages, defined by Adam Smith in his *Lectures on jurisprudence* (1762) as Primitive, Pastoral, Agrarian and Commercial.[30] Various modifications of this model were produced but the basic structural concept remained a central and influential component of the school's philosophy, together with Smith's particular emphasis on the economic regulation of social establishments. In theory, the concepts of property and self-interest would encourage the individual to break away from the nomadic clan or tribe, and to establish settlements and a system of protective rights. In his influential *Essay on the history of civil society* (1767), Adam Ferguson described how childlike loyalty to the head of the clan, which caused the individual to bond unselfishly and irrationally to his community, is gradually replaced by a mature instinct towards self-preservation and self-interest, factors which regulate the community as a whole, and which are eventually co-ordinated with the general interest by the moderating forces of the state and legislature. Rationalism thus prevails over blind loyalties, and modern society is guided by the *consensus gentium* rather than force.[31]

The Scottish school of Smith, Adam Ferguson, Robertson and Stewart created templates first and obviously, for economics, but secondly, for history and historiography. Progress between the stages of civilization was seen as inevitable, but not necessarily uniform or straightforward: hence the existence of societies in an arrested state or retrogressive stage of development, such as Scotland's own pockets of 'primitivism' in the Highlands. This aspect of Enlightenment thought formed the basis for the emergence of conjectural history, later to be adopted by nineteenth-century embryonic anthropology as the Comparative Method. Any section of society which had not yet progressed from a primitive to a civilized stage of development provided the necessary key to 'remembering' the condition in which mature society had previously existed, and from which the advancement of society might be measured. 'If, in advanced years,' wrote Adam Ferguson, 'we would form a just notion of our progress from the cradle, we must have recourse to the nursery; and from the example

---

30 See J. Rendall, *The origins of the Scottish Enlightenment* (1978), pp. 141–2. 31 For context and summary of Adam Ferguson's philosophy see J.W. Burrow, *Evolution and society* (1966), p. 11.

of those who are still in the period of life we mean to describe, take our representation of past manners, that cannot, in any other way, be recalled'.[32]

In its attention to discrete stages of progress rather than organic evolution, and in its stress on the economic rather than any 'spiritual' condition of the people, conjectural history and Scottish Enlightenment philosophy provided a rational structure for understanding the past, undercutting the romantic cult of the primitive and crucially, shifting focus from racial to economic determinants in the explanation of social traditions, customs and behaviour. To counter this anti-humanist stance, which promoted – as Adam Smith's *Wealth of nations* has been taken to do – the 'invisible hand' of financial regulation in society, Scottish philosophers kept faith with the notion that human intervention in the form of virtue would keep a mechanistic ruthlessness at bay: inevitable economic and social transition retained a space for a humanist sense of individual responsibility.

Almost immediately, literary fiction became a primary conduit for these ideas. In the school of sentimental fiction, Henry Brooke's *The fool of quality*, serialized between 1765 and 1770, has been read as a study of civic humanism and the organic moral community, and similar preoccupations have been noted in the work of Henry MacKenzie, Tobias Smollet, Hugh Blair and James Fordyce, novelists who shared to varying degrees, a concern with the relationship between the 'man of feeling' and the civic body to which he belongs.[33] But the romantic and historical novelist Walter Scott was the most influential and far-reaching fictional exponent of Scottish Enlightenment concepts. If his Victorian profile was that of a nostalgic medievalist, Scott has been read by more recent critics as a staunch conservative, attempting to re-invent in his fiction a gapped and politically inflammatory past, or as a proto-modernist whose highly strategic narrative self-consciousness reflects on the fractured and recalcitrant condition of history itself.[34] But most authoritatively, his fiction offered an analysis of the transition from feudal authority to market economy, the evolution of commercial and civic man, and the gradual hegemony of bourgeois capital over that of landed aristocracy. His historical sensibility was instinctively comparativist, an impulse famously encapsulated in the alternative title of *Waverley* (1814) –

---

32 *An essay on the history of civil society* (1793), pp. 146–7. Samuel Ferguson was familiar with the work of Adam Ferguson: see his letter to William Smith O'Brien (Smith O'Brien Papers, NLI vol. 432, p. 907).   33 On Smollet and MacKenzie in this respect, see N. Phillopson, 'The Scottish Enlightenment', p. 20, and on Mackenzie and Brooke see J. Dwyer, 'Enlightened spectators and classical moralists: sympathetic relations in eighteenth-century Scotland' in his *Sociability and society*, pp. 103–5. For general commentary on the philosophical content of these novelists, see G. Kelly, *English fiction of the Romantic period* (1989).   34 Scott attended classes held by Dugald Stewart, professor of Moral Philosophy and chief popularizer of Adam Smith, at Edinburgh University. See both K. Sutherland, 'Fictional Economies' and D. Forbes, 'The rationalism of Walter Scott' (1953).

'Tis sixty years since' – and illustrated dramatically by what the author described as the 'moral lessons' which would be drawn from his treatment of the Highland/Lowland schism in the novel.[35]

Scott remains the best known of the many writers identified by Katie Trumpener as belonging to a precise literary community, generated within the relationship between Ireland and Scotland in the early nineteenth-century. This 'transperipheral Irish-Scottish public sphere', sustained by the mutual interests of publishers, reviewers and readers, aligned the work of Edgeworth, Maturin, Morgan and the Banim brothers alongside that of Scott, John Galt, Charlotte Smith, Caroline Lamb and Susan Ferrier. These writers were united by the need to develop a literary form suited, in both philosophical and generic terms, to the matter of their respective nations, and capable of registering the vast and irreconcilable anomalies in socio-economic development characteristic of both Ireland and Scotland. The form in which this was initially achieved was the national tale, identified by Trumpener as a prototype of 'romance proper', and an indirect product of Enlightenment models of comparative analysis, from Montesquieu's contrasted cultural geographies to the four-stage historical model of social evolution developed by the Scottish Enlightenment. With its highly analytical devices (such as the telescoping of a clan 'feud' or the illumination of an archetypal and perhaps legendary figure), the national tale could accommodate 'representative' markers of differing stages of progress, raising tangential questions on the ethics of improvement or the limits of responsibility. What the authors of the national tale begin to explore, claims Trumpener, is 'the coexistence of multiple layers of time in place, and the discontinuities of place in time', not in terms of idiosyncratic crisis but as anomalies common to any society, through which the valued ideals of civility, morality and social virtue can be articulated and tested.[36]

Within this context, Ferguson's attempt to write a series of national tales appears as a straightforward legacy of the fusion between the pervasive models of the Scottish Enlightenment's historical philosophy and the timely consolidation of a specific genre of historical fiction. Scott was inevitably the linchpin, his reputation, at the time of his death in 1832, at its highest point, and his Irish disciples including the writers James McHenry, W.H. Maxwell and Matthew Archdeacon.[37] When Ferguson wrote of his ideal to 'raise the native elements of Irish story to a dignified level', or as he also put it, into 'the realm of legitimate history', he invoked Scott as his authority and as a guarantee of

---

35 *Waverley* (1981), p. 5, p. 340. 36 *Bardic nationalism*, p. 137, p. 151. 37 See J. Cahalan, *The Irish novel* (1988), p. 26. Cahalan also discusses Scott's influence on the novels of the Banim brothers in *Great hatred, little room: the Irish historical novel* (1983), chapter 1.

authenticity. Writing in 1836, he described Ireland as 'the richest mine of romantic and historical material in Europe, which would be served not by coarse burlesque on national humour, nor in frivolous representations of passing events or characters' but by the responsible treatment of a writer such as Scott.[38]

These of course, were barbed comments, for Ferguson was consciously defying a school of exploitative romance – specifically that led by the writers Thomas Crofton Croker and Charles Lever – which was seen to have travestied the country's history and character, using its peculiar juxtaposition of cultivation and grotesquery in order to forge a 'curiosity' for an English readership.[39] Against this grain, Scott's fiction provided a template for what seemed to be a scientific approach to the past. Ferguson highlighted what he saw as the aberrant social composition of Ireland in his 1836 commentary on the nature of Irish society, and the language employed here testifies to his attempts to maintain the register of the historical comparativist. 'We are peculiarly in a transition state', he wrote. 'Our present condition combines the characteristics of many epochs [...] You can take your stand, as it were, on the line of junction and lay your hand on one side on barbarism, on the other on the perfection of civilization.' Rather than aestheticized as a romantic and exotic anomaly, the country is assessed in terms of its regional variations on a scale of social maturity and is presented as a geographical and physiological canvas against which the progress of civilization may be measured. Touring Ireland is a speculative exercise, Ferguson insisted, 'like going backwards and forwards through the rooms of a well-arranged historical museum'.[40]

It was of course, customary in the period to invoke the contrast between barbarism and civility as a means of reinforcing a nineteenth-century evolutionary idealism. But Ferguson was deeply attached to such ideas as a viable historical paradigm for Ireland. The same language informs much of his speculation on societal and racial evolution during the 1830s; it dominates his 1834 essays on James Hardiman's *Irish Minstrelsy*, and re-emerges in his introduction to the 'Versions from the Irish' section in his collection *Lays of the western Gael* (1864), where his apology for certain compositions refers to the contrast between the

---

38 'Attractions of Ireland, no. 2 – scenery and society', *DUM* 8 (Sept. 1836), 330; see also *SSFID*, vol. 1, p. 4 and p. 139.   39 Thomas Crofton Croker's *Fairy legends and traditions of the south of Ireland* was attacked in the *Ulster Magazine* 3 (12 Nov. 1834), 125, as a travesty of nationality. Charles Lever's *Popular tales and legends of the Irish peasantry* was likewise condemned in the *Dublin Penny Journal* as a work in which 'the creations of fancy have been substituted for the realities of life', 2 (1832), 329–30.   40 'Attractions of Ireland, no. 3 – society', *DUM* 8 (Dec. 1836), 658. Compare the description given by the Scottish historian Sir James Mackintosh; 'We can now examine almost every variety of character, manners, opinions and feelings and prejudices of mankind into which they can be thrown either by the rudeness of barbarism or by the capricious corruptions of refinement [...] History [...] is now a museum, in which specimens of every variety of human nature may be studied.' *The law of nature and the law of nations* (1798), in *The miscellaneous works* (1846), vol. 3, p. 60.

ruder age in which they were written and the advanced civilization in which they are now presented. What it indicates is that at the very least, he had absorbed fragments of a Scottish social philosophy, endorsing an Enlightenment view of the Irish condition as transitional and fluid, rather than a Romanticist determinism which regarded it as a fixed phenomenon and a colonial aberration.

The *Hibernian nights' entertainments* are of interest then, because they represent the young writer's attempt to construe an Irish nation in these terms, recognizing the inevitability of social transition from itinerant clan society to mature self-regulating government, and from the passions of feudal leadership to the rationalism of civic responsibility. The tales making up the series effectively trace the development of Irish culture and society from pre-conquest to Elizabethan Ireland, but their emphasis is increasingly on the processes of social and economic determinism which ultimately produced Ireland's nineteenth-century social conglomeration. Admittedly, the early tales in the sequence are limited in scope, with a sense of recuperative rather than speculative historiography. 'The return of Claneboy', written while Ferguson was still in Belfast, is topographically exhaustive in its details of his native Antrim.[41] The second published tale, 'Shane O'Neill's last amour', is more adventurous but again lacks depth, while 'The sons of Usnach', a treatment of the Deirdre legend, is little more a literal rendition of Theophilus O'Flanagan's eighteenth-century manuscript version of the same.[42] As his fictional venture matured, however, Ferguson began to combine his basic interest in romantic historical conflicts with an increased attention to the social scenarios of each narrative, highlighting material conditions as much, if not more than, the dramatic and romantic events of the plot. The portraits of pre-Christian and medieval Ireland which are produced in 'The captive of Killeshin' and 'Corby MacGillmore' combine inter-tribal strife with a sustained commentary on the economic foundations of clanship, while 'The rebellion of Silken Thomas' and 'Rosabel of Ross' contain elaborate reconstructions of sixteenth-century market and trade economies.

Clearly, the young writer gradually sensed the widening philosophical scope of his fictional project, a factor reinforced by the publishing history of the tales. The *Hibernian nights' entertainments* are best known in the three-volume posthumous 1887 version edited, re-arranged and footnoted by Lady Ferguson, whose efforts gave the impression of coherence and completeness to what was in fact an unfinished fictional experiment.[43] But this edition also removes the publication con-

---

41 See Denman on this point in relation to the Ordnance Survey Commission, *Samuel Ferguson*, p. 41. 42 Denman, *Samuel Ferguson*, p. 44. 43 All quotations are from M.C. Ferguson's three-volume edition of the *Hibernian nights' entertainments* (1897). Ferguson's use of the *Thousand and one nights* model was in fact a remarkably common literary device of the period: see P. Caracciolo (ed.), *The Arabian Nights in English literature* (1988), and also W.J. McCormack's comments on the significance of the Arabian model in the tales, in Deane (ed.), *Field Day*, vol. 1, p. 1185.

text – and crucially, the Scottish dimension – from the works. The tales were initiated in response to the encouragement of the publisher William Blackwood, in Edinburgh, and the first two stories were published in *Blackwood's* in December 1833 and February 1834 respectively. Ferguson appears to have been confident of his success with further fictional contributions, writing to Blackwood in June 1833 of a 'projected series', which he intended for publication in the same magazine.[44] *Blackwood's* failed to accommodate five further tales however, and these were serialized instead in Ferguson's alternative outlet, the newly-established *Dublin University Magazine*, between December 1834 and May 1836.

Here, the stories were presented under the title of *Hibernian nights' entertainments*, and a frame-tale linking the episodes was introduced. This latter innovation undoubtedly marks Ferguson's transition from purely restorative historical fiction to a conceptual use of his material. A prologue to the story of 'The sons of Usnach' informs the reader that Turlogh O'Brien, bard of the O'Neill, has secretly infiltrated Dublin castle in the winter of 1592, in order to relieve the tedium of three incarcerated Irish princes, Red Hugh O'Donnell and Art and Henry O'Neill, by telling stories to help pass the hours of their imprisonment. The structure, which recalls Scott's frequent use of a prefatory story or 'disclaimer', self-consciously draws attention to the discrepancies between different historical periods, as if to dramatize the author's contrived move from a 'literal' historicity towards conjectural fiction.[45] The tales become 'entertainments' which, while aspiring to a historical status, also acknowledge their own fictitiousness, a duality stressed by the interruptive exchanges between Turlogh and the three princes, in which the historical material of the tales is challenged and evaluated. They provide a moral and educational resource, important not for the 'small hinges' of historical detail but to highlight the social distance between past and present: when the princes interrupt and query the narrative, the bard Turlogh reminds them of 'the strange usages of different times and nations' which they must consider in their response to the stories.

The narrative function shifts considerably therefore; the tales lose their purchase on any ideas of historical verity, but gain a foothold in the construction of a perspective on history itself. And the paradigm of enlightenment progressivism within which the later tales operate becomes clearly visible. The tale of 'Corby MacGillmore', for example, plays on the juxtaposition of two differing stages of societal and economic transition. Set in Antrim at the beginning of the fifteenth century, this narrative traces the eventual extinction of a

---

[44] Ferguson to William Blackwood, 3 June 1833, NLS MS 4035 f211.   [45] See, for example, Scott's introductory preface to *The betrothed* (1825), which illustrates his ironic view of the relationship between history and fiction, and the frame-tales used in both *The fair maid of Perth* (1828) and *The fortunes of Nigel* (1822).

pagan tribe living on the outskirts of a Christian community. There are close resemblances to Scott's 1817 novel *Rob Roy*, in which the author's conflation of legend and socio-economic conjecture served to furnish what he described as 'an interesting chapter, not on Highland manners alone, but on every stage of society in which the people of a primitive and half-civilized tribe are brought into contact with a nation in which civilization and polity have attained complete superiority'.[46] Like the ancient McGregor clan of the Scottish tale, Corby McGillmore's outlawed tribe, which plunders neighbouring settlements for iron, is fast declining as a result of its isolation and, it is implied, obsolete social ethics, into savagery. Though excluded from society, it is constantly brought into contact with civilization through its rapacious exploits and the secret marriage of MacGillmore to the daughter of an enemy Christian chieftain. Meanwhile an external, speculative perspective on events is provided by Brother Virgil, a Christian friar who, finding himself by chance in MacGillmore's hidden camp, welcomes the opportunity to 'observe more closely the manners of the strange people among whom it had been his mishap thus to be cast'.

Virgil identifies MacGillmore as a romantic noble savage; though wild and ruthless he is possessed of a 'natural piety', a phrase which Ferguson was to scatter through his 1834 discussion of Irish society in the Hardiman review.[47] Through Virgil's perceptions of this tendency in the chieftain, the trajectory of historical evolution to which the tribe must conform is endorsed. Transition may necessitate conflict and sacrifice, but its inevitability is never in question. McGillmore is clearly an archetype: as in Scott, all the warring clans and their charismatic but ruthless leaders are upheld as anomalies; the romantic but ultimately doomed residue of a former stage of history, whose societal basis is now giving way. The life of the clan is 'imagined' rather as the conjectural historian might visualize his own previous incarnation at the edges of the contemporary civilized world, in a decisive shift from historical chronicle to historical conjecture, as it were, and with a distinguishable attempt on the part of the author to indicate the universal pattern of determinism which exists beneath the dynamics of the fiction.

The representative aspect of characters such as MacGillmore is key to their function in the *Hibernian nights' entertainments*. When actual historical events and characters impinge on a tale Ferguson refers to them only tangentially. 'The rebellion of Silken Thomas' thus treats an episode in Irish history less as a specific political narrative, and more – as would Scott – as a tale of manners slanted towards the general illustration of the demise of feudal autonomy and the rise of an urban market economy. This tale, the most sophisticated and

---

46 *Rob Roy* (1893), p. 54. 47 'Hardiman's *Irish Minstrelsy*, No. 3', *DUM* 4 (Oct. 1834), 452.

artistically coherent of the series, is based on the 1534 revolt of Thomas Fitzgerald, son of the lord deputy, the earl of Kildare, against Henry VIII's authority in Ireland. The story was a popular one and was retold in at least two different versions in the *Dublin Penny Journal* between 1834 and 1835, but Ferguson seems to have relied on the version of the incident given by the Holinshed chronicler Richard Stanihurst in 1577.[48] He expands on this account considerably, but also, significantly, shifts the dramatic emphasis from the insurrection against the crown to the power struggle which it initiated between the old, military, feudal regime represented by Fitzgerald, and the ascendant authority of Dublin's merchant-traders.

This particular conflict was of course a key element of Scottish Enlightenment economic philosophy. The legacy of Adam Smith had given currency to an understanding of the crucial stage of transition from a power structure based on deference and traditional allegiances to one founded upon the self-regulation of the market-place, in a shift from agrarian to urban authority. Commerce, Smith believed, encouraged a society to develop political maturity and to establish effective legislative institutions. In addition to increasing both cultivation and wealth within the community, commerce introduced order and good government, and led to an emphasis on the liberty and security of individuals who had previously existed in a state of war with their neighbours and dependency on their superiors. The dissemination of wealth urged the individual towards self-protectiveness, which in turn promoted stability within society as a whole, as the bonds of affection sustaining a patriarchal or clan-based regime were eroded and replaced by the authority of the independent citizen. Transition towards a 'polished' commercial basis accelerated the decay of the old social order, while morally enriching that of the new.

Again it is almost certain that Ferguson's reading of the late Middle Ages in Ireland in these terms was mediated by Scott, and in this case by Scott's presentation of a similar conflict in one of the Cannongate Chronicles, *The fair maid of Perth* (1828).[49] Set in the fourteenth century, Scott's novel recreates a power struggle between the craftsmen and burghers of Perth and the feudal aristocracy of Scotland. Like *Waverley*, the novel highlights the corruption of the feudal regime as it begins to lose governmental legitimacy to the claims of an emergent bourgeoisie, dependent not upon tradition or deference but on self-protective values rooted in capital and commerce. *The fair maid of Perth* thus drama-

---

48 It is difficult to be precise with regard to Ferguson's sources for the tales. Possibilities range from Charles O'Connor's Latin translation of the Annals of the Four Masters, the Book of Howth, the Ulster Annals and the chronicles of Stanihurst, Ware and Campion. See William Hodder, 'Ferguson: his literary sources' (1987), pp. 57–66. 49 Ferguson alludes to this work in order to illustrate the meaning of the term 'fosterage' in his third *Irish Minstrelsy* review article, *DUM* 4 (Oct. 1834), 452. There are numerous similarities between the two works.

tized almost programmatically the speculative economics Smith had bequeathed to Dugald Stewart and the other popularizers of his writings, and in doing so provided a suitable template for Ferguson's sixteenth-century tale of conflict around the Pale.

The hero of 'The rebellion of Silken Thomas' is not the Geraldine renegade himself but the knight Sir John Talbot, (the name inevitably echoes Scott's Colonel Talbot in *Waverley*), who interacts with individuals and events drawn directly from historical sources. An archetypal middle-man, Talbot is an unassuming, unremarkable soldier who becomes torn in his allegiances between two opposing forces when his engagement to the daughter of a Dublin merchant clashes with his responsibility to Fitzgerald's militia. Ferguson begins by establishing the economic context of these events, but the scene of commercial stability, industry and prosperity with which the narrative opens is disrupted almost immediately by the announcement that Fitzgerald's son Thomas intends to surrender his allegiance to the crown in protest at the (reported) execution of his father in London. While the military might of the rebel forces assembles itself Talbot is dispatched to the city authorities to demand access to the castle and its artillery, and the centre of conflict is transferred to the threat which is posed by a military insurrection to the stability of property and trade in the capital.

As in the power-struggle illustrated by *The fair maid of Perth*, the action of the tale is dominated by the citizenry identifying itself, staking its claim for legitimate democratic self-government, and asserting its status as a merchant class in opposition to the pre-eminence of the aristocratic regime. The priority of commerce over militarism is constantly invoked, with money, trade and commodities representing an alternative system of authority to that of Fitzgerald. The citizens, having suffered the attempts of the rebels to dominate them, remain resilient and persistent in their instinct towards merchant life, and the news that the Dublin siege has finally ended is conveyed to Talbot by the fact that traders and their livestock have been seen again on the open road. The decline of the displaced aristocrats and Fitzgerald's rebel army is accelerated, finally, by an act of betrayal which transgresses the code of *gossipred* or fosterage within the clan, the breakdown of old social bonds marking another step towards a bourgeois democratic ascendancy. As the traditional allegiances on which Fitzgerald relies give way, the nobility of the country finds it must submit to the practices of the new social contract, and become subject to a civil government ruled by the market-place.

The *Hibernian nights' entertainments* are, claims Leerssen, 'a remarkable effort at that almost impossible genre, an Irish historical novel'.[50] The impossibility

---

50 *Remembrance and imagination*, p. 184.

of Ferguson's task seems to have weighed too heavily upon him, and not surprisingly perhaps, after producing only fourteen of his intended twenty-one night episodes he abandoned the series. The tales remain significant however, as a filter for the many influences – literary, political and philosophical – of his early career. Crucially, they illuminate his familiarity with the linguistic currency of a speculative anthropology derived from Scottish Enlightenment principles, a familiarity too extensive to be attributed only coincidentally to a cursory reading of Scott. What emerges is a sense of the young writer's affiliation to a precise literary culture steeped in the general legacy of Scottish philosophy, and his readiness to translate those perspectives into the parameters of the national tale. In this context, Ferguson's attempt to impose a rational structure on Ireland's past prefigures the kind of pressure he would experience throughout his life in his struggle to accommodate the aberrations of his country in literary, and in his own terms 'legitimate' form.

Furthermore, Ferguson's apparent instinct towards a liberal evolutionary paradigm which ultimately prioritized the ascendancy of a civic, self-governing bourgeois community must also be read into his later engagements with ideological oppositionists in Dublin and specifically, against the grain of the language of the Hardiman review. The *Hibernian nights' entertainments* suggest that Ferguson's sense of Ireland's social constitution owed a great deal more to an eighteenth-century tradition of progressive enlightenment liberalism than to the calcified racial formulations of Victorian popular culture, while the evolutionary paradigm which they negotiate undermines Ó'Tuathaigh's assessment that 'Ferguson's model society is socially static; the dynamics of social change, not to speak of social conflict, are either ignored or simply not noticed'.[51] On the contrary, his understanding of the relationship between cultures as transitional according to historical evolution, rather than rather than fixed according to crude racial determinants, was highly influential in shaping his view of the connection not only between Ireland and England, but also between the urban centre of Dublin and the rural hinterlands of the country.

Finally, the tales may be regarded as an illuminating trajectory of Ferguson's cultural origins, within an inspirational but volatile Belfast circle still closely linked to Scottish intellectual tradition. The question they raise therefore, concerns the extent to which he remained attached to this legacy after his move to Dublin. Did he abandon the *Hibernian nights' entertainments* along with his 'Northern' values; the radical inheritance of lowland Antrim, the inclusive pedagogy of the Belfast Academical Institution, the spirited language and politics of O'Hagan and the *Ulster Magazine*? One might easily conclude that Dublin's

---

[51] 'Sir Samuel Ferguson – poet and ideologue' (1987), p. 11.

Tory Unionist agenda demanded a different style of cultural idealism and that Ferguson adapted accordingly, but this reading overlooks a number of strains and tendencies which continued to emerge in his writing. First, there is the persistence with which he looked to Edinburgh for inspiration in his efforts to stimulate a cultural hierarchy within Dublin, and as a model for the kind of stable civic culture he later sought in a Dublin intellectual network. Secondly, his attempt to rationalize the fractures in Ireland's societal constitution would remain, for the most part, invested in Enlightenment concepts of monogenetic progressivism, rather than in imperialist stereotype, a nuance in his historical perspective which underwrote his increasing interest in Irish antiquarianism. And finally, the impact of his origins is reflected in the difficulty with which he affiliated himself to Isaac Butt and the *Dublin University Magazine*. As the next chapter will suggest, what the Hardiman review represents is no *bravura* statement of Ascendancy hegemony, but the traumatic, contradictory and uneven result of Ferguson's attempts to insinuate himself into the Dublin scene while retaining in essence, the values and proclivities of his Northern liberal heritage.

CHAPTER TWO

The *Irish Minstrelsy* review, 1834

In one of his Ordnance Survey letters of November 1834, the Irish scholar John O'Donovan remarked:

> I find from the last number of the University Mag. that Master Ferguson is hammering away at Hardiman. He is partly right but too severe. Old Torlogh Carolan never received such a castigation before. We may expect a similar castigation from abler pens, nor will our accuracy or love of truth afford us protection; for critics can ridicule truth and accuracy as well as falsehood and blunders![1]

In 1831 the historian James Hardiman, a Catholic writer and antiquarian, published a volume of translations from seventeenth and eighteenth-century Gaelic sources, entitled *Irish Minstrelsy, or Bardic remains of Ireland*. The collection included a selection of Jacobite *reliques*, sentimental ballads, bacchanalia and a number of compositions attributed to the poet Carolan, and the book as a whole represented an attempt to popularize an oral and bardic literary inheritance through the combined efforts of a team of translators. In addition, Hardiman intended the *Irish Minstrelsy* to address the political sensibilities of a contemporary readership, and in his notes and editorial commentary framed the translations within the suffering and penal subjugation of post-Reformation Ireland. 'Great is the retribution which England owes this ill-treated land', he wrote. 'May the errors of the past be remembered as warnings for the future.'[2] In the sensitive wake of Catholic Emancipation Hardiman's language was antagonistic if not openly provocative, harnessing to the *Minstrelsy* a determining subtext which annexed Gaelic Ireland as an exclusively Catholic, nationalist possession.

Ferguson's extensive review of Hardiman's book originated in a suggestion by William Blackwood in 1833 that he explore some of the Gaelic manuscripts held in London libraries, a research task which immediately aroused the young writer's interest. 'As you anticipate', he wrote to Blackwood in November of that year, 'I find ample material for a series on the *Irish Minstrelsy*.' He enclosed with

1 Ordnance Survey letters: County Fermanagh, 17 Nov. 1834. 2 J. Hardiman (ed.), *Irish Minstrelsy*, vol. 1, p. 138.

this letter the first two articles of his intended series on the subject, of which he explained: 'I tried at first with as grave a treatment as I could give it, but I found that no other style than that I have adopted would answer.'[3] Blackwood failed to find a place for the essays in the Edinburgh magazine, however, discouraged perhaps by their tone or by the limited appeal of their content to a non-Irish readership, and Ferguson was obliged to transfer the rejected articles to the newly-established *Dublin University Magazine*, where the series eventually ran to four pieces published between April and November of 1834.

As John O'Donovan observed, Ferguson was vociferous in his denunciation of Hardiman. He took issue with the style and quality of the translations which the *Minstrelsy* team had produced, and while appreciating the fact that the project was governed by a desire to rehabilitate Irish bardic material within an English-speaking population, deplored the resultant lapse into the conventionalism of schoolroom poetry. 'We regret that while we applaud the purpose, we must unequivocally condemn the execution', he wrote. 'All the versifiers seem to have been actuated by a morbid desire, neither healthy nor honest, to elevate the tone of the original to a pitch of refined poetic art altogether foreign from the whole genius and rationale of its composition.'[4] Furnishing his argument with examples of stylistic mismanagement in several individual pieces, he exposed in the translations a disregard for accuracy and a lack of feeling for Irish composition and rhythm.

The translation issue provided, in turn, a springboard for a series of connected preoccupations, as Ferguson sought to undermine what he identified as the editor's pervasive political bias. Hardiman's narrative of English repression was displaced by his own study of the causal relationship between Irish character and the country's retarded social development. As in the *Hibernian nights' entertainments* he depicted Ireland as a transitional society, which had been arrested in its progress towards constitutional maturity by tendencies inherent within the native Irish population. Decrying the clan mentality which persisted under a tyrannical Roman Catholic hierarchy, he outlined his vision of a new all-embracing nation, and transformed the review into an impassioned plea for

---

3 Ferguson's communications with Blackwood on the subject are in his letter of 5 November, 1833, NLS MS 4035 f213. He refers in his fourth article to his research in the Lambeth and Cotton manuscripts, 'Irish Minstrelsy, no. 4', *DUM* 4 (Dec. 1834), 516. Questions as to the standard of his Irish persist. He had been engaged in his own translation work since the previous year, when he wrote to the antiquarian George Petrie, '[p]ray make my respects to O'Donovan, and tell him I have begun Irish, and have translated all I want of Hardiman' (cited M.C. Ferguson, *SSFID*, vol. 1, p. 46). There is little doubt, however, that he used cribs for much of his translation work: included in a 1910 Belfast Museum catalogue of Ferguson memorabilia is a copy of a translation of an old Ossianic tale, made by Eugene O'Curry for Ferguson, on which the poet based his 1861 poem 'The Cromlech on Howth'. In the case of the Hardiman translations his wife records that he was aided by schoolfriends Fox and O'Hagan, *SSFID* vol. 1, p. 36. R. Welch discusses Ferguson as a translator in *A history of verse translation from the Irish* (1988), pp. 90–101. 4 'Irish Minstrelsy, no. 3', *DUM* 4 (Nov. 1834), 435n.

Protestant participation in Ireland's cultural heritage. By way of conclusion to the series he provided an appendix containing his own versions of particular poems, pitting his skill and sensitivity against what he perceived as Hardiman's aesthetic irresponsibility.

Ferguson's review of Hardiman has been drawn out repeatedly by critics anxious to establish the battle-lines of nineteenth-century cultural politics. While the essays have attracted some praise for their critical and cultural adventurism, the prevailing response has been a cynical one, based on the premise that Ferguson's governing intention was to sequester the material of Gaelic culture on behalf of a hegemonic Protestant Ascendancy. Seamus Deane, for example, while applauding Ferguson's idealism, has insisted that the policy of cultural inclusiveness advocated by the review masks the writer's anxieties concerning the instability of the country and the threat of Catholic insurrection to the Union. By shifting the dispute over Catholic claims to the level of literature, Ferguson was attempting to create a feeling of mutual compatibility between Protestant and Catholic, thereby neutralizing the threat posed by a separatist Celtic identity as a basis for Catholic insurrection.[5] Like Deane, Leerssen has some praise for Ferguson's skills, describing the review as 'brilliantly-argued', but primarily, he sees the piece as a naïve challenge to Hardiman's claim to the material culture of Ireland as the exclusive territory of Catholic nationalism. Ferguson attempts to recover possession and priority, through criticizing Hardiman's translators and offering his own (better) versions of Gaelic poetry, in a process described elsewhere by Tom Dunne as 'the colonization of Gaelic literature in the interests of the Anglo-Irish Ascendancy'.[6] And in more aggressive terms, Cairns and Richards have used the Hardiman review to confirm their belief that Ferguson's pursuit of Gaelic literature was rooted entirely in the interests of his Ascendancy allies. What was advocated, they suggest, 'was little less than an act of cultural appropriation; an attempt to structure discussion and interpretation of the cultural products of Ireland's past'.[7]

From this perspective, the review appears contaminated by bigotry and shaped by a glaring racial primitivism. It reads as a systematic endorsement of a Protestant Ascendancy agenda, or worse, as base sectarianism channelled into a self-conscious and premeditated policy of cultural exploitation, in the interests of a specifically demarcated caste. The overtly nationalist and Catholic ethos represented by Hardiman could only be negated through the

---

5 *A short history*, p. 69. 6 Leerssen comments at length on the review, *Remembrance and imagination*, pp. 181–5. See Dunne's comments in 'Haunted by history: Irish Romantic writing, 1800–50', in R. Porter and M. Teich (eds), *Romanticism in national context* (1988), p. 83. 7 *Writing Ireland*, p. 30.

Ascendancy's manipulation of his resources, within the pernicious schema proposed by Ireland's colonial élite. In these terms, Ferguson is seen to have assumed the role of Ascendancy apologist and imperial strategist in a straightforward collaboration with the Protestant junta of the *Dublin University Magazine*. As Cairns and Richards would see it, the 1834 review is therefore seminal to a discourse of Celticism established by the work of the eighteenth-century antiquarians of the Royal Irish Academy, and supplemented in the nineteenth century by the work of the Ordnance Survey, as part of an ongoing plan 'to ensure that this emerging strategic formation of texts could be mobilized to the advantage of the Ascendancy'.[8] Ferguson's project was devised therefore, purely in the interests of Anglo-Irish supremacy and imperial hegemony; his literary sympathies were harnessed to and governed by this overarching political concern.

The timing of the review – published in a particularly sectarian *DUM* during 1834 – inevitably adds to its potential as a document of imperial strategy. The high political temperature of the 1830s, in the wake of Catholic Emancipation, was forcefully registered in Coleridge's 1830 treatise *On the constitution of church and state*. Seeking to cement the relationship between English nation, state and religion, Coleridge's livid response to the proposal that the houses of parliament be opened to Roman Catholics drew long-term precedents from Burke and a tradition of Romantic constitutional conservatism in order to reinforce the country's existing institutions against any encroachment of a Catholic hierarchy. The Coleridgean shadow thus appears to fall quite naturally over Ferguson's claims for inclusiveness: together with other unionist political theorists, David Lloyd asserts, Ferguson 'began to envisage a gradual evolutionary process by which Catholic Irish sentiments could be weaned from "primitive" loyalty to clan and faction and be attached instead to king and constitution'.[9] His project for the rapprochement of Protestant and Catholic within the national community, as the Hardiman review would have it, was merely the cultural manipulation of affairs towards this political end.

If this critical reading of the Hardiman review cannot be reversed, then it should at least be mitigated by a recognition of the uneasy, knee-jerk rhetoric, theoretical eclecticism and indeed, inconsistency which in fact characterize the articles. Ferguson's speculative social analysis is distinctly second-hand and his account of Ireland's retarded evolution is little more than a flirtation with political and ethnological frameworks in widespread circulation at this time. His indulgent conjecture on social evolution is derivative of the continuing historicist debate on civic development which permeated Anglo-Irish policy during

---

8 Ibid., p. 30. 9 *Nationalism and minor literature* (1987), pp. 56–7.

this period, and the attempt to graft this on to an apologia for constitutional stability is distinctly ham-fisted. Understandably, commentators looking for polemic have invested the articles with significance – W.J. McCormack, for example, describes them as 'a charter document in the history of Anglo-Irish literature' – but realistically, the idea that Ferguson had embarked by 1834 on a shrewd and calculated Ascendancy propaganda campaign is unlikely.[10] The political gestures of the review are ingratiating rather than defiant, highlighting the author's need to negotiate a fissured readership, rather than confirming his ability to proselytize on behalf of a distinct and pre-existent hegemony.

More important, the publishing context of the articles weighs against their authority. The review was written at the instigation of William Blackwood and destined for the Scottish journal, a factor with relevance for its style and subject matter. Its speculative theorizing on social development and the nature of government in Ireland was in keeping with *Blackwood's* long-running but generally abstract interest in the progress of the imperial peripheries – for example, the condition of the West Indies or Sierra Leone. When William Blackwood refused the articles, the newly-established *Dublin University Magazine* was clearly regarded as a poor option for Ferguson who, still in touch with his Northern circle and writing from the distance of his London law terms, was far from comfortable with the factionalist tendencies of the journal. Against this background, the Hardiman articles read as an awkward splicing of ideological perspectives, their appeal to Irish Protestants exposing, ironically, the contradictions rather consensus within that constituency.

If the Hardiman review has anything substantial to offer, it lies in Ferguson's attempts to articulate the basis of an Irish civic state. In the third article in particular, his analysis of Ireland's faulty social transition and resultant social irregularity dovetails into the concurrent preoccupations of the *Hibernian nights' entertainments*, but also provides the foundation for a vision of an Irish civic community underpinned by Adam Ferguson as much as Coleridge. Beneath the territorial skirmish which the exchange with Hardiman fore-grounded lies a clumsy but essentially well-meaning attempt to interpolate into the complex cultural *realpolitik* of 1830s Ireland the progressivist and educationalist philosophies of the Scottish Enlightenment, and a tradition of civic idealism dating back to Aristotle. Ferguson's efforts to sustain such a language within the critical parameters of a Protestant unionist imperialist mindset undoubtedly testify to his naivety at the time, but also hint at his ideological distance from a coterie his critics have too readily supposed him to represent.

---

10 *From Burke to Beckett*, p. 140.

ISAAC BUTT AND THE *DUM*

Ferguson was twenty-four at the time of writing the Hardiman review, and the essays, with their derivative conflation of conjectural and constitutional theory, waspish commentary and sentimental hyperbole, are tantamount to the rhetorical gymnastics of the trainee barrister. True, his translations are well executed, and create a repository of phrases appropriate to the emergent cause of Irish Protestant cultural nationalism, but the project is characterized by opportunism and intellectual bravado. Much of the review consists of point scoring against Hardiman and the 'petty anti-Anglicanism' of his annotations.[11] This was Ferguson's first major critical venture, and it would seem that his anxiety to gain some leverage in the increasingly influential circles of literary journalism weighed heavily on his prose.

This was not, however, an area for individuality. The conventions of reviewing, together with the principles of house style and collective responsibility fostered by individual journals were well established.[12] And Ferguson's apprenticeship to *Blackwood's Edinburgh Magazine*, which had a reputation for scurrility and savagery, obviously influenced his early style. The Scottish journal's character was stamped clearly on the ludic diversions of the '*Noctes Ambrosianæ*', a series of mock 'coffee-house' debates composed by several of *Blackwood's* senior contributors, including William Maginn and John Gibson Lockhart. Ferguson clung to the coat-tails of this group during his early association with the magazine, and his endeavours to develop an appropriately derisive style are evident in an unpublished verse satire which he sent to Blackwood in 1832. Entitled 'Captain North's log: on board the good ship *Maga*', the lampoon comprises an attack on James Tait, who had recently launched *Tait's Edinburgh Magazine* as a Whig counterpart to the Tory *Blackwood's*.[13] The satire is unsophisticated, even crass, but it reveals Ferguson as the young hack eager to ingratiate himself with the editorial hierarchy of 'Maga', as the *Blackwood's* journal was known.

The 1832 skit also draws attention to the homage paid by Ferguson to 'Christopher North', otherwise John Wilson, professor of Moral Philosophy

---

11 '*Irish Minstrelsy*, no. 3', *DUM* 4 (Nov. 1834), 515. G. Smyth in particular notes the abrasiveness of the review, and comments that 'it is difficult to see how Ferguson might reconcile the virulence of his discourse with the consensus which was his ostensible goal', *Decolonisation and criticism*, p. 221n.   12 For background on the nineteenth-century periodical and its conventions, see J. Shattock and M. Wolff (eds), *The Victorian periodical press* (1982); J. Gross, *The rise and fall of the man of letters* (1969), and R. Wellek, *A history of modern criticism* (1965), vol. 3.   13 Ferguson to William Blackwood, 1 April 1832, NLS MS 4890. Ferguson wrote to his brother John to tell him of his first contacts with the *Blackwood's* set. 'I spent ten days delightfully in Edinburgh. Wilson asked me to Ambrose's, where I had a "nox Ambrosiana", and introduced me to his family [...] I must get myself introduced to Lockhart and [Leigh] Hunt (who has my manuscript still) before I leave town if possible, both being in their opposite ways men of high character.' Cited M.C. Ferguson, *SSFID*, vol. 1, pp. 25–6.

at Edinburgh University and the magazine's leading contributor. North was officially acknowledged and celebrated as a mentor of the *DUM*, with the Irish magazine's editorial persona Anthony Poplar proclaiming him as a father figure in the opening article of the first issue.[14] Independently however, the young and impressionable Ferguson developed a deep respect for the vicious Scottish critic, to whom he frequently sent his regards through Blackwood, and of whose reputation he was highly conscious, writing on one occasion of his anxiety that the savage pen of the 'professor' might lacerate a friend's recent contribution to the magazine. Ferguson was attentive to the pugnacious style of North's reviews, noting in 1832 his particularly damning attack on Tennyson's recent *Poems, chiefly lyrical*. Tennyson's work was dealt with in oblique but scathing terms before North toned down the rancour and applied himself to the subject with greater delicacy in the concluding section of his assessment. Ferguson wrote to Alexander Blackwood: 'Tennyson may be well pleased with the last half of his notice which gave me a pleasant surprise as I had seen only the severe introduction and was trembling for a writer whom I admire so much.'[15]

The shadow of North is therefore perceptible behind the brash dismissals and critical affectations which characterize Ferguson's attacks on Hardiman and his translators, and indeed the general context of critical and journalistic tradition in which the Hardiman review must be located helps to explain his expansiveness and abrasiveness. As noted earlier, Ferguson mentioned to Blackwood that the review provided him with an opportunity to experiment with differing 'treatments', and the stylistic collage of humourist, advocate, historian and hack results in a highly self-conscious exercise in the dynamics of the literary review. Not surprisingly, Ferguson came to regret his critical high-handedness, writing nine years later to Hardiman: 'I have often felt since I first had the pleasure of knowing you personally, that your treatment of me as a friend, after the petulant – tho' really not ill-designed attack on your first publication in which I had been engaged shortly before, ought to give me a lesson in forebearance and good feeling in after-life.'[16]

This near-apology serves to highlight the split between private and public roles which affected literary journalism in general and Ferguson in particular in the early years of his career. Nineteenth-century periodical journalism was very much about conformity to a collective ethos. While certain established critics such as North achieved individual notoriety, writers were generally bound by the practices of anonymity and collective responsibility to which most jour-

---

[14] Anon., 'The present crisis: a dialogue', *DUM* 1 (Jan. 1833) 2. The *Wellesley Index* lists Samuel O'Sullivan as the author.   [15] North's review of Tennyson appeared in *Blackwood's* 31 (May 1832), 721–41. See Ferguson's letters to Alexander Blackwood, 8 May 1832, NLS MS 4032, f255, and 11 Mar. 1834, NLS MS 4038, f239.   [16] Ferguson to Hardiman, 28 Aug. 1843, RIA MS 12N 20.

nals adhered. The review platform created a vehicle for the individual ego, but in overall deference to the identity of the magazine. Inevitably, anonymity was frequently breached with the use of sobriquets and initials, or with the inclusion of stylistic and personal hints in the text itself. At the same time, the preservation of anonymity was important to a young and relatively insecure journalist struggling to maintain a professional life outside the magazine or journal.[17] The convention of the editorial first-person plural theoretically determined the relationship between the editorial board and the contributors by conveying the submission of individual identities to an overall consensus. Critics were heavily dependent on this arrangement, not least because it provided both protection and a centralized source of 'enormous and overbearing authority'.[18]

These conventions underline the systematic means though which Ferguson as an individual contributor was aligned with the interests of the *Dublin University Magazine*. Launched in 1833 as the organ of intellectual Irish Toryism, the *DUM* littered its early essays and editorials with the first person plural, and in his study of the journal John McBride suggests that such articles were 'designed to foster a collective mystique, a sense of solidarity between magazine and reader by the use of the imperious or sometimes quite intimate editorial "we"'.[19] By such means the *DUM* sought to disguise its own insecurity: one estimate suggests that less than a quarter of some one hundred and fifty Irish periodicals launched between 1800 and 1848 lasted more than a year.[20] While the magazine derived authority from its close imitation of *Blackwood's Edinburgh Magazine* in both content and format, it desperately needed to define an ethos and cement a readership through the plural pronouns of its text.

It was important too, that this homogenizing procedure carried the magazine's political agenda, for the *DUM* was concerned to forge a consensus from interests which many regarded as conflicting: on one hand the journal was patriotically committed to Irish culture and history, but on the other it sought to express an aggressive unionist response to the growing self-confidence of the Catholic population after emancipation.[21] The use of the first person plural was necessary, therefore, as a safeguard against the emergence of visible inter-

---

17 J. Shattock, *Politics and reviewers*, p. 16; see also J.P. Klancher, *The making of English reading audiences* (1987), p. 51. Ferguson's anxieties in this respect were occasionally heightened, as is indicated his letter to Robert Blackwood in 1838 concerning the manuscript of his lampoon on the Leitrim parish priest and preacher Father Tom Maguire, 'Father Tom and the Pope', at a time when he was about to be called to the Irish Bar. 'I am very desirous not to be known as the author', he wrote. 'It will be laid at Carleton's door or at Maxwell's and they can both bear the implication'. Ferguson to Alexander Blackwood, 28 Mar. 1838, NLS MS 4046 f155. See Denman, *Samuel Ferguson*, pp. 52–4, on the background to the piece in the context of anti-Catholic squibs of the 1830s. 18 J. Woolford, 'Periodicals and the practice of literary criticism, 1855–64', in *Politics and reviewers*, p. 115. 19 'The *Dublin University Magazine*', vol. 1, p. 118. 20 B. Hayley, 'Irish periodicals from the Union to the *Nation*' (1976), 83. 21 See 'New Year's Day, or our first number', *DUM* 1 (Jan. 1833), 87, for Stanford's editorial on patriotism (attrib. *Wellesley Index*).

nal tensions. In the light of this system of enforced consensus it has been assumed that Ferguson was fundamentally coherent with *DUM* policy even as it developed into vehement anti-Catholicism. The four *Irish Minstrelsy* articles are unsigned, with only the poems in the concluding appendix appearing under the initials 'S.F.' Ferguson's frequent, almost emphatic use of the editorial first person plural would seem to reinforce the notion that the *Irish Minstrelsy* review was articulating for the readership views close to the heart of *DUM* policy. Indeed, the piece has been read as a manifesto for the magazine itself, and John McBride insists that the transfer of the first two articles from the Scottish to the Irish journal was crucial to their meaning and success: if the first installment of Ferguson's analysis had been published in *Blackwood's*, he argues, 'its tone would seem no less passionate, but the piece would not possess the contextual relevance it holds as a direct address to the Protestant nation in their own journal. The tenets of the review are at the very centre of the magazine's social and cultural preoccupations and the piece further establishes this centrality.'[22] So closely aligned is the language to a *DUM* house-rhetoric that it hints at the super-imposition of a register and phraseology guaranteed to be acceptable to the editorial board.

In public, therefore, the Hardiman review and the *DUM* coalesce but in private, the idea of a consensus is seriously undermined by aspects of Ferguson's relationship with the journal, which he regarded as a very poor relation to *Blackwood's*. It was not unusual for the two magazines to share contributors – Samuel O'Sullivan and John Anster, for example, wrote at various times for both – but Ferguson continued to give priority to the Edinburgh journal.[23] McBride's claim obscures the fact that the material of at least the first half of the review was intended to appeal to a Scottish and English audience and was penned by an author psychologically distanced from Ireland, viewing the country from a detached vantage point. Ferguson's interest in Gaelic material originated in Belfast in the context of Ulster Presbyterian radicalism and in the company of liberals and nationalists such as Teeling and O'Hagan, while his research into the *Minstrelsy* sources was instigated at the suggestion of William Blackwood in Scotland and undertaken in London. His continued relationship with these external authorities disrupts the centrality of the articles to a Dublin

---

22 'The *Dublin University Magazine*', vol. 1, pp. 116–17.   23 In a letter written from Belfast, Ferguson offered the review to Blackwood, stating that 'you will find in No. 1 of the *Minstrelsy* that I have said some things perhaps too broadly', and suggesting the need for corrections at the proof stage; 15 Nov. 1833, NLS MS 4032 f215. He wrote again in January sending something 'which I hope you will like better than the *Minstrelsy*'; NLS MS 4038 f235. Denman points out that Ferguson initially regarded the *DUM* as a 'second string to his bow' (*Samuel Ferguson*, p. 17), but in fact throughout his career he continued to defer to the Scottish journal as the primary option for his material: as late as 1867 he stated in a letter to John Blackwood, 'I have a feeling of loyalty which makes it my duty to give you the refusal of [the poem] "Megesdra"': NLS MS 4220 f153.

unionist exercise. Peter Denman has observed evidence of possible cosmetic revision in several places following the transfer of the material to Ireland, but nonetheless Ferguson's original publication context still looms as an invisible presence in the text.[24]

More significantly the concept of the Hardiman review as a seminal *DUM* manifesto, confirming the harmonious union of both editorial and authorial will, is upset by Ferguson's difficult relationship with the magazine in 1834, as editorial control passed from Charles Stuart Stanford to unionist barrister and Trinity College professor of Law Isaac Butt. His transition from the comparatively broad intellectual panoply of the conservative *Blackwood's* to the narrow sectarian corridor of the *DUM* was by no means smooth, as his personal political sentiments clashed with the extremist policies advocated by the journal. Ferguson believed that Butt had introduced to the previously moderate voice of the *DUM* a raucous Orangeism, solicited and encouraged by a hard line editorial board dominated by Samuel and Mortimer O'Sullivan. In August 1834 he voiced this complaint in an extensive letter to his friend R.J. Tennant in Belfast:

> Let me solicit your good offices in enabling me to withstand the force of high orange bigotry against which I have just declared war. The case stands thus. I have been for some time an efficient contributor to the *University Magazine*. The editorship has lately passed from the hands of Stanford, a liberal and gentlemanly man, into those of Mr Butt, a servile and officious tool of the most intolerantly truculent of the Brunswick priests.

Butt, Ferguson continued, was bound in obedience to the will of a 'clerical conclave' which had formulated a noxious policy statement, a 'modest falsetto [...] which is to be brayed by all the donkeys of the Orange press', and which he quoted as follows: 'Roman Catholicism, however abused cannot be rendered less pernicious in its effects on Civil Society by any reform short of the Protestantism of the Established Church of Ireland.' Ferguson's reaction to the proposed item was one of unmitigated fury:

> On the rampant absurdity of this brutal dogma I need not dwell; you alone perceive its hideous deformity, and will I am sure aid me in my efforts which I am now making to trample it into the ruin of smothering denunciation. I have withdrawn from all connection with the concern until Butt either resigns or recants. The proprietors feel that I am

---

24 Denman speculates on the probable composition dates of the essays, and discusses Ferguson's possible revisions of the first two on the transfer to the *DUM*, *Samuel Ferguson*, p. 20.

right, and would be glad to oust Butt, were it not that they dread the power of his instigators and abettors. I would publish the correspondence I have had on the subject but that I feel the public would attribute it to chagrin at Butt's refusal to admit my sentiments.

The solution, Ferguson continued, was that his friends should review the forthcoming number of the magazine – containing the article in which a version of the offending passage was to appear – and make known their objections to the expression of any such principle. They were also urged to condone the views he himself expressed in his review of the writers Samuel Lover and William Carleton, which was due to appear in the same issue. This done, 'I believe that the proprietors would be much less terrified by the threats of our protestant inquisitors and that I would have much less difficulty in vindicating my right to constant and uncontested admission in their pages.'[25]

The row was relatively short-lived: by the 24 August, Ferguson was able to write to Tennant informing him that 'the maniacs have recanted and I predominate'.[26] But the victory was far from conclusive. In the September issue of the magazine a vehement denunciation of Catholic Ireland appeared in an article written by Mortimer O'Sullivan, in which 'popery' is systematically condemned for causing national disaffection, for elevating the power of the priesthood and for degrading the population into blind submission. The readership is advised that 'it should be the grand and paramount object of the British government and the British public to effectuate its extermination by every honest and Christian means'. This was not an isolated incident moreover, but part of a sustained campaign against Roman Catholicism orchestrated in conjunction with a defence of Protestant extremism, as the *DUM* under Butt's editorship took on the role of apologist for Orangeism.[27]

Ferguson was to remain at odds with the *DUM* for the next ten years. Having informed Tennant that he intended to 'cut politics' from his magazine work after the row with Butt, he restricted his contributions to literature and landscape. Privately, he continued to express his alienation from the journal in letters to Alexander Blackwood, stating in 1837 that he had not 'employed my pen in those pages for some years back, nor do I mean to do so while the chief ambition of their conductor seems to be to ridicule and make little of his own country and countrymen'. A year later, with reference to his failure to offer con-

---

25 Ferguson to R.J. Tennant, 21 August, 1834, PRONI MS D1748/c/197/6. Ferguson was to become much closer to Isaac Butt in later life, when the latter's politics became more moderate. In 1876, after Butt was 'blackballed' from the Royal Irish Academy, Ferguson penned for him a 'consolatory sonnet': *SSFID*, vol. 1, p. 31. 26 24 Aug. 1834, PRONI MS D1748/c/197/7. 27 Anon. 'On the Roman Catholic religion in Ireland', *DUM* 4 (Sept. 1834), 312. *Wellesley Index* cites Mortimer O'Sullivan as the author.

tributions to the *DUM*, he wrote that 'I have not had any connection with that Establishment for some time, and don't think it likely that I will renew the connection'. In 1841, in the course of a summary of local newspapers and their politics, he described the magazine as 'another of the organs of the Extreme party, but I have had nothing to do with it for some years'. The relationship was to deteriorate even further when the editorship passed to Charles Lever in 1842. Lever's championing of Thackeray, whose *Irish sketch book* was published in the same year, was to incense Ferguson beyond measure, ultimately pushing him further towards the welcoming and sympathetic circle of Davis and the *Nation*.[28]

This, then, was the private history of what appeared in public to be a harmonious affiliation. The conflict with Butt took place halfway through the serialization of the Hardiman articles, undermining any possibility of a consensus. Content to follow the moderate party line of Protestant Tory patriotism espoused under Stanford, Ferguson's dismay at his successor's sectarianism places his review of Hardiman in a peculiar juxtaposition to the *DUM*'s directive. It might even be suggested that far from professing the aims of a cohesive Protestant unit, the third Hardiman article – dramatically different in style from the first two – is actually an attempt to mitigate the extremism to which the magazine was headed. The language thus combines post-Emancipation crowd-pleasing stabs at Roman Catholic superstition – gestures not uncommon in *Blackwood's* and *de rigueur* in the *DUM* – with a panicked attempt to maintain more liberal appeals to inclusiveness and tolerance. Ferguson's concluding points, such as the expression of sympathy for both Catholic subjugation and Protestant suffering which accompanies the lament 'Timoleague', or his envisaging of a 'neutral spot of ground', recorded in the notes to 'The fair hills of holy Ireland', are both, in effect, palliative: ultimately any brash statement of Protestant superiority is replaced with hints of the private sentiments hitherto lost in public rhetoric. The confident language of the Hardiman review is entirely illusory; no coherent Protestant mission to appropriate a native culture, merely a balancing act as the young writer attempted to reconcile the conflicting demands of cultural sensibility and career interest.

The insecurity of his situation in the early 1830s is a reminder that much of Ferguson's early work must be treated with caution, and read for style as much as substance. In this respect, the Hardiman review forms a category which includes two earlier *DUM* contributions. In January of 1834, Ferguson's 'Inaugural ode for the new year' purports to be rousing loyalist war-cry, but its reduction to stilted Spenserian stanzas suggests a literary or historical curio rather than

---

28 Blackwood letters, n.d. 1837, NLS MS 4044 f213; 28 Mar. 1838, NLS MS 4046 f155; 29 Jan. 1841, NLS MS 4056 f15; 3 June 1843, NLS MS 4065 f247.   29 *DUM* 2 (Nov. 1833), 589.

an explicit exercise in propaganda. 'A dialogue between the Head and Heart of an Irish Protestant', published in November 1833, is more ebullient but just as conventionalized. In the debate, 'Heart' is in sympathy with native Catholic Ireland and 'Head' at odds with it, fearful of revolution and loss of Protestant control, but confident of the right to nationality:

Head:
'Protestant Ascendancy, which promised to make us another England, is by the fraud and violence of traitors, rendered ineffectual for good or evil, and come after it what may, whether a Popish Establishment, a tolerating French philosophical morality, or Deism at large, Ireland never can be that which Protestant Ascendancy might have made her. Yet stripped as we are of power and privilege, neither Whig tyranny nor Popish malice can deprive us of our birthright, which is the love of Ireland.'[29]

The position taken by 'Head' has subsequently been identified by critics as Ferguson's own stance. For Robert O'Driscoll, the abstract rule of Ferguson's intellectual powers leads to his 'instinctive, almost irresponsible, youthful effulgences on the privileges of Protestantism, his distrust of the Catholic clergy, and his disgust at constant attempts at rebellion' in the work, while David Lloyd describes how the author closes the dialogue with an appeal 'to engage in a struggle with the growing body of Catholic and incipiently nationalist opinion which would call into question the right of the Anglo-Irish to consider themselves Irish and would encourage the antagonism of the common people against the Ascendancy'.[30] In their identification of author and text both readings overlook the generic or structural traditions of the dialogue, however, and obscure the extent to which Ferguson, the trainee barrister, was rehearsing an argument from the sidelines. Thus, he invokes a highly formulaic eighteenth-century debate between reason and passion, suggesting precedents drawn from David Hume and Adam Ferguson.[31] By working within a very recognizable literary and philo-

---

30 O'Driscoll, pp. 19–20; Lloyd, *Nationalism and minor literature*, p. 155.   31 Ferguson evokes Hume in his phrase, the 'ascendancy of the heart' (*'Irish Minstrelsy*, no. 2', *DUM* 4, Aug. 1834, 161). Hume's use of the dialogue form relied on the idea of rehearsing and articulating contradictory positions, without necessarily identifying with either, or to represent frustration, ambivalence and despair; 'Head' playing devil's advocate in order to elicit exaggerated sympathies from 'Heart'. See J.R. Smitten, 'Hume's Dialogues concerning natural religion as social discourse', in J. Dwyer and R.B. Sher (eds), *Sociability and society*. Adam Ferguson also made frequent use of the reason/passion convention; consider for example his statement that to be learned and to have an 'ascendant' among men is to distinguish 'the promptitude of head from the ardour and sensibility of the heart', *Essay on the history of civil society* (1793), Section 5; 'Of intellectual powers', p. 47. Ó Tuaithaigh has suggested that the 'Dialogue' is an echo of the

sophical tradition, Ferguson was examining the contradictions of his culture and society from a stylized, rhetorical and political distance. In the immediate wake of the Reform Bill, and as Repeal agitation surged, the 'Dialogue' was composed, as Peter Denman has rightly suggested, 'to engage with the issues of the moment, rather than to offer itself as a portrait of the artist'.[32]

Both articles underline the anxieties the writer was beginning to experience outside the liberal consensus of Belfast, and together with the Hardiman review they represent his means of enquiry into political sentiments to which he was not necessarily committed. The response to Hardiman cannot be regarded as Ferguson's compliant reproduction of *DUM* ideology, and his ubiquitous invocation of the editorial 'we' operates as a device idealizing an imagined consensus rather than confirming an existing one. His intended Scottish destination makes it unlikely that his articles were written as a direct and specific counter to Protestant extremism in the *DUM* but his review nonetheless offers a palliative, for the subtext to an overt condemnation of Catholic cultural monopolization is an anxious readjustment of aggressive Protestant perspectives. His continuing reliance on outside support, from Tennant in the comparatively liberal pocket of Belfast and more symbolically perhaps, from a Scottish tradition secure in its own 'national' heritage, reinforces an image of the young Ferguson as an isolated activist covering up the lack of any decisive internal mandate. A decade or so later in a letter to William Smith O'Brien, Thomas McNevin would refer jokingly to Isaac Butt and Samuel Ferguson as 'Orange Young Ireland', but in 1834, any such conflation was out of the question.[33]

CLAN, STATE, AND NATIONAL CHARACTER

Early in 1835, shortly after he moved back to Dublin from London, Ferguson wrote to Tennant in Belfast, '[t]here is a host of fine fellows in Dublin who will do something for the honour of their country yet, if they get but moderate encouragement. In many respects I am one of the least able, but in inextinguishable ardour for the cultivation of an Irish taste I am behind no man.'[34] Certainly, few would doubt his enthusiasm and tenacity. But what exactly did Ferguson understand an 'Irish taste' to be? And how was his investment in a cul-

---

views of the main protagonists – notably Grattan and Fitzgibbon – in the debate on the Union in 1800 ('Sir Samuel Ferguson'). Ferguson was also aware of the theological use of the dialogue form: compare his own 'Two voices – a dialogue between conscience and the intellectual soul', *Poems* (1880). 32 *Samuel Ferguson*, p. 3. Denman discusses the work here with reference to Ferguson's detachment as an Ulster Presbyterian and to the wider context of radical politics pursued by 'British democrats' such as Hume and Cobbett. 33 O'Brien Papers, NLI MS 2291. Cited G.C. Duffy, *Young Ireland* (1880) pp. 503–4. 34 Ferguson to R.J. Tennant, 25 Jan. 1835, PRONI MS D1748/c/197/11.

tural 'Irishness' to remain distinct from reliance on an ethnological 'Irishness' determined and shaped by the weight of constitutional and imperial policy? Ferguson's writing in the early 1830s suggests confusion on both issues, and the Hardiman review is dogged by his unsuccessful attempts to secure the volatile concepts of national character and authenticity within the flux of contemporary – and indeed, not so contemporary – debates on these subjects.

The easiest place to start, of course, was to define what 'Irishness' was not. Ferguson's concern with the many travesties and shallow burlesques of national character in literary circulation is registered in his September 1834 article on Samuel Lover and William Carleton. Entitled 'Irish storyists', the piece draws a pointed contrast between Lover's *Legends and stories of Ireland*, published in 1834, and the third edition of Carleton's *Traits and stories of the Irish peasantry*, issued in the same year. In this review, Lover is denounced as a panderer to the whims of the metropolis, a charlatan who has grotesquely misrepresented his subject, and Carleton, meanwhile, congratulated for drawing on his close experience of the Irish peasant to give a 'true vindication of national character'. Carleton is exemplary in his loyalty to the Irish, having sacrificed a quiet life of ease and dignity to become, Ferguson claims, 'a friendless man of letters struggling to elevate the character of an ungrateful country, by waging war as well against the stupid prejudices of her national condemners, as against the ignorance and bigotry, and vicious superstition of her sons'. His only flaw consists in his recourse to 'squalid verisimilitude' in descriptions of peasant poverty, a tendency Ferguson rejects as an irrelevance:

> What though the blight of national calamity has, in some districts, left the Irish peasant, in physical culture, little better than the beast of the field, degenerate in stature, in aspect semi-brutalized – and, even as we write, we see the wanderers of Connaught, ragged, diminutive and of abortive feature, the mis-creations of hardship and neglect, crowding to the quays, upon their weary way to the English harvest – what though in food and raiment these poor Irishmen be the raggedest remnant of humanity that ever fluttered its fantastic wretchedness in the chill air of contempt, yet there is scarce one among them in whose breast, naked and sunburnt though it be, his nation's genius has not placed a perennial fountain of affections, deep, pure, and inexhaustible; but, to the superficial anecdotist, secret as the subterranean flow of springs beneath the desert.[35]

---

35 Irish storyists – Lover and Carleton', *DUM* 4 (Sept. 1834), 299 and 303.

Here 'Irishness' is established as a constant, a boundless source of emotional resilience in the face of economic deprivation. Carleton's Irishman is thus redeemed from any connection with Lover's glib sketches, but sheltered too, from the implications of the author's heightened realism.

Clearly, the passage displays a tendency towards racial essentialism, and this aspect of the 'Irish storyists' review underlies the central preoccupations of the attack on Hardiman. In its stylistic transformations of Irish poetry, and more, its political location of Ireland's literary effects, Hardiman's publication undermined the possibility of a distinct and immutable Irish personality. This is exemplified in the battle over the identity of Turlogh O'Carolan, the eighteenth-century blind musician and bard whose attributed canon dominates the *Minstrelsy* collection. Where Hardiman presents Carolan as a rational, elegant and sophisticated versifier who unconsciously imitated the Troubadour poets, Ferguson successfully recasts the bard as an irrational and melancholy romantic – emotional, indulgent and poetically spontaneous – an Irish Robert Burns. Hardiman defends Carolan against charges of drunkenness, with the added explanation that the Irish have sought refuge in alcohol largely as a result of their oppression since the eighteenth century and the imposition of the penal laws. In return, Ferguson presents a lengthy legalistic case drawing on documentary evidence to prove what he insists is a racial tendency towards indulgence and insobriety unrelated to Ireland's political history. Whatever ground Hardiman gains for his model of a justly aggrieved nation through his symbolic use of the figure of Carolan is undercut by his reviewer's rapid restoration of the bard to his role as a familiar Celtic type.

The case is taken further with the issue of translation. In his review, Ferguson objects to the manner in which the *Minstrelsy* poems have been, as Máire Mhac an tSaoi would later put it, 'bowdlerized and drawing-roomized out of all semblance of reality or genuine feeling'.[36] Through the process of translation all indications of a national, 'subterranean' character have been erased, and Hardiman is held responsible for versions which obscure rather than testify to the essence of national character. 'It must be plain to every reader that [the] pieces are more valuable as keys to Irish sentiment than as elegant additions to polite literature', Ferguson observes. Hardiman's misunderstanding of this fact has resulted in translations which deny their original sources, and his translators are individually accused of travesty. D'Alton is guilty of 'pretension'; Curran 'Saxonises, interpolates, mangles'; Furlong, 'in raciness, in naiveté, in quaint expression, falls short of the original'.[37] In each instance the loss of the remote and refractory elements of the material in Irish is emphasized, the increased accessibility and uniformity of Hardiman's texts disregarded.

36 'Introduction', *Irish Minstrelsy* (1971), p. 6.

The critique implies the existence of qualities in the original literature which have remained hidden to the Hardiman project, but which Ferguson's deeper sensitivity is able to manifest. In his consideration of Irish love poetry he attempts to re-establish the causal link between the material's naive, spontaneous intensity and an indelible national character. These lyrics exhibit 'nothing impure, nothing licentious in their languishing but savage sincerity', he insists. The characteristics of amatory poetry in Ireland are an indication of a national spirit, for 'in its association with the despondency of conscious degradation, and the recklessness of desperate content, is partly to be found the origin of that wild, mournful, incondite, yet not uncouth, sentiment which distinguishes the national songs of Ireland from those of perhaps any other nation in the world'.[38] Through the extension of the poetry to the national personality, recognizable traits of Irish character are highlighted, confirming the sympathetic but idealized portrait which Ferguson offered in his review of Lover and Carleton. Like Carolan, the poetry itself is vital evidence of an authentic and discernible national personality.

Ferguson's exposition of this quintessential Irishness and his comments on the refractory nature of Gaelic literature have led David Lloyd to suggest that his deliberate intention is 'to encounter Gaelic poetry in its foreignness' in order to establish the recalcitrant and inassimilable qualities of the Celt. This represents, in Lloyd's view, an exercise in cultural aesthetics which is part of a conscious policy exercised on behalf of the imperial state, and which locates Ferguson within a specific Celticist tradition as notoriously manifest in Matthew Arnold's 1867 lecture 'On the study of Celtic literature'. Where Hardiman had engaged in what Lloyd describes as 'quite a restrained attack on the devastation of Irish culture under English rule', Ferguson responded with 'an attempt, through a synthesis of aesthetic and ethnological criticism, to appropriate Hardiman's material to a conservative vision of the political resolution to Ireland's problems which markedly prefigures Arnold's'. The political machinations here are evident, it seems, for what is intended is the establishment of a malleable Celtic personality, subject to the coercions of the Empire. Ferguson's criticisms of Hardiman's translations are seen to consolidate a distinct Irish

---

37 'Irish Minstrelsy, no. 3', *DUM* 4 (Oct. 1834), 453–4; 453n. Compare Ferguson's 1867 review of Matthew Arnold's 'On the study of Celtic literature', in which he accuses Arnold of labouring his case, basing his argument for distinct racial characteristics on mis-styled translations of Celtic originals. 'There is an impossibility of preserving style in accurate translation, and when the translator, to catch the style, deviates at all from the line of accuracy – as Macpherson did with a success which would have been complete had he but candidly admitted the liberties he took with his original – what is gained in effect is lost in confidence.' *Athenaeum*, 2072 (3 July 1867), 45–6. This review is not included in Denman's bibliography but is made on the basis of a reference by M.C. Ferguson, *SSFID*, vol. 2, p. 87, and substantiated by numerous internal allusions in the piece.   38 'Irish Minstrelsy, no. 2', *DUM* 4 (Aug. 1834), 154.

personality or Celtic type, 'an index of a characteristic of the Irish genius which, insofar as it is represented as "living", makes it entirely assimilable not only to English poetry, but, more importantly, to the English constitution'.[39] The governing purpose of Ferguson's text is thus the vindication of imperial hegemony upon the basis of an aesthetic and ethnological construct.

Lloyd is persuasive on the logistics of this process in general, but weak on the real significance – or lack of it – in Ferguson's work. Ferguson's attitude was by no means a significant departure from what had become a fairly standard convention in translation: from the late eighteenth-century Ascendancy patriots and Charlotte Brooke, who offered her 1789 *Reliques of Irish poetry* 'to throw some light on the antiquities of this country' to the Catholic J.J. Callanan whose 1823 translations in *Blackwood's* were presented, he avowed, 'more as literary curiosities than on any other account', the recalcitrant nature of Irish material had been emphasized and its essential Gaelic 'difference' highlighted through explanatory footnotes or exegetical commentary. In this respect Ferguson's Hardiman review merely subscribed to what Leerssen has highlighted as a long-established literary and philological cult of the primitive in the study of a Gaelic heritage, adding little to the immediate dynamics of any Celticist political strategy.[40]

Moreover, Lloyd's tendency to read backwards, from Arnold to Ferguson, has the effect of establishing Ferguson as the dynamic originator of an imperial strategy rather than a relatively insignificant subscriber to the kind of ethnophilosophical debates on national character with which his readership was more than familiar. Like the *Hibernian nights' entertainments*, Ferguson's review of Hardiman draws on traditions of eighteenth-century anthropology, but in its rambling speculation on racial primitivism and stunted social development it also engages with the most common clichés of early nineteenth-century public debate on race. Its bifurcation in this respect is very much of the time, marking the point of suture between the tail-end of enlightenment comparativism and the beginnings of Victorian essentialism. Amidst the diffuse streams of enquiry initiated in the light of imperial expansion and continental research during the first half of the century, controversy raged between the former, characterized by theorists of monogenism and environmental determinism, and the latter, whose polygenist beliefs began to gain the upper hand. To a large extent, writes Nancy Stepan, 'the story of racial science in Britain between 1800 and 1850 is the story of desperate attempts to rebut polygenism, and the eventual acceptance of popular quasi-polygenist prejudices in the language of science'.[41]

---

39 'Arnold, Ferguson, Schiller', p. 155. 40 C. Brooke, 'Preface', *Reliques of Irish poetry* (1789). J.J. Callanan published six translated poems in *Blackwood's* in 1823: this comment is cited by M.F. McCarthy in his editorial introduction to *The poems of J.J. Callanan* (1861), pp. 93–4. See R. Welch, *A history of verse translation*, pp. 34–43 on Brooke, and pp. 59–61 on Callanan. 41 *The idea of race in science* (1982), p. 30. For further discussion of racial typography in relation to Ireland, see

Inevitably, the background to the debate was charged with politics, as the liberal philosophies and egalitarian doctrines of the enlightenment were squeezed by imperial policy-makers seeking justification for expansion or slavery, or simply by conservatives fearful of French revolutionary optimism, 'a defensive reaction', suggests one commentator, 'against the idea of equality on the part of groups whose unquestioned class superiority was being undercut by the social changes of the nineteenth century'.[42] And largely because of its immediate relevance, speculation on racial origins moved quickly from its theoretical platforms into the public domain, pointing to a level of popular interest in the subject which was both politically dynamic and, in journalistic terms, highly topical, many years before Darwin's revelations. While the proliferating anthropological, archaeological and linguistic commentaries on the subject were increasingly complex, the underlying questions were straightforward. Were racial characteristics the product of different climatic and environmental conditions which, over time, altered dramatically the basic human form and mentality? Or were they the visible evidence of essential and ineluctable differences between the races? Were civilization and intellectual maturity the goals to which all races might aspire? Or were only certain races capable of such achievements, together with the social responsibilities they entailed?

Ferguson's response to the issue is therefore intelligible as a point of intersection at which his scientific interest in social evolution and comparative anthropology fused with the more fashionable tenets of imperialist ideology. On a simplified level, the *Irish Minstrelsy* articles may be regarded as an essentialist response to Hardiman's determinist position; in other words, as an attempt by Ferguson to reduce to racial fundamentalism the claims which Hardiman had made on the grounds of political and economic deprivation. Disquieted by Hardiman's inference that Irish inadequacies were the result of English domination, he undermines a determinist argument and affirms with confidence that nationality is indelible, distinctive, and undiminished by external conditions, endorsing, as Leerssen points out, a belief in ethnic, inborn racial essentialism. We believe, he states:

> that the great proportion of the characteristics of a people are inherent, not fictitious; and that there are as essential differences between the genius's [sic] as between the physical appearances of nations. We

L. Gibbons, 'Race against time: racial discourse and Irish history', in his *Transformations in Irish culture* (1996), and C. Morash, 'Celticism: between race and nation' (1998). 42 G.W. Stocking, *Race, culture and evolution* (1968), p. 36. Stocking provides a detailed discussion of the theoretical background to the debate between environmentalism and determinism, with reference to the monogenist leanings of ethnological scientists such as James Cowles Prichard, whose *Researches into the physical history of Man* was published in 1813, and to the French polygenist tradition led by George Cuvier (1769–1832). More generally on nineteenth-century anthropological science see P. Bowler, *The invention of progress* (1989).

> believe that no dissipating continuance of defeat, danger, famine, or misgovernment, could ever, without the absolute infusion of Milesian blood, Hibernicize the English peasant; and that no stultifying operation of mere security, plenty, or laborious regularity could ever, without actual physical transubstantiation, reduce the native Irishman to the stolid standard of the sober Saxon.[43]

This delineation confirms the racial principle introduced by Ferguson's analysis of Hardiman's translations, and picks up on the romantic appeal of racial opposites which Scott, in the famous introduction to the 1830 edition of *Ivanhoe*, had emphasized in distinguishing between the Norman and Saxon races of England.[44] Ferguson's response to Hardiman thus endorses an essentialism which, carried to its logical conclusion, would provide the foundations for aesthetic and political systems alike.

The display of intellectual confidence in the above passage has led to its frequent citation as evidence of Ferguson's belief in racial absolutes, but in fact he was far from decisive on the matter. Just as public opinion wavered on the subject, so Ferguson's own perspective shifted from this to monogenist and environmentalist positions on the Irish character. The passage quoted earlier from his 1834 review of Lover and Carleton indicates that he had forged a compromise between his recognition of the effect of economic degradation on the Irish peasant, and his desire to promote the notion of an irreducible Irishness. Two years later he had shifted ground towards an environmentalist perspective much more in keeping with his affiliation to Scottish intellectual tradition.[45] In one of a series of articles on Irish society published in the *DUM* in 1836, Ferguson insists that the mental and physical features of the Irish and English are not fixed racial phenomena:

> Take the most intelligent yeomanry of England; transplant them to the bogs and mountains; outlaw them, and isolate them, and if they leave their fastnesses in search of education or of subsistence, hunt them back to their hovels with indignity and violence; pursue this course for but a very few generations, and the noble-featured race with which the experiment was begun will have deteriorated into a wide-mouthed, flat-nosed, low-browed and hollow-eyed rabble, poor in person and pitiable

---

[43] 'Irish Minstrelsy, no. 2', *DUM* 4 (Aug. 1834), 154–5. See Leerssen's comments on this passage, *Remembrance and imagination*, p. 185. [44] See A. Fleishman, *The English historical novel* (1971), p. 26. [45] The position is summarized by the Scottish historian William Robertson: 'If we suppose two tribes, though placed in the most remote regions of the globe, to live in a climate of the same temperature, to be in the same state of society and to resemble each other in the degrees of their improvement, they must feel the same wants and exert the same endeavours to supply them.' Cited G. McMaster, *Scott and society* (1981), p. 56.

in intellect. A spare potato diet for seven years would reduce Hyperion himself to a satyr.[46]

Here, racial essence gives way to climatic and environmental determinism, and throughout the essay, poverty and economic deprivation are stressed as the governing factors at the heart of Irish 'difference'. In the light of the 1836 essay, the essentialist rhetoric of the Hardiman review comes to lack conviction, reflecting merely the philosophical and political confusion behind Ferguson's intellectual posturing.

Overall then, the derivative nature of Ferguson's comments on the racial essence of 'Irishness' offsets the political impact in the review. And his analysis of the country's flawed constitutional history, dealt with mainly in the third article of the series, is equally formulaic. Ireland's historical and social evolution is analyzed in terms of a causal link between the emotionalism of Irish character and the conditions of government in the country. The connection between this native tendency and permanent governmental inadequacy had already been expressed in dramatic terms by the persona of 'Head' in his 'Dialogue between the Head and Heart of an Irish Protestant' of 1833, and the *Minstrelsy* piece picks up the theme. 'It is to the excess of natural piety developing itself in loyal attachment to principles subversive of reason and independence, that we would trace the tardiness, nay, sometimes the retrogression of civilization and prosperity in Ireland', he explains. 'Natural piety we would define as the religion of humanity, the faith of the affections, the susceptibility of involuntary attachments to arbitrary relations in society.'[47] A hangover from the clan system of fosterage or *gossipred*, natural piety and the resultant tendency towards blind social attachments remained the central weakness in Ireland's civil transition. As a result the country had missed legitimate stages of social development, having been unable to progress from clan rule to mature constitution, and having switched its affections instead from clan chief to 'clan Rome'. Against the continuing domination of the Roman Catholic church, 'the lingering tyranny of a debasing priestcraft', the counterbalance of a British Protestant government is implied as a necessity.[48]

Such an expression seems repugnant by contemporary standards, but of course, in the 1830s it was both commonplace and even comparatively restrained

---

46 'Attractions of Ireland, no. 3 – society', *DUM* 8 (Dec. 1836), 666. Ferguson's ideas on race were to change frequently during his career: see his article 'The Celtic-Scythic progress', *DUM* 34 (Mar. 1852), 277–91. 47 '*Irish Minstrelsy*, no. 3', *DUM* 4 (Oct. 1834), 448. See the views expressed by 'Head' in the 1833 'Dialogue', in relation to Elizabethan Ireland. As discussed in chapter one, Ferguson provided a fictional illustration of the historical necessity of clan-solidarity in his 1835 *Hibernian nights'* tale 'Corby McGillmore', in which the clan chief McGillmore is described as possessing an essential 'natural piety', a devout commitment to his clan. 48 '*Irish Minstrelsy*, no. 3', *DUM* 4 (Oct. 1834), 460, 452, 447.

when compared with the sentiments expressed by the O'Sullivan brothers and other *DUM* stalwarts. Ferguson's argument was distinctly old hat. The connections between national character and government had been debated repeatedly since the mid-eighteenth century. In his essay 'Of national characters', the Scottish philosopher David Hume rejected environmental determinism and emphasized instead what he described as the moral causes which determined national genius; the circumstances of living and working which rendered a set of manners peculiar to a race, including the economic conditions of existence and, crucially, the nature of government.[49] Even more specifically in terms of Ferguson's intellectual background, the Scottish historical philosopher Adam Ferguson had explored the subject at length in his *Essay on the history of civil society* (1767). In a section entitled 'The principles of union among mankind', he highlighted the tendency among primitive people to retain irrationally strong bonds with their kin on the basis of loyalty: 'It is, in short, from this principle alone that we can account for the obstinate attachment of a savage to his unsettled and defenceless tribe, when temptations on the side of ease and of safety might induce him to fly from famine and danger.'[50] This strength of affection, though engendered in times of difficulty, remained a feature of tribal life for a long time after famine, hostilities or warfare ended, preventing a more natural transition from the rule of feudal lord to monarch, and, eventually, to commercial interest as a safeguard of rights and property.

This theory of clanship was applied specifically to Ireland when, in 1824, *Blackwood's* regular contributor Thomas Crofton Croker produced his *Researches in the south of Ireland*, a text with which Ferguson was familiar. 'An Irishman is the sport of his feelings', wrote Croker, in his opening chapter on 'History and national character'. 'With passions the most violent and sensitive, he is alternatively the child of despondency or of levity.' In the context of Ireland's peculiar development, the long-term effects of a clan-based regime on the native personality are evident:

> The rough and honest independence of the English cottager speaks the freedom he has so long enjoyed, and when really injured his appeal to the laws for redress and protection marks their impartiality and just administration. The witty servility of the Irish peasantry, mingled with occasional bursts of desperation and revenge – the devoted yet visionary patriotism – the romantic sense of honour, and improvident yet unalterable attachments, are evidence of a conquest without system, an

---

49 *Essays moral and political* (1904), pp. 144–8. See Leerssen's comments on Hume in this respect, *Mere Irish*, pp. 27–31.
50 *Essay on the history of civil society*, Section II, 'The history of political establishments', p. 31.

irregular government, and the remains of feudal clanship, the barbarous and arbitrary organization of a warlike people.[51]

Following this assertion with a lengthy description of the native customs of *gossipred*, or fosterage, and *tanistry*, or the law of succession in native Irish self-government, Croker concludes that while the Irish have in the past exhibited potential for advancement they have also suffered 'the want of superiors to direct and encourage their labours, and to whom they might with confidence look up for support'. The case for external government is thus once again cemented to popular theories of civil transition and national character, in a formulation which would provide a mainstay of unionist ideology throughout the century.

Ferguson's analysis is fairly perfunctory, by comparison. Because of their tendency towards strong clan loyalties, he suggests, the Irish failed to transfer their affections to a ruling monarch, thereby missing out on a vital 'middle-stage' of civil development. Without this stage, the country has no basis for transition towards a modern state:

> [T]his has been the reason why we find the principles of the revolution operating so inefficiently on a nation not yet free from the reluctant sway of patriarchal loyalty; and hence it has come to pass, that Irish society, at the present day, exhibits those anomalous features of mixed crudeness and maturity which are but the representatives of two different stages of society, whose antagonist principles have hitherto found no mutual means of reconcilement [...] Strange anomaly in history, that a country should for two thousand years, continue in the same grade of civil advancement, retarded from the next by the very excess of characteristics most essential to its assumption, and finally subdued by a people so far in advance of her own that after centuries of fellow citizenship, the two races are still unable to amalgamate from the want of these intermediate steps on the civil scale – steps forgotten by the one and never taken by the other.

Ireland has suffered throughout her history from 'an ascendancy of the heart', a quality which, while lending sentimentality to the Irish character and passion to Irish poetry, has essentially prevented the country's advancement towards complete civilization and the capacity for self-government.[52]

The argument was already a tired one. However legitimate its basis in eighteenth-century speculative anthropology, by 1834 its popularization in Scott's

---

51 *Researches in the south of Ireland*, p. 13; p. 2. Ferguson refers to Croker's work in 'Attractions of Ireland, no. 1', *DUM* 8 (July 1836), 113.   52 'Irish Minstrelsy, no. 3', *DUM* 4 (Oct 1834), 451; 'Irish Minstrelsy, no. 2', *DUM* 4 (Aug. 1834), 160.

novels and party-political journalism had dulled its effect: it certainly does *not* represent what Eagleton describes as 'an intriguing theory of Irish history' originally formulated in the Hardiman review.[53] There is a sense too, that Ferguson is unwilling to follow up the precise constitutional implications of his socio-historical analysis. Where Coleridge prefaced his 1830 *Treatise* with a precise definition of his terms and ideals, Ferguson's instinct is to frame his discussion in the safer rhetoric of eighteenth-century civic idealism and the imagery of an Augustan pastoral idyll. 'What constitutes a state?' he asks, in the opening of the third article; not industrial prowess, but 'bold men and chaste women [...] the elements of a nation'. In place of Coleridge's projected political infrastructure, he offers only an abstruse concept of Irish virtue: 'virtue, evading alike the spurns of power and the trampling march of superstition, has risen, is rising, indomitable as the nation it redeems'. Irish greatness will be built on the civilized arts, on great works and social improvements, and on sheer strength of character:

> Instinctive piety, to lay the only sure foundations of human morals and immortal hopes; constitutional loyalty, to preserve the civil compact inviolate, legitimate affection, to ensure public virtue and private happiness; endless humour, to quicken social intercourse, and last, and save one attribute best, indomitable love of country to consolidate the whole.[54]

The language of the passage is distinctly more Adam Smith than Samuel Taylor Coleridge, its touchstones of sociability and sensibility directly related to the Scottish intellectual inheritance which remained a subtext to Ferguson's uneasy Dublin debut. Again, the Hardiman review exceeds the boundaries of literary antiquarianism and engenders a struggle to splice together competing ideologies in an awkward and premature apologia.

The author of the Hardiman review had absorbed discursive elements of the major constitutional debate surrounding the issue of Catholic Emancipation, but his ability to process and utilize such material effectively on a political level was evidently limited: in 1834 Ferguson simply lacked, for all his stylistic exuberance, the philosophical and political credibility which Lloyd and others have attributed to him retrospectively. If the review articles constitute any kind of unionist propaganda document, it is an unwieldly one, less than clear in its aims, less than original in its choice of terms. Certainly the issues of national character and self-government were at the very heart of imperialist sensibility, but so readily available to all that in Ferguson's hands, they are hardly revelatory. At best, the Hardiman review is an amalgam; the young writer's excitement at dis-

---

53 *Scholars and rebels*, p. 66.   54 'Irish Minstrelsy, no. 3', *DUM* 4 (Oct. 1834), 447 and 467.

covering a national Irish literary heritage, combined with his absorbed ideas of Enlightenment ethnology, grafted on to a populist sectarian currency.

What then, can be learned from the piece? The inconsistency in the language of the articles is certainly telling. Leerssen claims to finds it difficult to believe that the Hardiman review was composed at the same time as its author embarked on the *Hibernian nights' entertainments*, but it is precisely the sense of a split discourse which undermines Ferguson's credibility as a commentator.[55] The lack of cohesion which characterizes the articles is underlined, furthermore, if one looks behind twentieth-century interpretations of Ferguson's motives to the nineteenth-century context of journalistic publishing within which he was trying to operate. The 1834 articles reveal both his vulnerability to warring influences in contemporary political and social philosophy, and his susceptibility to the vagaries of journalistic style. His comments on the weakness of the Irish clan mentality and the pernicious influence of the Roman Catholic hierarchy reflect his adoption of a common discourse rather than the evolution of a personal credo; these were panicked attempts to satisfy in public the Orange extremists whom he denigrated in private. And while most commentators accept that his appendix of translations constitutes a significant document in Irish literary history, the prefatory material has little authority, marred by hollow rhetorical gestures and theoretical eclecticism. An over-enthusiastic collage of literary, political and historical experimentation, it cannot be regarded either as a tenable personal policy statement or as a consummate Ascendancy manifesto.

More secure conclusions may be drawn from two aspects of the Hardiman confrontation. First, Ferguson had successfully tested the strength of his own journalistic talent and the parameters of the literary review. He never again attempted a project as ambitious or as evangelical as the *Irish Minstrelsy* series, and his future contributions to the *DUM* were undoubtedly more cautious and restrained. Secondly, he had begun to tackle the intellectual and artistic challenge of defining Ireland and Irishness. Against the internal tensions of the Protestant intelligentsia and the wider sense of political uncertainty within the country as a whole, he was determined to stabilize some kind of identity, and his attempts to find images and representations of rural and urban Ireland were to continue throughout the 1830s. The review of the *Irish Minstrelsy* collection ushered in what is best described not as a Celticist conspiracy but as a period of intense national self-consciousness. In studies ranging from geology, antiquities, literature and topography, Ferguson was to intensify his plan to make the island and identity of Ireland accessible to its disparate social groups, and in doing so, to consolidate on the emergent concept of a stable, civic intelligentsia in the capital.

55 *Remembrance and imagination*, p. 184.

CHAPTER THREE

The 'Attractions of Ireland'

Slemish is one great joint of that spine of mountain that runs between the vale of Glenwhirry on one side, and that of Broughshane on the other, heaved over its fellows so high, and so abruptly, that to the eye of one standing on its highest point, the platform of its summit is alone visible, like a green island underfoot, floating a thousand feet above the middle of Country Antrim, for from that point neither base nor side can be seen, but all around, from Louth upon the south, to the hills of the Causeway upon the north, and from the mountains of Argyleshire and Galloway upon the east to the Western highlands of Derry and Tyrone, everything lies under view as on a map.[1]

Ferguson's tale 'The return of Claneboy', from which this description is taken, tells of the journey made by Yellow Hugh O'Neill to recover from the third earl of Ulster the land of his birthright. Before the onset of hostilities, O'Neill surveys the terrain from the top of Slemish mountain, where he questions his guide on the names of the unfamiliar loughs and regions. The story initially appeared in *Blackwood's* in December of 1833, seven months after the first of the new Ordnance Survey charts of Ireland was presented to King William IV. By the third decade of the nineteenth century the project to provide a six-inch map of Ireland was at its height. Throughout the north-east where Ferguson's tale is set, on the mountain peaks of Divis, Sawel and Slemish, the sappers of the Royal Engineers had set up their theodolites, ready to translate trigonometry into cartography.[2]

The mapping of Ireland provided an appropriate point of confluence for Ferguson's various engagements in the 1830s, as his creative response to Irish history and landscape dovetailed with his semi-professional engagements in topographical research and travel writing. The stories of the *Hibernian nights' entertainments* are, as Denman remarks, topographically specific to the point at which they seem to require a road-map, with place-names 'driven into the text like so

---

[1] *Hibernian nights' entertainments*, vol. 1, p. 49. [2] J.H. Andrews, *A paper landscape* (1975), p. 90. Unless otherwise stated, I have used Andrews as my main source of information on the Survey.

many stakes, as if to fasten it on to a storied landscape'.[3] And the shaping of the tales according to the fashionable dictates of picturesque romance reflects their close relationship to the burgeoning conventions of commercial middle-class leisure pursuits, in travel, landscape sketching and engraving.[4] The series sits quite naturally therefore, alongside its author's parallel commitments in the middle years of the decade; first, to the Topographical Department of the Ordnance Survey, and secondly to a range of commercial publishers – Curry, Knight, Fisher and others – anxious to cash in on the vogue for the exploration and depiction of Ireland in a flurry of guidebooks and travelogues.

A substantial part of Ferguson's work in the period was thus occasioned by the fusion of cartographical empiricism with picturesque tourism. While both were offshoots of imperialism's grand design, and certainly, the Ordnance Survey project as a whole remained within the remit of an acquisitive colonial mentality, their particular function at a local level and in a Dublin context is a useful indication of the bourgeois instincts of the Irish capital. In conjunction, they provided the means by which rural experience could be contained and determined by urban interests, specifically, the administrative, regulatory and recreational interests of a new middle class. The old relationships between aristocratic estate owner and the land were gradually giving way to a new series of connections between rural periphery and urban administration, as municipal and franchise reform took effect and the regions of the British Isles became increasingly accessible. Like antiquarianism and archaeology, fashions for topography and tourism were related as much to the development of middle-class cultural practice as to imperial ideologies. The creation and management of an Irish 'countryside' were essential to the definition and indeed, delimitation of an urban centre, and important too, to the development of a civic sensibility inextricable from an urban identity. Again, therefore, the structures and formulae through which Ferguson began to engage with the matter of Ireland have class implications, and highlight at the same time the extent to which the representation of Ireland was determined by commercial, rather than specifically political, interest.

---

3 *Samuel Ferguson*, p. 42. 4 By the 1830s the term 'picturesque' was frequently applied to fiction: the author of an anonymous article in *Blackwood's* in April 1833 complained that 'it seems to be the established maxim among the new and picturesque style of historical romance, that literal truth in matters of fact is not only to be laid aside where it might derange the plot, or disturb the philosophic unity of conception, but that it should be violated *ad libitum* by the author, merely, like the emperors of heroic tragedy, "to shew his arbitrary power"'; 3 (April 1833), 624. Scott's fiction in particular was described as 'picturesque', and in his introduction to the 1831 edition of *The fortunes of Nigel* he provided a definition of the term in relation to historical romance: '[t]he most picturesque period in history is that when the ancient rough and wild manners of a barbarous age are just becoming innovated upon, and contrasted by, the illuminations of increased or revived learning, and the instructions of renewed or reformed religion. The strong contrast produced by the opposition of ancient manners to those who are genuinely subduing them affords the light and shadows necessary to give effect to a fictitious narrative': *Works*, vol. 26, pp. 6–8.

The Ordnance Survey of Ireland conducted between 1824 and 1836 represented the most definitive attempt to date to rationalize the Irish terrain and provide cartographical records adequate to the requirements of an expanding economic and legislative administration. The new system was intended to cater for the evaluation of rates and tax, the improvement of road and railway engineering, the demarcation of parliamentary and municipal boundaries, the facilitation of geological research and even the drainage of Irish bogland, the latter a pipe dream of several nineteenth-century land-economists.[5] The Survey Commission inevitably represented one of many activities during the 1830s initiated by the expansion of state administration and intervention in Ireland, as the government introduced a number of measures directed towards the rationalization of church, education, welfare and law in the country. In September 1831 the Whig government established funds and policy for a national system of elementary education in Ireland; by 1835 ten district asylums had been built under the auspices of the lord lieutenant; in May 1836 the Irish Constabulary Act expanded the role of a centralized police force and salaried magistracy, and in July 1838 the Irish poor law extended the English system to Ireland, dividing the country into one hundred and thirty separate 'unions'. Culminating in the population census in 1841, the decade was dominated by increased official involvement in rural areas and by the expanded presence of a centralized authority in all aspects of Irish public life.[6]

While this process was by no means unique to Ireland, the use of the country as a 'laboratory' for administrative experimentation has nonetheless been remarked upon by historians of the period.[7] David Lloyd, for example, has emphasized the extent to which the process was a means of reinforcing the Union, as 'the anomalous condition of Ireland within Great Britain; already evident in its poverty, Catholicism, different social structures and so forth, led the administration in Dublin to measures of internal integration that involved a pattern of deliberate state interference which long preceded any comparable developments in any other parts of the British isles'.[8] But while the Ordnance Survey of Ireland can be glossed in such terms, it was also a remarkable exercise in social documentation and indeed, cultural anthropology, part of the impulse towards empirical enquiry which characterized British policy in the early nineteenth century, as the 'condition of the people' question focussed the attention of statisticians and policy makers. In addressing the condition of the

---

5 See Andrews, *A paper landscape*, p. 138. 6 See F.S.L. Lyons, *Ireland since the Famine* (1971), pp. 65–6; R.F. Foster, *Modern Ireland*, p. 290. 7 Lyons, p. 65. See also O. MacDonagh, *Ireland: the Union and its aftermath* (1977), pp. 35–52. 8 *Nationalism and minor literature*, p. 56. See also J.B. Harley, 'Maps, knowledge, and power' (1988), on the relationship between cartography and imperial ideology, and A. Smith, 'Landscapes of power in nineteenth-century Ireland' (1998).

Irish people, the Ordnance Survey in Ireland expanded far beyond a purely utilitarian premise. Under the auspices of Captain Thomas Larcom and the designated Topographical Department of the Survey, the mapping project developed into a pioneering and monumental study of Irish environment, cultural history and social conditions.

Larcom's predecessor at the head of the project, Colonel Thomas Colby, had initiated efforts to attend to such matters as the history of Irish place-names, but Larcom's succession to the post in 1824 led to a huge increase in the range of data collected. His immersion in the work, for which he set himself the task of learning Irish, and his vow to register the land not only as a physical entity but also in terms of the character and circumstances of its inhabitants, earned him great respect in the Commission. As Andrews points out with reference to the reading material which appeared in the Captain's library at his Mountjoy headquarters, this personal enthusiasm was closely bound up with the general '*connais-toi toi-meme*' philosophy of a western European movement, which led in the early 1830s to the formation of the Moral and Statistical Society of France, the Statistical Society of London, the Statistical Department of the Board of Trade, and the statistical section of the British Association. In this respect Larcom represented very much the values of the Enlightenment, filtered through a utilitarian and rational bureaucracy.[9]

The list of additional tasks which Larcom compiled and circulated amongst his officers in 1832 included series of questions on the habits and traditions of the people of each county, their living conditions, feast-days and holidays, religious practices, manners and means of recreation. Inevitably the work-load increased dramatically, as this accessory to the Survey expanded beyond the capabilities of the original workforce, and Larcom, who had already enlisted the aid of the Irish-language scholar John O'Donovan in 1828, found it necessary to draw further upon the resources of a non-military network of researchers. The Topographical Department of the Ordnance Survey was therefore established in order to co-ordinate a team of local experts, headed by O'Donovan as toponymic field adviser, and the antiquarian and artist George Petrie. This team would work on the documentation of Irish place-names, and collect material relating to historical artefacts and antiquities of each locality, ultimately producing a comprehensive 'Memoir' of information relating to each county covered by the mapping Survey.

The Topographical Department thus encouraged the professionalization of a group of men whose amateur preoccupations with Ireland as an object of

---

9 Andrews, p. 147. See also Larcom papers, NLI LP 7550. Larcom's investigative agenda may be compared to the similar list for travellers produced by the Royal Society; see T.M. Curley, *Samuel Johnson and the age of travel* (1976), p. 197.

study now received official recognition. And at this stage Samuel Ferguson became connected with the project. His contact with the Department developed as a result of his interest in Irish antiquities, which was strengthened during this period as he later explained, 'by the intimacy which sprang up between me and the late Dr George Petrie, then engaged in the preparation of materials for the Ordnance Survey Memoir'. In Petrie's study, Ferguson recalled, he became acquainted with the Gaelic scholars John O'Donovan and Eugene O'Curry, and the poet James Clarence Mangan, all of whom were employed at the Department's headquarters in Petrie's Great Charles Street home.[10] Ferguson himself was never officially employed on the Survey: at least, his name does not appear on Larcom's pay lists for the years 1830 to 1839, but nonetheless he was closely involved with the work, forwarding information to Petrie who thanked him accordingly – 'You are worth a whole regiment of such fellows as Ledwich and Vallancey' – and compiling material on County Antrim, in which he took a personal interest.[11]

The circle which resulted from this process of recruitment, official and unofficial, was crucial to Ferguson's sense of civic potential in the capital. Inevitably, the project has invited contemporary scepticism: Eagleton has complained that the camaraderie of the scholars represented in fact, 'a class structure in miniature', with the Catholic elements, O'Donovan and Mangan, simply serving as 'subalterns to the gentry' and being patronized accordingly.[12] In fact, no such clear lines of demarcation are visible. There is speculation that Petrie, for example, was Catholic by birth if Protestant by inclination, and Ferguson's position was simply that of an impecunious and rather lowly research assistant. John O'Donovan, on the other hand, was regarded and respected by all parties as the superior intelligence of the project, and subsequent letters and exchanges between members of the group, including Larcom, suggest little, if anything, in the way of an exploitative class hierarchy.[13]

More to the point is the question of the Memoir's political alignment. As has been noted, Ferguson's engagement with the Ordnance Survey has been cited as evidence of his strategic collusion with imperialism, but in fairness it is impossible to categorize the contribution of the Topographical Department in secure political terms. On one hand, the values of the Department were fre-

---

10 See M.C. Ferguson, *SSFID*, vol. 1, p. 60. 11 Larcom papers, NLI LP 7553. An entry for 12 May, 1842 gives an account of employees from 1830 to 1842; M.C. Ferguson, *SSFID*, vol. 1, p. 46. See also Petrie's letters, 30 Oct. 1833, RIA MS 12n 22, p. 17. Edward Ledwich and Charles Vallancey were noted eighteenth-century antiquarian scholars. 12 *Scholars and rebels*, pp. 130–1. 13 See P. Murray, 'George Petrie 1798–1866', vol. 1, p. 396. M.C. Ferguson writes of the close friendship between her husband and John O'Donovan, and the two men corresponded frequently on antiquarian and other matters; *SSFID* vol. 1, pp. 76–7. O'Donovan's letters to Larcom suggest a similar closeness. See P.M. MacSweeney, *A group of nation builders* (1913), and C. Ó Lochlainn, 'John O'Donovan and Colonel Larcom', *Irish Booklover*, 29 (1945).

quently identified with Irish self-assertion and reclamation. Referring to Thomas Davis's enthusiastic response to the nationalist potential of the Survey, Andrews states that 'it was felt in some quarters that the historical and social section of the Memoir might have an exacerbating effect on Irish patriotic feeling and so accentuate the divisions between planter and native, Protestant and Catholic, government and governed'.[14] Indeed, in an extreme case an anonymous contemporary, signing himself simply 'a Protestant Conservative', wrote to the commissioners in May of 1842 to complain of what he identified as closet 'papistry' supposedly going on behind the scenes of the Department's office.[15] Yet at the same time the *imperial* initiative behind the Survey's Topographical Department was repeatedly cited in defence of the project. When the British government suspended funding for the Memoir research in 1842, pleas for a reversal of the chancellor's decision were made on grounds designed to appeal to the security and authority of the Empire. In 1843, William Rowan Hamilton's open letter defending the Ordnance Survey Memoir rejected the charge that revived historical interest would be exploited for seditious purposes, and insisted that a failure to foster such an endeavour was in itself a dangerous lapse, for 'nothing can be more mischievous than the present vague state of our knowledge of ancient Ireland. The political events of former times may be quoted by any party, and turned with equal facility to their purposes, while from the general ignorance that prevails of the real character of these events, the public are unable to detect their falacy' [sic].[16]

The work of the Topographical Department was politically ambiguous therefore, a fact reflected in the heterodox political and religious composition of the team assembled by Petrie and O'Donovan, and reinforced by the unofficial network of scholarly interest on which it capitalized. If the Irish Ordnance Survey was a colonialist power apparatus, the Memoir it fostered was distinctly *national* in its alignment, and Ferguson's affiliation to it is a representative instance of his work falling between the two poles of national incentive and imperial design, apparently without contradiction.

More pertinently, his involvement must also be understood in terms of the local value of the project. In the context of his general interests and writings

---

14 Andrews, *A paper landscape*, p. 173. 15 Cited Andrews, p. 142; Larcom papers, 2 May, 1842, NLI LP 7553. 16 See Larcom papers, NLI LP 7553; W.R. Hamilton, letter on the Ordnance Survey Memoir, 1843. Similar justification of the Survey appeared in an article published in the *DUM* in April 1844, following the official cancellation of the Memoir. The author laments the speed with which Irish relics and antiquities are disappearing in 'the shipwreck of time', and compares the solicitude of the French government to its heritage, before going on to promote the research as being firmly within the interests of the British kingdom as a whole – a guard against general moral decline and a prop to the integrity of the Empire. The article is included by Lady Ferguson in her list of her husband's published writings, and though the attribution has been justifiably queried by Denman (*Samuel Ferguson*, p. 202), the piece is nonetheless in keeping with the position he advocated throughout his 1836 articles.

during the 1830s, the Memoir was more important as a social than a political agency, consolidating as it did a scholarly fraternity based in the capital, and defining itself largely through its intellectual and scientific commitment to regional and rural Ireland. In many respects, the Memoir team represented the natural evolution of a company already engaged in historical pursuits, walking tours, sketching trips, and constant correspondence on matters of linguistic and cultural interest. It coheres too, with the forceful social dynamics of intellectual and cultural collaboration in the period, when the whole concept of antiquarian and historical research as a civic responsibility was germane to cities throughout the British Isles, representing 'an alternative cultural force of amazing vigour, an attachment to local identity motivated in many ways by the same sentiments as that civic pride which spurred on the town-hall and sewer-builders of the later nineteenth century'.[17] In other words, the consolidation of a civic identity through such honourable engagement with the past and the landscape was as much the purpose of research as the production of scholarly information. And in civic terms therefore, the topographical team, much more than the editors and contributors of the *DUM*, began to supply the model of informed responsibility which Ferguson had derived from Scotland, and which he wished to find in Dublin.

A version of this idealism can certainly be detected in Ferguson's persistent claim for a new ascendancy in Dublin, based on an intellectual and cultural meritocracy. If, in the first half of the nineteenth century, the city was in danger of appearing provincial and second-rate, it needed to reclaim civic status without recourse to the increasingly bankrupt symbols of an old, land-based aristocracy, through the medium of a cultivated, professional urban hegemony. Petrie, O'Donovan and the Ordnance Survey topographical team were merely a section of a larger group of activists, listed individually in the third of Ferguson's 1836 articles on Ireland, entitled 'Society'. Here, Ferguson turns for his sources of native intellectual and cultural aspiration to the members and associates of the Royal Irish Academy; the scientists Humphrey Lloyd and Joseph Portlock, the mathematician Sir William Hamilton; James Pim the engineer, the chemist John Apjohn, William Stokes the physician and the writers Caesar Otway, William Carleton and John Anster.[18] This gallery of achievers is presented as a new nobility, deeply committed to the spirit of enquiry, to literature, art and science, but unlike its absentee predecessor, committed also to Dublin and the health of the nation as a whole.

17 P. Levine, *The amateur and the professional*, p. 61. 18 'Attractions of Ireland, no. 2 – scenery and society', *DUM* 8 (Sept. 1836), 332. Under the presidency of Bartholomew Lloyd and, after 1837, of William Rowan Hamilton, the RIA was seen to enjoy a 'golden age' of achievement: see T. Ó'Raifeartaigh (ed.), *The Royal Irish Academy* (1987).

Ferguson's comments on the social dynamics of research *per se* reinforce the value he placed on the Ordnance Survey, not as an isolated phenomenon but as a representative element in a new and emergent national self-assertiveness. A passage outlining his vision of the country's future illustrates how his concept of national integrity had become inextricable from the dynamic ego of the scholar or scientist, valiantly extending knowledge from the centre to the regions in the name of progress. 'The development of a new national genius is an era in the history of human life', he wrote. 'Our day for distinction may also be approaching':

> Hitherto we have been scientifically the most neglected country in Europe. All our wants in that respect are now supplied at once. Geography, topography, statistics, and natural and civil history are all in operation at the present moment for our benefit. Nor is it in theoretical science alone that our wants are about being so fully supplied. Great works, the result of scientific enquiry are everywhere in operation, opening up the country and bringing the members of our family, as it were, under one roof. Level roads are laid down where a few years since were nought but steep and rocky bridle paths; bridges of solid masonry supplant the unstable stepping stones that served to bear the last generation from bank to bank of mountain torrents, out of one wild into another; harbours open their wide-spread arms to shelter the distressed merchantman where formerly an inhospitable coast presented its ironbound front to the breakers of a tempestuous sea. We are exercising a new industry, and with wealth we are acquiring that self-respect which will soon demand leisure for the luxury of intellectual employment. Every step in the progress from facilitated intercourse and increased knowledge of our selves and our resources to self-respect and intellectual competition is pregnant with importance. The introduction of a new breed of cattle is fraught with interest to the farmer; the discovery of a new generator excites all the attention of the mechanist; the appearance of a new star would be hailed by the astronomer with rapture – how much closer does it come home to the educated man to see a young nation entering the lists of intellectual competition, striking out paths of enquiry hitherto untrodden, creating styles and schools hitherto unimagined – perhaps in the collision of intellects throwing light upon questions till then involved in undissipated darkness. If there be any power or originality in the Irish mind, it is now or shortly that it must begin to show itself forth.[19]

---

19 'The Attractions of Ireland, no. 3 – society', *DUM* 8 (Dec. 1836), 662.

Written in 1836, while its author was deeply involved with the work of the Ordnance Survey Memoir, the passage is a confident hymn to the progress which would secure the values of empiricism and science within the parameters of Irish national interest. True, Ferguson's confidence still hinged largely on the Ascendancy-dominated Royal Irish Academy as the nerve centre of intellectual progress, but at least his language had shifted from the hollow sectarianism of the Hardiman review to an engaged and inclusive optimism. Indeed, the articulation of 'a young nation' in these terms would shortly attract the interest of Charles Gavan Duffy, who was to recommend Ferguson's 1836 articles on Ireland to Thomas Carlyle, as a useful preparation for his Irish tour.[20]

TOPOGRAPHY, TRAVEL AND THE PICTURESQUE

If the Ordnance Survey symbolized the scientific containment and management of a rural hinterland by an urban administration, the parallel aesthetic management of the countryside was manifest in the expanding cult of the picturesque. Like other cities of the British Isles, Dublin developed during the first half of the nineteenth century a vogue for travel through the rural regions of Ireland, as demographic changes and the processes of industrialization and urbanization produced a moneyed and leisured middle class eager to appropriate for itself a lost rural idyll. The picturesque represented the shifting of landscape and topographical art into a new and characteristically bourgeois social sphere, from a private to a public domain. And like the Ordnance Survey, the conventions of the picturesque demanded the ritualistic inspection of the country from a series of vantage points, establishing a highly formal apparatus within which the landscape was contained, observed and controlled. The picturesque was essentially a means of imposing order, an aesthetic means of policing and administering the rural landscape from the industrial centre, as 'the picturesque of the tourists became a rule precisely analogous to the developing bureaucracy of professional surveyors and overseers'.[21]

From the latter half of the eighteenth century, the idea of the picturesque emerged as a primary component of artistic and social discourse. The change was conceptual as much as social. In a discernible break from the conventions of the Sublime, which subjugated the individual to the domination and supremacy of 'Nature', the picturesque mode endowed the artist with a sense

---

20 Denman, *Samuel Ferguson*, p. 33. In 1850 Carlyle wrote to William Allingham to recommend 'The Irish Counties' in the *Penny Cyclopaedia* 'by one S. Ferguson of Dublin'; *Allingham's letters* (1911), p. 130. 21 A. Liu, *Wordsworth: the sense of history* (1989), p. 99.

of precedence and power over the landscape. It stressed the formalizing authority of the observer, whose preconceived ideal restrained the natural world and determined the value of the countryside. A scene was judged 'picturesque' if it was conducive to the ordering eye of the sketcher: landscape was appreciated in terms of its representational potential or, as defined by the chief apologist of the picturesque, William Gilpin, according to that which will 'please from some quality capable of being illustrated in a picture'.[22] Nature was no longer a finished and autonomous phenomenon but a subject to be manipulated and completed by the observer. The experience of the natural world had become the mediated apprehension of 'landscape' as something predetermined by the requirements of art, its defects and irregularities smoothed out and softened. John Barrell notes that

> a person of much education in the eighteenth century would have found it very hard, not merely to describe land, but also to see it, and even to think of it as a visual phenomenon, except as mediated by particular notions of form. The words 'landscape', 'scene', and to a lesser extent 'prospect' [...] demanded, in short, that the land be thought of as itself composed into the formal patterns which previously a landscape painter would have been thought of as himself imposing on it.[23]

From an ideological perspective the paradox is an appealing one. With its promotion of the individual over and above the observed terrain, the picturesque signified that civilization was in control of what had become in the wake of industrialization, an alien territory. 'Nature' was the ultimate unknown quantity, but recreating the rural environment in the picturesque image – restraining and disciplining the landscape through formalized visual representation – established an anthropocentric aesthetic and in effect, a means of imaginative colonization. For the amateur sketchers and landscape connoisseurs who followed this doctrine, the picturesque appropriation of the countryside through specific and regimented methods was tantamount to the psychological sequestration of the rural terrain and the extension of an urban authority.

In Ireland as elsewhere in Europe, the aesthetic colonization of the land was characterized by the fad for landscape gardening. Maria Edgeworth's 1812 novel *The Absentee* describes Lord Colambre's visit to a manor pretentiously entitled 'Tusculum' in the Dublin suburbs, where the *nouveau-riche* Mrs Raffarty out-

---

22 See U. Price, *Essays on the picturesque* (1794) and W. Gilpin, *Essays on picturesque beauty, picturesque travel and sketching landscape* (1794), Essay 1, p. 3. A. Bermingham analyses the relationship between the picturesque and commercial reproduction, *Landscape and ideology* (1987), p. 84.   23 *The idea of landscape* (1972), pp. 2–3.

lines her fashionable aesthetic philosophy while showing her visitor around her estate, stressing her hatred of straight lines, uniformity and formality. On the neighbouring estate of the fashionable Lord and Lady Killpatrick, meanwhile, the picturesque cultivation of the tenantry has been taken to extremes. 'They had built ornamented, picturesque cottages, within view of their park; and favourite followers of the family, people with half a century's habit of indolence and dirt, were promoted to these fine dwellings.'[24] The rural fiction of the picturesque was largely created through such pretence, the creation of a natural world which highlighted its own contrivance. 'The picturesque-lover – busily doctoring his garden to resemble wild nature – really, however, desired the illusion of remote landscape recently touched only by the hand of time.'[25]

The affectations satirized by Edgeworth in her fiction of Irish fashionable life had become by the early nineteenth century a widespread feature of middle-class convention. Whereas classical landscape painting in the European tradition, as represented in Ireland by the painters William Ashford or James Arthur O'Connor, was limited to the aristocrat commissioner or the exhibition-goer, the popular style of the picturesque was amenable to print culture; easily, cheaply reproducible and accessible to literate society. Encountering the rural 'other' was no longer the prerogative of a minority but the privilege of a newly urbanized middle class concerned with defining its own status through its response to the countryside. In common with the inhabitants of other cities in the British Isles therefore, Dubliners in the 1830s pursued the picturesque, just as they pursued the range of bourgeois interests in theatre, civic architecture, or the municipal museums and galleries which signalled a new class predominance. With better transport systems and increased leisure time, tourism within one's own country was seen as desirable, especially after the Napoleonic wars discouraged travel to the continent. Having been toured successively by foreigners, from Arthur Young to William Wordsworth, the Ireland of the 1830s was 'consumed' by a domestic contingent for which it served an important function of self-definition.

This pattern had been well established elsewhere. The English lake district in particular had helped to standardize the concept of the rural retreat, and indeed to provide a blueprint for the phenomenon. The picturesque tour, like the art of picturesque sketching, set a discipline through which the individual's experience of the landscape was carefully and precisely regulated. Thomas West's *Guide to the lakes*, published in 1799, presented a landscape already familiar from the writings of William Gilpin, and furnished the quintessential system for a

---

24 *The Absentee* (1910), p. 170; p. 181. W.J. McCormack comments on Edgeworth's novel in this respect in *Ascendancy and tradition*, pp. 133–5. See also the discussion of the landscape gardening vogue in Ireland in E. Malins and the Knight of Glin, *Lost demesnes* (1976).   25 J.W. Foster, 'The topographical tradition', *Colonial consequences* (1991), p. 19.

rewarding observation of the land through a series of predetermined 'stations' or viewing points. The procedure was quickly adopted by others, including Wordsworth in his influential *Guide through the district of the lakes*, in its fifth edition by 1835.[26] By the 1830s the appropriation of expanses of countryside expressly for the recreation of the city dweller had precedents throughout the British Isles. The English Lake District was perhaps the best known prototype but as Esther Moir points out, 'the lakes were only setting the pattern which was to be followed elsewhere – stretches of country laid aside, as escape for the town-weary, a reminder of that older world upon which an urban civilization was relentlessly encroaching'.[27] The notion of escape was chimerical: tourists simply carried their urban values with them, and the presence of the city was constantly felt in dialectic with the rustic world.

This version of the urban/rural relationship became a cliché of visual representation in the period. Several paintings – English and Irish – portray the smoke and chimneys of the town in the distance from the green open spaces of the countryside. Constable's 'London from Hampstead Heath' can be compared to William Ashford's 'Dublin from Chapelizod' and Petrie's 'Belfast from Turf Lodge': all three recreate the city as a faint memory for those who have rediscovered a rural idyll. At a more commercial level, the picturesque tour initiated major developments in the representation of landscape, with new publishers rushing to reproduce the countryside, pictorially and graphically, as a marketable commodity for the consumption of the Dublin middle classes. During the 1830s and 1840s, advances in the development of steel engraving combined with a vogue for travel writing and pictures, leading to a wealth of illustrated travel books. For the first time 'the interested reader could, from a variety of publications, gain an impression of Irish scenery without leaving his fireside'.[28]

It is hardly surprising that Ferguson, short of money in the capital and ready to take on lucrative employment while he studied for the Bar, became involved in the process. In July 1837 he wrote to Alexander Blackwood, expressing his frustration at the 'weight of the topographical engagement' which had kept him from rhyming and romance, a comment which refers to more than one venture in addition to his work for the Ordnance Survey Memoir.[29] In 1835 he assisted with material for *The new picture of Dublin or A stranger's guide to the Irish metropolis*, issued by the publisher William Curry as one of a series of Irish tour-guides, and in the same year he was commissioned to prepare statistics for the Irish Topographical Branch of *Knight's Penny Cyclopaedia*.[30] Such activities

26 On Wordsworth, the picturesque and the Benthamite panopticon see A. Liu, *Wordsworth*, p. 103, p. 114.   27 *The discovery of Britain* (1964), p. 156.   28 M.R. Booth, 'Irish landscape in the Victorian theatre' (1997), p. 163.   29 Ferguson to Alexander Blackwood, 3 July, 1837, NLS MS 4044 f213.   30 Ferguson is acknowledged as a contributor on p. 2 of the prefatory advertisement to Curry's *New picture of Dublin* (1835). He alludes to his work for *Knight's*

appear to have been kept at a distance from his poetic endeavours and were geared towards supplying the pecuniary rather than the creative needs of the young writer. In 1836 he capitalized on the work, when he published a series of articles entitled the 'Attractions of Ireland' in the *DUM*. This comprised three essays; the first a geological survey of the country, the second a description of Irish scenery with an extended portrait of County Wicklow and the third an anthropological study of the physiognomical and cultural variations in Irish society as encountered on an imaginary regional tour. It was an exercise dedicated to the educated observer, a celebration of the visual opportunities on offer not only to the tourist but to the economist or philosopher, who would find in the country a wealth of material for scrutiny. Ireland, Ferguson effused, was a pageant, 'open to the inspection of all [...] everywhere presenting some permanent feature of interest – some constant subject of speculation; a panorama, indeed, of physical nature, a theatre of life'.[31]

The 'Attractions of Ireland' articles grew out of Ferguson's various topographical engagements therefore, and indeed they function as an extended advertisement for Curry's publications, including the *New guide book to the whole of Ireland* of 1836. Additionally, they form a highly imitative contribution to the spate of scientific and philosophical commentaries on the country which emerged during the period, typified by Archibald Alison's series, 'Ireland', which ran in *Blackwood's* from 1834 to 1835. Ferguson's articles are highly conventional, picking up the fusion of sublime impressionism and utilitarian evaluation set by eighteenth-century surveyors Arthur Young and William Cobbett, and incorporating numerous references to previous scientific, aesthetic and cultural commentators on Ireland.[32] Allusions to these predecessors provide an authoritative gloss on his own commentary: together they form a textual inheritance which he interposes

---

Penny Cyclopaedia in a letter to R.J. Tennant, 25 Jan. 1835, PRONI MS D1748/C/197/11. Short of material for the latter, he wrote to Tennant in Belfast requesting a copy of the Statutes of the town but at the same time urging discretion on the matter. 'I have no intention to make my honourable employment known very extensively', he informed his friend; 'I mention it to you merely that you may know what use I have for the information.' Ferguson was also caught up in the wave of resentment which followed the publication of Samuel Lewis's *Topographical dictionary of Ireland*, in 1837; see his letter to Robert Blackwood, 9 Aug. 1838, NLS MS 4046 f161. 31 'The Attractions of Ireland, no. 3 – society' *DUM* 8 (Dec. 1836), 658. These three articles were serialized as 'no. 1 – scenery' (July 1836), 112–31; 'no. 2 – scenery and society' (Sept. 1836), 315–33; and 'no. 3 – society' (Dec. 1836), 658–75. 32 These range from agricultural surveyors and land-economists, as represented by Richard Griffiths, the geologist, civil engineer and commissioner of Irish land valuation, to the amateur gentlemen tourists whose various works are cited, including Thomas Crofton Croker (*Researches in the south of Ireland*, 1824); Henry Inglis (*A journey throughout Ireland in 1834*, 1836); C.O. or Caesar Otway, *Sketches in Ireland* 1827), and Sir Jonah Barrington, (*Personal sketches of Ireland* 1827/1832). Additionally there are references to Richard Twiss (*A tour in Ireland in 1775*, 1776) and, on a less complimentary note, to the purveyor of 'caricature and conscious prostitution', as Ferguson terms him, John Barrow (*A tour round Ireland*, 1836). Finally there are incidental allusions to the literary exponents of the country; William Carleton, whose *Traits and stories* had begun to appear in the *DUM* in 1833, and the poets Thomas Moore and William Drennan.

between himself and his subject; a specific allusive chain, as Ferguson quotes from Thomas Crofton Croker who in turn has cited Edmund Spenser, or refers to Henry Inglis who in turn drew upon the agricultural surveyor Arthur Young. Where the review of Hardiman in 1834 was discernibly shaped by the conventions of journalistic literary criticism, the 'Attractions of Ireland' text appropriates and manipulates the phraseology of the rural tour, as its author intersperses geological analysis with scenic rapture or anthropological speculation, toying with the nuances and mannerisms of each. The vista at Killarney is contained in the terminology of the picturesque tourist, the Giant's Causeway in County Antrim described in laborious geological detail. Echoing his evocation of the Irish peasant, in his 1834 review of Lover and Carleton, Ferguson depicts a peasant funeral by superimposing picturesque figuration on determinist physiognomy, in an account of environmental conditions in the locale between Carlingford and Newry:

> You look around and find yourself in a desolate tract of bogs spread out at a great elevation among surrounding mountains. A crowd of people, we will say, are crossing by a rough track through the morass towards the main road. Suppose it is a funeral: the eye is first struck by the bright red cloaks of the women, relieved by the black peat hags through which the little procession winds. The ear is next startled by the wild cadence of the Irish cry. And now we distinguish the long grey great coats of the men floating loosely around limbs cased in short breeches which are open at the knee: their hats, broad at the crown and overhanging, are slouched over their eyes; their brown throats are bare; their gait is loose and lounging, but they are a well-grown and athletic set of men; the women, for the most part bare-headed; but some have white and coloured handkerchiefs wrapped round their coal-black hair. They are now so near that you can distinguish their features, but alas, what a change is here! These open projecting mouths, with their prominent teeth and exposed gulls, these high cheekbones, and depressed noses, bear barbarism in their very front.[33]

Such examples abound in the articles, combining to produce material fluent in a conventional language. The impression created is of Ireland as a text already read; a country which is still exotic but no longer uncharted. If in reality, the terrain outside Dublin remained an amorphous, inscrutable mass, on the page it was manageable and coherent. By the 1830s, it had been subdued by the for-

---

33 'The Attractions of Ireland, no. 3 – society', 666–7.

mulaic writings of a long, interwoven succession of travel writers, and determined according to the schema of the privileged urban viewer.

The assumption of metropolitan values and the aspiration towards an urban self-consciousness is central to the 1836 articles, which systematically juxtapose rural with urban, region with capital. And Ferguson makes a point of distinguishing Dublin from the primitive decrepitude of the regions, employing such distinction to reinforce the refinement of his adopted city. For the educated observer:

> all nature abounds with enjoyment; but nowhere, we venture to say, will that enjoyment be obtained by such a man more fully, more expeditiously, more cheaply, or more safely than in our own country – nay, at our own capital. Of all the northern capitals, Dublin indeed seems to us the best situated in this respect; for while the city itself stands in a plain as rich and cultivated as high civilisation can make it, a single day's march will bring an active citizen where he may roam about the length of a summer's morning, not only out of sight of the habitations of men, but in full view of the eyrie and within hearing of the scream of the eagle.[34]

The rural excursion had become the hallmark of urban sophistication, and Ferguson's role of internal 'tourist' becomes a signifier of urban bourgeois values. Rural Ireland was an accepted commodity, but the practice of touring it, sketching it and writing about it in the picturesque idiom clearly defined one as a leisured member of the urban bourgeoisie. As the detached observer gained a superiority through the process of surveillance, so did the city assume authority and stability from its creation of a rural opposite; its replacement of an unknown quantity with recognizable formulae. The 'Attractions of Ireland' articles are part therefore, of a broad dialectic between the capital and the regions of Ireland. They refer to a public, rather than a personal response to the Irish countryside, to the shaping of the distinctive urban sensibility through which their author underlined his identification with Dublin.

GEORGE PETRIE AND THE IRISH PICTURESQUE TOURIST

From the rationalizing and administrative activities typified by the work of the Ordnance Survey Commission to the aesthetic reproduction of the country-

---

34 'The Attractions of Ireland, no. 2 – scenery and society', 333 and 315.

side according to the restraining conventions of the commercial picturesque, a pattern emerged through which the rural hinterland was systematically brought into focus by an urban enclave.[35] The artistic parallel to scientific procedure deserves emphasis in this respect, particularly in relation to the Survey, which, in addition to its mathematical apportionment of the landscape, developed its own artistic initiative. In the provision of topographical and antiquarian records the role of the sketcher was vital, and as a result of this combination of requirements the artist and antiquarian George Petrie proved a major influence both on Ferguson and on the reading public as a whole, in terms of perceptions of the country. Petrie was officially appointed to the Topographical Department in 1835, but his contributions to it through his interaction with O'Donovan had begun some years earlier.[36] One of the leading Irish antiquarians of his generation, he brought to the Survey team not only his historical knowledge but also his skills as an artist, which were channelled into producing records of ruins and antiquities, much praised by Ferguson for their authenticity in his review of Petrie's *Ecclesiastical architecture in Ireland*, in 1845.[37]

Alarmed at the decay he had observed during his tours around the country, Petrie underlined the need for a pictorial record of antiquarian sites. In a letter to Larcom expressing this opinion, he lamented that the churches of County Galway, for example, had become more dilapidated since his last visit than he had thought possible over a century. 'And if I had not sketched so much three years since, very little would be known hereafter on the antiquities of the place. Even the Irish inscriptions have been destroyed or the flags carried away. And this shows the necessity of having a draughtsman with the topographer.'[38]

Petrie's artistic contributions were valuable, therefore, to the historical dimension of the Survey, but his influence extended far beyond this, through his domination of commercial topographical illustration and landscape painting. From 1819 onwards he was employed in the provision of hundreds of sketches for Irish travel guides, including James Norris Brewer's *Beauties of Ireland* (1820), Thomas Cromwell's *Excursions in Ireland* (1820), and George Newenham Wright's *Guides to Wicklow and Killarney* (1822). In collaboration with fellow artists Andrew Nichol and Henry O'Neill he also provided material for illustrated guides to Wicklow and the Antrim Coast. There was little scope for stylistic individuality in the work however, and the publishers' commissions were spe-

---

35 The terms are used here according to the framework established by M. Hechter, *Internal colonialism: the Celtic fringe in British national development* (1975), p. 143. The 1842 census estimated that only one fifth of the Irish population lived in towns or villages. See T.W. Freeman's analysis, 'Land and people, c.1841' (1989).   36 For Petrie's life and work see P. Murray, 'George Petrie 1789–1866', W. Stokes, *The life and labours in archaeology of George Petrie* (1868), and E. Crooke, *Politics, archaeology and the creation of a national museum*, chapter 4.   37 'Petrie's round towers', *DUM* 25 (April 1845), 379–96.   38 Petrie to Larcom, 20 Aug. 1839, NLI LP 7550.

cific. 'My feeling, as well I believe as your own, would rather incline highly to ruins; interesting from architectural character or picturesque features', wrote his publisher Brewer in 1825, setting Petrie's brief for the *Beauties of Ireland*.[39]

The extent to which this satisfied Petrie's personal artistic leanings is questionable: the transition from the classical landscape tradition of the Royal Dublin Society School in which he had trained with Francis Danby and James Arthur O'Connor to the more lucrative field of topographical illustration was perhaps not effected without compromise. In such work he was clearly bound to the criteria set by public taste for the picturesque at the expense no doubt, of more fulfilling excursions into the romantic sublime.[40] But in fact, even Petrie's exhibited landscape work, including his early scenes of 'Glendalough and 'Glenmalure' in 1815, or later his 'Last round of pilgrims at Clonmacnoise' and 'Saint Bridget's Well, Clare' in the late 1820s, suggest that his interest in the derelict remnants of the Gaelic past imbued his non-commissioned art with a strong romantic tendency, easily translatable into a commercial picturesque. When he toured Ireland sketching for the Ordnance Survey his reports to Larcom illustrated his tendency to present the country in terms of its most nostalgic and crepuscular qualities.[41] And these were the properties disseminated to a wide audience during the 1830s through Petrie's regular pen-and-ink illustrations of ruins and antiquities in the *Dublin Penny Journal*. Praising the artist's contributions, his biographer William Stokes cites from the magazine an anonymous article celebrating the enduring image of the country he had established:

> If we were desirous of giving a stranger a true idea of Ireland [...] we should conduct him to one of our green open landscapes, where the dark and ruined castle, seated on some rocky height, or the round tower, with its little parent church, in some sequestered valley, would be the only features to arrest his attention; and of such a scene we should say emphatically, 'this is Ireland!'[42]

Such an image was pervasive and enduring. In 1866, the year of Petrie's death, the *Dublin Saturday Magazine* described how 'his simplest sketch assumed the char-

---

39 J.N. Brewer to Petrie, 26 Aug. 1826, NLI MS 789, no. 46. 40 See P. Murray, 'George Petrie', on this point, vol. 1, p. 21. 41 Lamenting the demise of romance in Connaught, for example, he praised 'the costumes of the women, so exquisitely beautiful and simple – exactly as if they had stepped out of the pictures of Raphael or Murillo. We shall soon have in their place cheap cotton gowns so odious to the lover of the picturesque, stays to destroy the grace and freedom of attitude that delights us every moment, and shoes and stockings to cramp the feet and give them corns and bunnions (sic), and deprive their grecian long toes of the classical proportions'. Petrie to Larcom, 24 Aug 1839, NLI MS 7550; cited P. Murray, vol. 1, p. 94. 42 Cited W. Stokes, *Life and labours*, p. 72.

acter of a painted poem: a green hillside, a shattered cross, a ruined watchtower, as treated by his genius, became the subject of a picture, the indescribable charm of which riveted the attention and set the imagination to work'.[43] In the public mind Petrie and the picturesque were interchangeable, as his vignettes became emblematic of an Ireland selectively viewed and romantically preserved.

Through his interest in art and his contact with Petrie, Ferguson once again appears on the amateur periphery of a professional discipline. In the 1830s he apprenticed himself to the artist in order to acquire the basis of a sketching technique suitable for the recording of antiquarian remains. Commenting on the close friendship they established, Lady Ferguson observes how profoundly her husband was influenced by the artist. Petrie offered Ferguson advice and encouragement in a series of letters and drawings on miscellaneous antiquities, and repeatedly, exhorted him to his sketchbook. 'For heaven's sake see it, and tell me and draw me all about it', he implored, in a letter referring to a church facade they had discussed. He instructed Ferguson too in the rudiments of sketching, passing on to him a reverence for detail and praising his progress: '[y]ou are certainly an admirable fellow – I say it soberly and without any joke', he wrote. 'Your letter describing [the church at] Ullard and the accompanying sketches are equally excellent, and when I give you a few lessons in foliage, which with the blessing of God I will most assuredly do, you will be a first-rate sketcher as well as antiquary.'[44]

Not surprisingly, this proximity to the discourse of picturesque art had a major impact on Ferguson's literary style and imaginative conception of Ireland. In the *Hibernian nights' entertainments*, his subscription to the laws of picturesque representation is evident in his descriptions of landscape, and in scenes which endorse in prose the crepuscular, static, antiquated Ireland produced by Petrie in a visual medium. Like Scott and his topographical illustrator Turner, Ferguson and Petrie shared an adherence to 'the romantic mystique of place, that is, to the perception of nature and human history in a topographical dimension'.[45] And all of this was sponsored and sanctioned by an urban commercialism which established the country's identity – and hence its value – through its features of picturesque antiquity. Ferguson's plea, in his 1836 articles, for the restoration and recollection of past generations 'summoned up by heroic monuments in every field', represents a genuine plea for historical responsibility, but one subject to the formulae of commercial taste and the dictates of artistic fashion.[46]

---

43 W. Stokes, p. 12. 44 M.C. Ferguson, *SSFID*, vol. 1, pp. 42–6. Lady Ferguson discusses Ferguson's sketches of ecclesiastical remains, as carried out under Petrie's tutelage. Some of Ferguson's landscape and ecclesiastical sketches are preserved with a collection of his papers in the Linenhall Library, Belfast, and in the Royal Irish Academy. 45 Turner was employed by Scott in 1818 to illustrate *Provincial antiquities and picturesque scenery of Scotland* (1819–26). See Finley, *Landscapes of memory*, chapter 1, and A. Holcomb, 'Scott and Turner' (1973), p. 211. 46 'The Attractions

The nexus of topography, antiquity and landscape became the basis on which Ireland was forged as a picturesque rural ideal, passive and depopulated; serving the interests of a middle-class urban culture but divested of any inherent political or social significance.[47]

Hence, 'The Attractions of Ireland' articles also serve to transfer the picturesque idiom from the antiquarian remains of bardic and medieval Ireland to a contemporary Irish landscape provided emblematically by County Wicklow. The county, with its dramatic scenery and celebrated beauty spots, was already well established as an accessible rural retreat for Dublin's middle classes. By the 1780s, 'a well-worn itinerary from Dublin led to Powerscourt with its mansion and waterfall, to the Glen of the Downs, that deep pass between the two long ranges of mountains, and to the Devil's Glen and Glendalough where the early Christian remains enhanced the landscape, both visually and conceptually'.[48] Few Irish counties were sketched and painted as frequently. George Barrett's 'Powerscourt Waterfall' (1760), James Arthur O'Connor's Wicklow landscapes of the 1820s, and Petrie's own early watercolours of Glendalough and Glenmalure were among the numerous exhibits which repeatedly depicted selected scenes. The travel-guide writers and the topographical illustrators who followed seized upon the picturesque potential of the area and marketed it to Dublin. In 1822, the Reverend George Newenham Wright published his *Guide to the county of Wicklow*, with engravings by George Petrie, a publication which anticipates in detail the visual and emotional agenda for the tourists of the 1830s. And in May of 1835 several passages from William Curry's *Guide to the county of Wicklow* featured in the *Dublin Penny Journal*, similarly espousing the conventions of picturesque etiquette; the careful selection of perspective, the regularization of emotional response and the use of pre-ordained viewing stations.[49]

Ferguson's treatment of Wicklow in the second of the 'Attractions' series is thus a formulaic account, but worth nothing, nonetheless, for the extent to which it underpins both picturesque convention and the reflexive elevation of an authoritative and progressive Dublin centre. 'We will now suppose our tourist, in addition to his qualifications as an engineer, endowed with more or less the eye of a painter', the section begins, before offering a description of the colouring of Djouce mountain. 'The cornfields then are just of the hue of emeralds, and the earth of the potatoes crossed by the colouring of the young crop makes a charming purple; then the moist atmosphere invests the rocks with tints of pink and violet, and the waters under the deep blue of summer

---

of Ireland, no. 2 – scenery and society', 331. **47** See W.J. McCormack's comments on Wordsworth's visit to Ireland in 1829 as an illustration of this relationship, *Ascendancy and tradition*, p. 37. **48** E. Malins and the Knight of Glin, p. 168. **49** See G.N. Wright, *A guide to the county of Wicklow* (1822), pp. 27–32.

skies are all cerulean, while distance blends and harmonizes the aerial perspective and distinguishes the whole.'[50] The true value of the county lies not in its intrinsic visual beauties, however, but in its availability for Dublin tourism and enterprise. Less than a day's journey away from the city, and even 'cheapened by the facility of access', as Ferguson suggests, Wicklow's popularity as a rural resort was greatly increased with the opening of the Dublin-Kingstown railway in 1834.[51] The construction of the new line had been celebrated by Ferguson in a previous *DUM* article, and hailed as a tribute to the engineer James Pim. Would this enterprise, so clearly emblematic of the advance of civilization in Ireland, eventually fail as other ventures had done?

> Or shall our delighted eyes behold the level line smooth as a garden walk, its granite sleepers steady as their native rock, and the clean metal rails themselves glaring like our own shoes in the sun; while, ever and anon, increasing from a dark point in the distance to the size of an over-hanging house-side, down comes the impetuous engine, whizzing and clanking and fuming like the black drudging demon of an enchanter [...] while all the broad breast of Killiney resounds to the blasting of the quarrymen, the mallet of the stone-cutter, and the busy tap of the builder's trowel – merchants bargaining, clerks cyphering, cranes and wagons groaning, and politics forgotten in the happy hurry of universal prosperity?[52]

For Ferguson the railway was a symbol of enterprise and industry, and of the continuing extension of urban technology into a rural landscape, a sentiment in keeping with his elevation of Wicklow as the ideal suburban excursion for the Dublin tourist. The building of road and rail further into the uncivilized reaches of the country would facilitate 'leisure for the luxury of intellectual employment', he claimed, creating a new, accessible environment for the modern traveller.

In this spirit he undertakes his own journey from urban sophistication into the retreat of the Wicklow mountains. Ferguson had visited the area in 1834 on a walking tour with the writer William Carleton, who later recalled in his autobiography only the fact that his companion had inscribed his poem 'The pretty girl of Lough Dan' in the visitors' album of an inn at which they had stayed. In the 'Attractions' piece, the visit is developed into a recreational tour. The opening section appears as a highly personal and intensely emotional piece of

---

50 'The Attractions of Ireland, no. 1 – scenery', 113; 'The Attractions of Ireland, no 2 – scenery and society', 320.
51 See T.W. Freeman, 'Land and people, c.1841', p. 259, and K. Murray, 'Dublin's first railway', p. 19. The new rail line was estimated to carry 4,000 people per day on the route south from the city.   52 'Hilloa our fancy: flight the first', *DUM* 3 (Jan. 1834), 27–8.

writing from the young poet; the Wicklow hills presented in a sequence of intimate dealings with the landscape, a quasi-religious communion with Nature. But the register is familiar, for just as the first and third of 'The Attractions of Ireland' articles adopted a particular posture – of the land economist or the anthropologist – so this middle section deliberately invokes the prose patterns of the tour-guide. Its author's invitation to the reader as 'imagined tourist' introduces a set of preconditions to the experience itself, as the geometric vision of the cartographer is replaced by simple descriptions which 'eyes unused to the theodolite can take in and remember without much exertion'. The resultant tour becomes an exercise, a process of formalized perception consciously invoking the customs of picturesque travel, and offers the reader only the itemized and conditioned responses of the urban tourist. The communion Ferguson describes merely reinforces a common practice, complete with conventional apostrophes and a ritualized emotional thrill.

The critic Jonathan Culler has suggested that one of the chief values of tourism lies in its semiotic function. 'The tourist is interested in everything as a sign of itself, an instance of a typical cultural practice.'[53] In the 1830s, the tourist role and its incorporated practices were public evidence of one's affiliation to a literate, leisured urban class, and indeed of the existence of such a class in the first place. Ferguson's Wicklow retreat and his use of the county as representative of rural Ireland pay homage to the urban myth which had created such an artefact. His response to the landscape is characterized by the same paradox which the 1836 articles exploit throughout; that any experience of Ireland based on individual and emotive values was simultaneously checked by conventions framed within a self-conscious public sphere, the location of the author within what Raymond Williams has described as the long history of the 'self-conscious observer' in landscape tradition.[54] Ferguson's use of a predetermined agenda, his exploitation of artistic prescription and his dependence upon the conventions of the tour underwrite his perspectives on the country at every stage.

The nature of the articles, and Ferguson's immersion in the discourse of bourgeois rural tourism to which they belong, offers further adjustment to concepts of class structure in nineteenth-century Ireland. They are a reminder of the formative middle-class sensibility which, in terms of taste, expression and self-definition, must be factored into discussions of the social and political ethos of Ireland in the 1830s. The general rush of publications in the period – publications determined for a domestic readership – points to the presence of an aspirant middle-class contingent for whom Ferguson and his contemporaries responded both commercially and ideologically. Like Petrie as an artist and

---

53 'The semiotics of tourism' in *Framing the sign* (1988), p. 155. 54 *The country and the city* (1973), p. 120.

illustrator, Ferguson as a writer manifests a curious but pertinent breaching – or more accurately a blurring – of boundaries, between the aristocratic scholarly élitism of the Royal Irish Academy and the commercially-oriented practices of an ascendant group of business and professional circles, just as his writing extended from refined cultural antiquarianism to the lucrative arena of travel writing and periodical hack work.

The 1836 articles acknowledge furthermore, an empirical impulse which found its symbolic co-ordinates in the operations of the Ordnance Survey. Ferguson's research for the Memoir, his support for the Survey as a whole and his topographical work during the 1830s combine to produce an intellectual endorsement of his private project to 'know' Ireland. Both aspects confirm the recurrent theme of 'The Attractions of Ireland'; the priority and status of Dublin as a credible urban centre which, as the context for an enterprising community of like-minded civic achievers, might to some degree withstand the wayward pull of sectarian and imperialist ideologies.

CHAPTER FOUR

Thomas Davis and the Protestant Repeal Association

In the late 1840s, Ferguson abandoned the Union and turned to Repeal. His political apostasy was short-lived but significant, marking the culmination of a decade of insecurity and flux. Increasingly estranged from the *Dublin University Magazine*, he began to move to the periphery of the dynamic Young Ireland circle, whose programme of cultural regeneration lessened his distrust of the Repeal movement as a whole. O'Connell had never won his approval, but the founders of the *Nation* newspaper seemed to promise a new and inclusive national identity for Ireland, one to which Ferguson could respond with enthusiasm and refer to with pride in the face of English caricature and ignorance. The contact between the writer and the *Nation* idealists served to fulfil needs on both sides as literary exchanges merged with ideological requirements. Within this relationship Ferguson found not only a fertile literary environment for his poetic material, which Charles Gavan Duffy was quick to assimilate into a neo-Celtic canon, but a new security in nationality, clearly marked in the exuberance and optimism of his 1845 article on the Scottish poet Robert Burns.

Ferguson's defection to Repeal was largely circumstantial, and the brotherhood promised by Duffy and the *Nation* provided the necessary cultural push. But in the context of his leanings towards a civic ideology, a further set of influences emerges, directly related to the professional confederacy of Dublin's legal network and institutions. Described as 'a safe, though not a brilliant advocate', his comparatively undistinguished legal career is nonetheless relevant to a full understanding of his cultural, political and civic sensibilities.[1] Two points are of particular significance. First, the specific class status of Irish barristers in the mid-nineteenth century provided Ferguson with professional co-ordinates in the Irish capital, and more, a *sense* of Dublin as a capital whose domestic institutions demanded protection in an era of prevailing centralization. Secondly, the political leanings of this group, which inherited a tradition of dissent established as far back as 1782, and which had officially registered its opposition to the Union in 1800, offer an important backdrop to Protestant Repeal. Ferguson's appointment as a barrister on the North-Eastern circuit court meanwhile, which

---

1 G.H. Smith, *The North East Bar* (1910), p. 84.

exposed him to the conditions of regional Ireland, also enabled him to maintain close acquaintance with a number of northern colleagues, whose nationalist political bearings deserve attention.

The figure providing a bridgehead between the two communities, political and legal, was Thomas Davis. One of Ferguson's Trinity College contemporaries, Davis was also called to the bar in 1838 but never addressed the Bench, and proved to be an ineffectual lawyer who 'got no business, and perhaps did not care to get any'.[2] But if his professional career was unsuccessful, his cultural activism was inspirational, and his iconic value for Ferguson – desperate to stabilize an acceptable image of cultivated middle-class Protestantism – immense. 'There is something in our feelings about this country that makes us brothers' he wrote to Davis in 1845.[3] Where his writings in the early 1830s had pleaded for Protestant participation in Ireland's cultural inheritance, his work in the following decade was preoccupied with defining the terms upon which that Protestantism should exist as a cultural and moral fraternity. For this, Davis provided a touchstone, in life a like-minded cultural nationalist, and in death a *tabula rasa* on which Ferguson would inscribe his vision of modern Irish Protestant civility.

Ferguson's leadership of the Protestant Repeal Association in 1848 thus brings together several key strands of engagement with Ireland. His rapprochement with Duffy and Young Ireland, his affiliation to a politically dynamic and independent professional body, in the form of the Dublin legal fraternity, and his concern to establish a place for Irish Protestantism – a concern inextricable from his relationship with Davis – all contributed to his sense that the country might indeed achieve its promise of civic, cultural and national integrity. What tipped him over the edge, towards a forceful and stated rejection of the Union, was, inevitably, the Famine. Deeply distressed by what he saw as English indifference to Irish suffering, he reacted vehemently against government mismanagement and insensitivity, the obstinate pursuit of political economy in place of practical relief. This, more than anything, shattered his confidence in the neighbouring island. 'I have no wish to see England unfortunate', he wrote to Aubrey de Vere in February 1848. 'I admire and esteem the English, but I cannot resist the impression that even in our own day, they may become very undesirable companions. In such an event we ought to be able to take care of ourselves.'[4]

THE LAW AND THE PROFESSIONS

The rise in status of the Irish legal profession during the first half of the nineteenth century was manifest in Ireland in the gradual formalization of legal

---

2 J.R. O'Flanagan, *The Irish Bar*, p. 418.   3 NLI MS 2644 f75.   4 21 Feb. 1848, NLI MS 13, 122–28.

training and practice. In 1830, the Law Society of Ireland was founded, and in 1839 Tristram Kennedy established the Dublin Law Institute for the education and examination of lawyers. True, Catholics were only admitted to the lower echelons of the profession at the end of the eighteenth century, and they remained a small component of the seven hundred or so barristers and almost two thousand solicitors and attorneys estimated to be working in 1839. In general however, the profession of barrister was comparatively accessible, particularly as the legal fraternity was seen to represent the gradual ascendancy of professional training over aristocracy and patronage. With its history of legal advocates from Grattan and Tone to O'Connell and Butt, it was also the obvious breeding ground for highly skilled political activists who campaigned on both sides of the Reform and Repeal debates. Steadily, the legal fraternity evolved into a vibrant political and social community, a formative intelligentsia which provided an alternative authority to the dominant Tory interest within the city, and a significant lobbying power on the political stage, as Dublin's Four Courts became 'the rallying point for all the aspiring talent in the country'.[5]

The Bar provided professional status, the legal profession representing in Ireland as elsewhere a companion to medicine and the church in the development of a culture of 'science and service'.[6] Even more than these two, it was closely identified with the emergence and consolidation of a distinct middle class, and – in the wake of the Union's devastation of Irish trade – a refuge for a new generation of would-be professionals. 'Our trade is annihilated – our manufactories are ruined', claimed the writer of one of the *Irish Quarterly Review*'s regular pro-Repeal editorials. 'For the past fifty years the Bar has been the goal of the ambitious scion of the middle classes in Ireland', and the natural resort therefore, for those 'seeking advancement' within a rapidly changing urban society.[7] The 1851 census in Ireland recorded a marked rise in membership of the profession, with 840 barristers – the 'upper branch' of the legal system – listed

---

5 C. Kenny, *Tristram Kennedy* (1996), pp. 68–72. Chapter three traces the 'surge of professionalism' in nineteenth-century legal practice in Ireland, and Kenny points out that this period of heightened activism coincided with the rise of the *Nation*. See also R.B. McDowell, 'The Irish courts of law, 1801–1914' (1956–7), on the structure and reorganization of the bar in the 1840s. For an account of political involvement, including the conservative impulse which was also active within the Irish legal fraternity as represented particularly by the work of Isaac Butt, see J. Hill, 'The legal profession and the defence of the *ancien régime* in Ireland, 1790–1840' (1990), and on the increased authority and lobbying power of the legal profession in both Britain and Ireland during this period, see P.J. Corfield, *Power and the professions* (1995). The resurgence of confidence in the Irish bar at the highest level is also noted by F. Elrington Ball who earmarks this period: '[w]hen Queen Victoria ascended the throne in the summer of 1837, the Irish judicial bench had completely recovered such loss of prestige as it had sustained at the time of the Union, and had reached high water-mark, if the criterion be the celebrity of its members': *The judges in Ireland* (1920), p. 279. 6 See E.J. Yeo, *The contest for social science* (1996), chapter 4. 7 'The present condition and future prospects of the Irish Bar', *Irish Quarterly Review* 1:4 (1851), 72–96. 8 See Corfield, pp. 31–3 on the implications and representation of the barristers and attorneys in the Irish census of 1851.

as working in the country.⁸ Status, of course, did not necessarily mean financial security, and younger members of the Bar were frequently impecunious, reduced to 'devilling', or preparing briefs for more senior colleagues. Lady Ferguson records that as a young barrister, her husband struggled to make sufficient income, finding like many of his peers a discrepancy between the high profile of the profession and the somewhat meagre standard of living it provided.⁹

The Bar provided a working community and social context within the capital. Members were expected to attend a requisite number of dinners at the King's Inns, to participate in Bar committee meetings, and to maintain a strict professional etiquette – outside their legal work barristers were not permitted to engage in any activity other than politics or writing.¹⁰ They published in their own journals, including, most notably, the *Irish Quarterly Review*, a vehemently national monthly periodical founded in 1849 and sustained for ten years on a staple diet of Irish politics, literature and culture. Outside Dublin meanwhile, the Bar fostered a national network of interest through the six regional circuit courts, each of which maintained a particular protocol. On the North-Eastern circuit, to which Ferguson was appointed in 1838, members were expected to perform socially as much as professionally, maintaining a gentlemanly ethos of 'debate and coffee-house exchange'.¹¹ Until 1859 they were required to attend nightly dinners involving heavily ritualized traditions of toasts, fines, singing and storytelling. Following a resolution passed in 1836, they were permitted to travel on public coaches rather than on horseback or the so-called 'Bar Waggon', but they were still expected to 'go in Professional costume' so as to remain distinct from other gentlemen, and to wear wigs and gowns at all times when on circuit business.¹²

The intimacy and idiosyncrasy of legal life in the capital and on circuit reinforces the extent to which the Bar can be seen as supporting a distinct professional community within nineteenth-century Ireland. It also raises the question of political tendencies within the legal fraternity. The profession had a tradition of political activism – its *alumni* including Grattan, Curran, Fitzgibbon and O'Connell – and a history of political independence, furnishing a Lawyers' Corps of Volunteers in 1782, and passing a motion against the Act of Union in 1800.¹³ A prevailing nationalist sentiment was, arguably, exacerbated by the

---

9 *SSFID*, vol. 1, p. 122. See also M.E. Daly's discussion of the financial problems of the legal profession in contrast to their significant social status in the city, *Dublin: the deposed capital* (1984), p. 133, and D. Hogan, *The legal profession*, p. 70. 10 Hogan, *The legal profession*, p. 9. 11 Corfield, p. 90. G.H. Smith records that Ferguson was admitted to the North-Eastern circuit Bar in 1839, not, as M.C. Ferguson states, the previous year. The six Irish circuits were Home, North-East, North-West, Connaught, Munster, Leinster. 12 G.H. Smith, *The North East Bar*, pp. 36–7. The controversial 1867 motion to continue the obligatory wearing of wig and gown on circuit was seconded by Samuel Ferguson. For life at the Bar see also R. Cock, 'The bar at assizes: barristers on three nineteenth-century circuits', *Kingston Law Review* 6 (1976), and W.H. Curran, *Sketches of the Irish Bar* (1855). 13 Hogan, *The legal pro-*

regulation requiring Irish trainee barristers to spend a year in residence at one of the four London Inns of Court. Gray's Inn in particular had a strong Irish membership, listing Thomas O'Hagan and Thomas Davis in its admission books for the early 1830s.[14] Following Emancipation, the legal profession was comparatively swift in opening its doors to Roman Catholics, as was evident in Michael O'Loghlen's appointment as first Catholic judge in 1835, and in the meteoric rise of Ferguson's close friend, Thomas O'Hagan, from the position of attorney general in 1861 to that of lord chancellor, in 1868. Through the high number of barristers and lawyers involved, particularly at committee level, the legal fraternity made up the largest professional grouping in the membership of the National Repeal movement.[15]

Overall therefore, the prevailing political tendency of the Irish bar was strongly independent and in many quarters overtly nationalist. Nowhere was this more clearly signalled than in the membership of the North-Eastern circuit, which was indelibly marked by links to the United Irishmen movement and 1798. The 'Father' of the circuit from 1836, Robert Holmes, whose first wife was a sister of Robert Emmet, had been arrested in 1798 on suspicion of involvement. Though released on that occasion, Holmes continued to draw inspiration from the legacy of the United Irishmen and maintained a high profile as an advocate for independence.[16] Other members of the circuit shared his background or views, including Ferguson's close friends from boyhood, Robert Gordon and Thomas O'Hagan; the former United Irishmen William Drennan and Henry Joy; and later, John O'Hagan, an intimate of the Young Irelanders.[17] These men, Ferguson's working partners from 1838 to 1867, when he retired from the Bar, provide an important and much overlooked counter to the supposed community of Isaac Butt and the *DUM*, and cast a very different political complexion on his national sensibility.

If the Bar's political hue had its roots in the traditions and events of the past, its political voice was galvanized, finally, by events of the present, and crucially by the policy of centralization which threatened to transfer the authority of the Irish law courts to London. Despite losing the ancient Gaelic Brehon laws since the founding of the King's Inns in the sixteenth century, the Irish

---

fession, p. 23, and G.H. Smith, p. 16. 14 Ferguson appears on the Lincoln's Inn *Admission Register* for 1831: 'Samuel Ferguson, (22), 3rd son of John Ferguson of Belfast, Co Antrim, gentleman'. The four London Inns were Gray's Inn, Lincoln's Inn, Inner Temple and Middle Temple. See J.R. Hill, who comments on the nationalizing effects of the exposure of Irish barristers to modernization and their position *vis à vis* their British counterparts, 'The intelligentsia and Irish nationalism in the 1840s', 73. 15 J.R. Hill, 'The Intelligentsia and Irish nationalism', 107. On the O'Loghlen family, Catholic representation and family networks in the legal fraternity during this period, see Hogan, *The legal profession*. 16 See O'Flanagan, p. 281. 17 See G.H. Smith, chapter 7. In 1887 John O'Hagan, who married Thomas O'Hagan's daughter, wrote 'The poetry of Sir Samuel Ferguson' as a tribute to his late colleague.

legal establishment had long prided itself on its independence as a distinct national institution.[18] By the early 1840s however, the progress of centralization was everywhere in evidence: the decades since the Union had already seen the merging of the two Exchequers, the Post Offices and the Board of Customs and Excise. With the legal system next in line for rationalization, the Irish law fraternity rebelled. In 1841, after Plunkett was replaced as lord chancellor – and therefore head of the judiciary – by Campbell, a Scottish lawyer, a meeting of the Bar registered its disapproval, and passed a resolution that 'inasmuch as all judicial appointments in England are made from the English Bar, so all judicial appointments in Ireland ought to be made from the Irish Bar'.[19] Their action signalled the beginning of a decade of resistance, as Ireland's lawyers fought to retain their practice, independence and status in a struggle which propelled many, Samuel Ferguson included, further along the path towards Repeal.

DAVIS, DUFFY AND THE 'NATION'

Thomas Carlyle, surprised in 1846 to find Ferguson 'so very national', identified in his Irish visitor a passion which was no doubt generated by the cultural and political excitement in Dublin in the early 1840s, but still rooted in a heavily contingent definition of nationhood.[20] Ferguson's negotiations with various individuals from the Young Ireland set represented the fortuitous collision of literary, professional and civic objectives, but his version of the nation remained tentative and provisional, ultimately at odds with the ideals articulated by Davis and his colleagues through the emotive nexus of race, language and education. The *Nation*'s emphasis on a nationality of 'the spirit as well as the letter' and on the crucial role of literature in this formation had much to appeal to Ferguson, who shared Davis's faith in the development of a cultural superstructure.[21] Their efforts coalesced therefore, despite the underlying bifurcation of their respective constitutional premises.

The timing of events was also influential. The engineering of a nationalist cultural programme by Davis and Charles Gavan Duffy coincided with Ferguson's increasing alienation from the *DUM* under the editorship of Charles

---

18 On the Brehon laws, see C. Kenny, *Tristram Kennedy*, preface. Ferguson was particularly interested in the Brehon laws from an antiquarian perspective: see his paper 'On the rudiments of the common law discoverable in the published portion of the *Senchus Mor*', *Transactions of the Royal Irish Academy*, xiv: 2, 'Polite literature and antiquities' (1867), 83–117. 19 Hogan, *The legal profession*, p. 58. In 1846, Irishman Maziere Brady was appointed as Lord Chancellor, and subsequent appointments were generally from the Irish bench; see McDowell, 'The Irish courts of law', 366. 20 Cited Duffy, *Four years*, p. 32. 21 The full prospectus for the *Nation* is given by Charles Gavan Duffy, *A short life of Thomas Davis*, pp. 56–7.

Lever. Ferguson had been enraged by what he regarded as malevolent caricature of the Irish in Thackeray's 1842 *Irish sketch book*, and wrote to Blackwood requesting space to condemn 'the contemptuous tone of the English pup' in the pages of the *Edinburgh Magazine*. He believed Lever's allegiance to and publication of Thackeray in the *DUM* were typical of an anti-Irish editorial policy pandering to the superficial tastes of the metropolis. The editorial committee was courting disaster. 'It is not improbable that the course they have been pursuing of late will lead to the establishment of a rival organ', Ferguson warned. Nothing did more to weaken the Conservative party in Ireland than their exhibition of contempt for their own country, and their eagerness to be laughed at and pitied. 'It may gratify the natural pride of superiority for the present, but it weakens British interests in the very quarters where their preservation is of most consequence to the maintenance and security of the Empire.'[22]

Ferguson was therefore open to those outside the *DUM*'s political sphere who were willing to take seriously his efforts to maintain dignity in Irish writing. When in 1845, Charles Gavan Duffy incorporated ten of his poems in the *Ballad poetry of Ireland*, he received a letter from Ferguson thanking him for the kind comments 'for which my own party has left me to wait a sufficiently long time', and adding that 'they are now doubly pleasing coming from your side of the house'. Furthermore the literary standards of the rival journal, which had been established in 1842, were proving to be closer to Ferguson's heart than those of his own magazine. 'I got a copy of the last *Nation* yesterday, and read it with very great interest', he wrote to Duffy. 'The writing is excellent; as good I think as it ever was, and the matter most important. With all my objections to the end you aim at, I must say that the *Nation* is the most creditable Irish organ.'[23] Though his estrangement from the *DUM* was at an end by 1844, the break in relations was enough to create an opportunity for Duffy and his enterprises to take hold.

The cultural agenda established by the protagonists of Young Ireland took some of its initial impetus from Belfast, where the journalist Charles Gavan Duffy claimed to have found a hidden liberalism within the Orange bastion. The enthusiasm of many of his northern friends for Irish history and antiquities increased his awareness of the resources lying dormant in Ireland's literary heritage, and during his time spent working with the Catholic magazine, the *Vindicator*, he considered the possibilities which might be opened up by a dedicated project. 'As a political journal the *Vindicator* was a success, but I longed to see it awaken an interest in native literature', he wrote. 'The fragments of

---

22 Ferguson to Blackwood, 3 June 1843, NLS MS 4065 f 247. For details of the quarrel with the *DUM*, see Denman, *Samuel Ferguson*, p. 62.   23 Duffy letters, 1 Aug. 1845, NLI MS 5756 f 463; 14 Mar. 1846, NLI MS 5756 f 311.

Celtic song which came down to us often in rude translations only, had been a constant joy to me, and I was persuaded that for a race whose public festivities were always enlivened by ballad poetry, chanted by minstrels and chiefs, song was an immense though greatly underrated force.' From these beginnings the literary manifesto of Young Ireland took shape. The *Nation*, established by Duffy, Davis and John Blake Dillon in 1842, strove to incorporate within a political programme a sense of national identity culled from literary texts, continuing what Duffy termed his experiment of 'appealing to an old bardic people in passionate popular verse'. The publication of *The spirit of the Nation* in 1843 confirmed the place of verse and song within the movement's programme for political education, and in doing so represented a defiant act of territorialization. 'When the *Nation* was established' Duffy later wrote, 'whatever could be called literature in this island belonged exclusively to the Tories. The *Dublin University Magazine* was read throughout the two islands, but it was more vehemently anti-national than the *Times*.'[24] Retrieving this viable and potentially explosive property was a therefore a critical step in the campaign for nationality.

What the *Nation* hoped to create was a readership linking an educated middle-class element to the O'Connellite masses. For this reason, Duffy's criteria for the texts included in his *Ballad poetry of Ireland* of 1845 sought to carve out a formula for a modern national mode, appealing to readers across a wide spectrum. In his introduction to the first edition of the volume he outlined his selection procedure. Old bardic material was excluded because translations of it were often 'un-Irish'. Street-songs were not appropriate as national songs, being suitable only to the *purlieus* of Cork or Dublin. What remained were the Anglo-Irish ballads; contemporary short lyrics or narrative poems which reproduced (and thereby signified the pre-existence of) an original national spirit, being 'the production of educated men, with English tongues but Irish hearts'. The resultant list – Griffin, Banim, Carleton, Callanan, Ferguson, Lover, Davis, Mangan, Walsh – provided a solid convocation of the kind of talent which had 'taught the native muse to become English without growing un-Irish in character', blending two worlds in a single, national idiom. Like Davis and Ferguson, Duffy took Burns as his model, depicting him as the cohesive bard who had united the local and universal, the primitive and sophisticated: the poet who 'wooed poetry from the salon and the library to become household among the poorest peasantry in Europe: elevated the uncouth dialect of his native hills to be familiar to fifty millions of men among the most powerful and united of modern nations.' The bonding process was enhanced by Duffy's indulgence in the kind of race-mongering which set parameters in Irish poetry until Yeats,

---

24 Duffy, *My life*, vol. 1, p. 55; p. 64; p. 69.

celebrating the 'strong passions of our nation', and the 'intense relish of the Celtic race for poetry of action and passion', or speaking of his race as 'so full of sensibility and impulsiveness', and thereby circumventing the reality of cultural and economic division within Ireland.[25]

The result is a pre-figuration of the 'Irish mode' later defined by Thomas MacDonagh, a poetic conglomeration encompassing peasantry and intelligentsia in an instant heritage, a swiftly manufactured and yet timeless national aesthetic.[26] In this way the 1840s movement was able to unite a range of classes within a single concept of identity, stressing the significance of race and language but eliding the complications of linguistic and historical fracture. David Lloyd has described how the Young Irelanders – a group dominated by members of the urban intelligentsia – were able to overcome their lack of organic connection with the people by invoking 'an alternative concept of organicism which rewrote discontinuity as continuity'.[27] As cultural policy it went far beyond anything Ferguson had achieved. And Ferguson too was harnessed to Duffy's agenda; remodelled as an unsung maverick committed to Irish culture in the face of unionist rejection. Duffy later recalled:

> It is proper to say that Samuel Ferguson had been at work on Irish literature long before Davis or the other writers of the *Nation*, but the *University Magazine*, to which his contributions commonly went, circulated among a class who had imperfect sympathy with his labours. In National stories and ballads and charming essays on the resources and attractions of the country he had anticipated much that was afterwards done in the *Nation*. But he had not reached the people, who knew so little of Ferguson that when I printed his fine ballads, 'Willy Gilliland' and 'Una Phelimy' in the *Ballad Poetry of Ireland*, a few years later, I was asked by educated people if the author was still living.[28]

Duffy responded to this perceived failure with a retrospective appropriation of Ferguson to the contemporary scene, weaving his miscellaneous poems into the fabric of the national spirit. In his introduction to the *Ballad poetry* he classes Ferguson's ballads with those of Scott, Burns and Southey, emphasizing his quality as a writer 'fired with a living and local interest [...] ventilated with the free air of the country'. And in apparent contradiction to the above suggestion that Ferguson was unknown even among educated readers, he added in a note

---

25 *Ballad poetry of Ireland* (1845), pp. 12–23. 26 MacDonagh describes this as 'the mode of a people to whom the ideal, the spiritual, the mystic, are the true', *Literature in Ireland* (1916) p. 8. See also MacDonagh's discussion of Ferguson, chapter 5. 27 *Nationalism and minor literature*, p. 68. 28 *My life*, vol. 1, p. 64n.

to the text that Ferguson's essays and historical tales published in the *DUM* 'have exercised a wide and powerful influence in nationalising the sentiments and pursuits of the literary and professional classes in this country'.[29]

Duffy's machinery was effective, and Ferguson showed little resistance, other than apparently remarking to a friend that 'some of these fellows long to stick their skeans into the bowels of the Saxon'.[30] The Young Irelanders were content meanwhile to appraise the elements of his writing which conformed to their ideal. John Mitchel later wrote to him from Paris, 'I have always been jealous of the fame of the individual who gave me in the days of my youth (helas!) the "Fairy Thorn" and "The Forging of the Anchor"'.[31] While Ferguson never wrote for the *Nation* he was thus deeply integrated into its literary programme, and his presence within the camp was doubtless seen as an encouragement to others of his class and political leanings. As the first edition of the *Ballad poetry* sold out, the success of its prescriptive editorial policy in this direction became apparent. 'Not a conservative of education but will read it and be brought nearer to Ireland by it', wrote Davis to Smith O'Brien.[32] Duffy's role in cementing interests through literary circles was therefore of paramount importance, long before any overt political concerns came to the surface.

The vitality of Ferguson's nationalism during the 1840s is illustrated by an Ulster-Scots verse letter, which he wrote for his friend Robert Gordon at the beginning of January, 1845. In the piece he describes his position as an unmarried man of thirty-five, bereft of wealth and fame, who can do no more than pledge himself to the Muse and to his country:

> For ilka day I'm growin' stranger
> To speak my mind in love or anger;
> And, hech! ere it be muckle langer,
> You'll see appearin'
> Some offerin's o' nae cauld haranguer
> Put out for Erin.
>
> Lord, for ae day o' service done her!
> Lord, for ane hour's sunlight upon her!
> Here, Fortune, tak' warld's wealth and honour,
> You're no' my debtor,
> Let me but rive ae link asunder
> O' Erin's fetter!

29 *Ballad poetry*, p. 32. 30 Cited Duffy, *My life*, vol. 1, p. 70. 31 20 Feb. 1886, NLI MS 3486 f 10. 32 Cited Duffy, *My life*, vol. 1, p. 90n. Negotiations do seem to have taken place with a view to Ferguson writing for the *Nation*. At one stage in 1847 Ferguson wrote to Duffy, 'If you would give me a place in the *Nation*, I would wish to speak my mind about the way the Magazine is going on'. 29 Apr. 1847, NLI MS 5757 p. 29.

> Let me but help to shape the sentence
> Will put the pith o' independence,
> O' self-respect in self-acquaintance,
> And manly pride
> Intil auld Eber-Scot's descendants -
> Take a' beside![33]

Ferguson's ardour for his country in the poem and his avowed intention to speak out warmly on her behalf convey a nationalist fervour, though admittedly, one which is constrained by expression in literary cliché. The apostrophe to the Muse and the personification of Ireland as feminine captive awaiting masculine rescue reduce the poet to the role of a courtly patriot whose valiant actions are restricted to the page. Sanitized by its own conventionalism, the verse-epistle is a gesture devoid of real political will. But at the same time, it touches on the implications of his attraction to Young Ireland. Against his consciousness of his 'five-and-thritty seasons' Ferguson could associate himself with the youthful spirit of an emergent national energy in Dublin circles. The poem suggests past frustrations and an overwhelming desire to give vent to emotion and self-expression, hinting at a new tendency in Ferguson towards a fluency of romantic feeling which had rarely surfaced in his self-contained poetry and ceremonious prose.

This revitalized enthusiasm revealed itself in a number of energetic pieces published in the *DUM* following his return to its list of contributors. In an article on Robert Burns in the spring of 1845, he offered an extended celebration of a national poetic voice, with a tone of confident jubilation in marked contrast to the reserved critical deliberation of earlier literary commentary on Carleton or Edgeworth:

> Where almost an angel from heaven would be disregarded in the obloquy and clamour of party or sectarian warfare, if a true poet arise, and speak according to his mission, he will undoubtedly be heard – even, as in old times, the bard could put an end to the battles of the Gauls, by shaking his chain of silence between the hosts. That such a man will someday arise among us, as Burns, sixty years since, arose amongst the Scotch, or as Berenger, in our own generation, has arisen among the Parisians – it is as reasonable, as it is conciliatory and cheering to expect.[34]

---

33 M.C. Ferguson, *SSFID*, vol. 1, pp. 125–6. The manuscript text of this poem is prefaced by a dedicatory letter to Robert Gordon. 34 'Robert Burns', *DUM* 25 (Jan. 1845), 67.

This prophetic passage, with its pseudo-scriptural register, is characteristic of the entire article. Such a poet would be furnished, Ferguson insists, by the middle classes of the Irish. In what seems a direct allusion to Young Ireland activity, he continues by celebrating a national genius which is now present in the country, as 'the young men becoming conscious of the possession of something not dreamt of before, as well as of the power of communicating these new feelings, begin to open their hearts to one another in generous sentiments of friendship, of manliness, of sympathising detestation of untruth, cowardice, oppression, meanness and treachery'. Drawing upon the Coleridgean distinction between Imagination and Fancy, he provides himself with a new critical apparatus which obliterates the narrow discriminations of the Hardiman review, creating a vast arena of literary possibility, in which poets such as James Clarence Mangan, Thomas D'Arcy M'Gee and Thomas Davis shine with originality and authenticity.[35] The example set by Burns had unleashed the channels of excitement which now ran between Ferguson and Young Ireland; the coherence and exuberance of the *Nation*, thrown into relief by the increasing dilettantism of the *DUM*, suddenly drew his minority interest into the proximity of a young, influential and dynamic national platform.

Ferguson's relationship with Young Ireland was cemented by individual contacts with Gavan Duffy, D'Arcy M'Gee and Mitchel, but above all with Davis. Despite his political reservations, Ferguson identified in Thomas Davis, the charismatic leader of the movement, ideal and essential qualities of educated Irish Protestant 'manliness'. The emphasis Davis placed on language, education and literature as major ideological components of his nationalism – preconditions rather than end results – meant that his programme was at least superficially compatible with a cultural nationalism rooted in literary endeavour, and in his communications with Davis Ferguson appealed to him without reference to any overarching teleological incompatibility. Rather, he tagged his expressions of national feeling to the journalistic, literary and cultural ventures they shared as common ground. In May of 1844 he wrote to Davis advising him to read an article he had written for *Saunders Magazine* on the subject of the Ordnance Survey memoir, in which he celebrated its stand against 'anti-Irish Irishmen'. A short time later he sent another letter promising Davis support for his proposal to be elected to the Royal Irish Academy, and adding 'I do hope to effect something for Ireland before very long'. By April of 1845, just a few months before Davis's death, Ferguson wrote to him again: having been called

---

35 'Robert Burns II', *DUM* 25 (Mar. 1845), 291. Coleridge makes this distinction in Section 12 of his *Biographia Literaria* (1817). Ferguson was to describe Thomas D'Arcy M'Gee as 'the greatest poet of them all', M.C. Ferguson, *SSIFD*, vol. 1, p. 146. Carlyle's 'On heroes, hero-worship, and the heroic in history' had been published in 1841, and there are obvious echoes of this text in Ferguson's treatment of Burns.

away suddenly to his father's death-bed he was unable to complete a proof-reading assignment on O'Connor's *History of the Irish Brigade*, a military history of Ireland, and turned to Davis as an able scholar and 'a gentleman', for help.[36]

Cultural and journalistic interests aside, central to Ferguson's identification with the Young Ireland ideologue was the policy engendered by Davis to redeem the Repeal movement from what Ferguson identified as its vulgar origins, and to wrest it out of the hands of the O'Connellite Catholic majority.[37] Removing this barrier to Protestant participation involved the erosion of religious polarities and the establishment of notions of tolerance and pluralism which might thrive under a national umbrella; a move which Davis attempted first in his attack on Trinity College, in his 1840 'Address to the Historical Society', and subsequently in his anonymous letters to the *Nation* published from 1842 to 1843. These essays, entitled 'Letters of a Protestant on Repeal', sought to highlight common ground between the two opposing sides, and were the beginnings of an effort by Repeal commentators to redress Protestant fears of a Roman Catholic ascendancy under an independent legislation. Davis stressed the necessity of Protestant participation in the movement and in any subsequent administration, carving out a place for Protestant responsibility in the future life of the nation.[38] And in the emphasis he placed on the Protestant voice, his approach to the Repeal question began to provide a basis for the definition of a modern Protestant identity, viable in and relevant to post-Emancipation Ireland.

This dovetailed almost perfectly with Ferguson's continuing struggle to characterize – indeed, even to find terminology for – an acceptable middle-class Irish Protestantism. As was suggested in the previous chapter, Ferguson's writing in the 1830s was geared towards stabilizing the identity of an urban intelligentsia. In the 1840s his strained manoeuvres between the language of religion, race and class exposed a continuing need to demarcate his caste; to find a means of expression which, like the Hardiman review's *ad hominum* to 'the Protestant wealth and intelligence' of Ireland would signify the existence of a unified contingent, historically rooted in the country but free from associations of decadence, absenteeism, Orangeism or Anglophilia. What was required was

---

36 Davis letters, 7 May 1844, NLI MS 2644 f 67; n.d. NLI MS 2644 f 71; 28 Apr. 1845, NLI MS 2644 f 75. Perhaps there was a veiled hint to Davis here, for Ferguson directed him towards his own forthcoming review of the book in the May issue of the *DUM*. In its opportunist conclusion this review is distinctly pro-Union. 'It is a pleasing reflection that both the Irish and Scotch can afford to look back on the times when they respectively marched under these banners, so hostile to England, without blushing for their old alliances or doubting of the stability of the new. Their new associations, by every consideration of interest, of circumstance, of language and natural affection, are those in which all can best work together for the public good and common honour of the United Kingdom.' 'O'Connor's *History of the Irish Brigade*', *DUM* 25 (May 1845), 608. 37 See Foster, *Modern Ireland* p. 317. For Ferguson's view of the 'vulgar' basis of Repeal politics, see the opening remarks of his article on Davis, *DUM* 29 (Feb. 1847), 190. 38 R. Davis, *The Young Ireland movement* (1987), pp. 25–35. On Davis's politics see also K. Molloy, 'Thomas Davis and the idea of the Irish nation' (1988).

a cultural rather than religious definition of a modern, intellectual Protestantism, and here the emergence of the Young Ireland leader was more than timely. Davis was the personification of a new creed, a secular Protestantism definable not simply as the increasingly besieged 'other' to an ascendant Catholicism but as a self-assertive intellectual, political and moral force. In suggesting that Thomas Davis was 'a Protestant only in culture' his biographer Richard Davis highlights his attractiveness to Ferguson, who sought stability in the notion of a civil hegemony or a cultural ascendancy bulwarked by religious traditions but not religious dogma.[39]

Ferguson's subsequent appropriation of Davis to his own cause is best illustrated by the text which, though frequently accepted as a straightforward lament, in fact conveys the ambiguity and complexity of his relationship with the nationalist leader. When Davis died of scarlatina in September of 1845, Ferguson's immediate response was to canonize him. From his own sickbed he wrote an elegy for the poet and sent it to Charles Gavan Duffy, who remembers how Ferguson had approached him. 'He read me fragments of a poem, the most Celtic in structure and spirit of all the elegies laid on the tomb of Davis. The last verse sounded like a prophecy; it was at any rate a powerful incentive to take up our task anew.' Two years later when the elegy was printed in the *Nation*, its place in the Young Ireland canon was confirmed.

> I walked through Ballinderry in the Spring-time,
> When the bud was on the tree;
> And I said, in every fresh-ploughed field beholding
> The sowers striding free,
> Scattering broadcast forth the corn in golden plenty
> On the quick seed-clasping soil,
> 'Even such this day among the fresh stirred hearts of Erin,
> Thomas Davis, is thy toil.'
>
> I sat by Ballyshannon in the Summer,
> And I saw the salmon leap;
> And I said, as I beheld the gallant creatures
> Spring glittering from the deep,
> Through the spray and through the prone heaps cleaving onwards
> To the calm clear streams above,
> 'So leap'st thou to thy native founts of freedom, Thomas Davis,
> In the brightness of thy strength and love.'

---

39 *The Young Ireland movement*, p. 26.

> I stood on Derrybawn in the Autumn,
> And I heard the eagle call
> With a clangorous cry of wrath and lamentation
> That filled the wide mountain hall,
> O'er the bare deserted place of his plundered eyrie;
> And I said, as he screamed and soared,
> 'So callest thou, thou wrathful-soaring Thomas Davis,
> For a nation's rights restored.'[40]

Subsequent commentators have endorsed Duffy's appraisal of the work by noting the Celtic qualities and affiliations of the lament.[41] Certainly, the poem reflects Ferguson's absorption of a stylistic and imaginative currency derived from versions from Gaelic sources. As an elegy it has an obvious precedent in the 'Lament for Owen Roe O'Neill' which Davis himself had translated, and it hints too, at several poems included by Ferguson in his appendix to the Hardiman review in 1834, including 'O'Hussey's ode to the Maguire'. Ferguson's portrayal of Davis as both the leaping salmon and the soaring eagle echoes the metaphoric presentation of the lost Chief Maguire by his grieving retainer: '[t]hough he were even a pleasant salmon in the unchainable sea,/Though he were a wild mountain eagle'.[42] Systematically allusive to the idioms of a translated Gaelic literary heritage, the poem's swift assimilation to the Young Ireland liturgy was straightforward.

This reading of the text should not obscure however, its possible relationships to classical tradition, in which the eagle was the bird of Jove, and more significantly, to Biblical sources. In Old Testament scripture the eagle was frequently invoked as a harbinger of wrath, vengeance and war, and as a symbol of the nation. In *Deuteronomy*: [t]he Lord shall bring a nation against thee from far, from the end of the earth, as swift as the eagle flieth, a nation whose tongue thou shalt not understand.' The personification of Davis as the sower in the first and fifth stanzas corresponds, meanwhile, to New Testament parable.[43]

---

40 M.C. Ferguson, *SSFID*, vol. 1, pp. 135–6. 41 Duffy's appraisal is cited by M.C. Ferguson, *SSFID*, vol. 1, p. 134. His evaluation of the lament's 'Celtic' qualities is echoed by Lady Ferguson who refers to 'its peculiar and characteristically Irish rhythm' (vol. 1, p. 137). Denman has asserted that though the poem is almost without parallel in its own century, 'it does have a tangential relationship with the Irish tradition of the *caoineadh*, or keen, the recited funeral lamentation best exemplified in the eighteenth-century "*Caoineadh Airt Ui Laoghaire*"'. Denman identifies within Ferguson's lament four characteristics of the Irish keen, and notes that the elegy is used as the opening poem in D.F. McCarthy's *Book of Irish ballads* (1874), concluding that it reveals Ferguson's 'intuitive feeling for Gaelic poetry, and his ability to marry it with the more formal requirements of poetry in English', *Samuel Ferguson*, p. 67. See also Colin Graham's commentary, *Ideologies of epic*, pp. 86–92. 42 R. Davis comments on how Davis's own translation of the 'Lament for Owen Roe O'Neill' established him as a patriotic poet, pp. 29–30. Ferguson's appendix to Hardiman's *Irish Minstrelsy* appears in the *DUM* 4 (Nov. 1834), 529–42. 43 Deut 28:49. For similar biblical usages see Isaiah 40:13; Deut 32:11; Jer 49:16; Hos 8:1; Job 39:27-30. Ferguson later uses the same image

While such allusions are masked by the poem's self-conscious conformity to the Young Ireland canon, they suggest nonetheless that the lament has a biblical orientation, and indeed, that it approaches the quality of a psalm. Ireland's Presbyterian planters were traditionally inspired by the Psalms, and particularly those of David, through which they symbolically allied themselves with the Israelites entering the Promised Land. Gréagóir Ó Dúill has suggested that this liturgical background in Ferguson's writing is frequently overlooked, arguing that it is 'one of the ironies of Ferguson's reputation that the influence of Presbyterian hymn-singing [...] should be commonly thought to derive from Irish language poetry'.[44] From this perspective however, the elegy for Davis underwrites its connection to a Gaelic literary tradition with a quasi-scriptural phraseology, linking the cadences of Protestant worship to the sentiments of a resurgent national virtue. This conflation of form and content is particularly marked in the closing stanza, which enumerates the qualities the inhabitants of Ireland should possess:

> Oh, brave young men, my love, my pride, my promise,
> 'Tis on you my hopes are set,
> In manliness, in kindliness, in virtue,
> To make Erin a nation yet;
> Self-respecting, self-relying, self-advancing,
> In union or in severance, free and strong;
> And if God grant this, then, under God, to Thomas Davis,
> Let the greater praise belong.

The biblical apparatus annexes the dead hero, stripped of his 'wrathful cry', for a new and unmistakably Protestant Ireland constructed on the basis of virtue, strength of character, national integrity and individual responsibility.

Crucially, this was the emphasis given to the poem on its publication in the *Dublin University Magazine* in February 1847, where it appeared with a prefatory essay on Davis written by Ferguson for the series 'Our portrait gallery'. A regular feature in the *DUM*, the 'gallery' provided an anthology of numerous contemporary personalities who were considered to be worthy successors to the luminaries of the previous 'Illustrious gallery', which included such figures as Swift,

---

to describe Aubrey de Vere's work on 'The legends of Saint Patrick': 'Mr de Vere moves, indeed, with an ample and easy gesture, and at times uplifts an almost irradiated brow as he follows the spiritual sower casting abroad the seeds of the faith among the savage clans', M.C. Ferguson, *SSFID*, vol. 2, p. 227.   44 Ó Dúill discusses the liturgical background to Ferguson's poetry in 'No rootless colonists: Samuel Ferguson and John Hewitt' (1991), p. 109. For general background on the Presbyterian use of the Psalms, see R.F.G. Holmes, *Our Irish Presbyterian heritage*, chapter 1.

Burke, and Grattan. In each case the subject was depicted so as to conform to a standard template, which emphasized valiant efforts made in the interests of Ireland but negated or ignored aspects of the individual's career transgressing the *DUM*'s political agenda. The series, which was intended to consolidate a sense of Ireland's social, intellectual and moral stability, frequently provided something of a laundering service therefore, and Ferguson's description of Davis must take into account the fact that he was writing within the established boundaries of this tradition. Even so, the essay on Davis elucidates the definitive criteria for what may be taken as Ferguson's national, Protestant ideal.

Ferguson's line of attack in the article consists in reducing Davis's major political tenet – repeal of the Union – to the level of a minor aberration from respectability. His introductory hierarchy of values is self-explanatory: Davis was 'a Protestant, a man of spirit, and an ardent lover of Ireland', who differed from his friends mainly in believing that it would be better for Ireland to separate from the Imperial Union, while they in turn considered it to be 'inestimably more for her advantage to remain with, and participate in the power and freedom of our great and free united Empire'. Having stated his priorities with regard to his subject, and having confirmed his own allegiances, using Davis as a platform, Ferguson concludes his introductory remarks with an assimilation of Davis to the Conservative intelligentsia for which he now speaks, describing him as the 'favourite of the élite of the intellectual world of Dublin'. His friends consulted him on everything, 'leaving the question of repeal to his own maturing judgement, which they never doubted would ultimately detach him from a design dangerous to Ireland's freedom and prosperity'. He was an Irish Arthur, sounding the 'intellectual *reveillé* of an entire people, coming to teach them 'justice, manliness and reliance on themselves'.[45]

Having offered this prelude Ferguson continues by enumerating the virtues of Davis which qualify him for inclusion in the 'Portrait gallery' series. The first and most important fact of his Protestantism is expanded upon at length: the Protestant is defined here as the true guardian of Irish independence, while the Catholic portrayed as a slave enthralled by Rome. 'We do not say that Protestantism is any passport either to the good will of worthy men, or to such honours as national services have a right to win from honest pens', he writes. 'But, in any question of national independence, the Protestant, or we should rather say the true Irish Catholic, stands on a very different footing from those whom, with every respect, we must designate as Italians.' The accusation is reinforced by a reference to the 1845 Colleges Bill, in which Catholic rejection of plans for integrated education was seen as evidence of control from Rome.[46]

[45] 'Thomas Davis', *DUM* 29 (Feb. 1847), 191.   [46] 'Thomas Davis', 192. In 1845 Peel's proposal to increase the

Ferguson continues his erosion of Catholicism by juxtaposing it with a confident burst of Protestant self-assertion. Again, he draws on the idea of the racial legitimacy of the Irish Protestant in order to fragment the concept of a unified Catholic Gaelic identity which had been the mainstay of O'Connellite political success:

> This is politically speaking a free country – a portion of one of the freest and mightiest nationalities in the world, self-contained and absolutely independent of all external authority. In whatever change may take place within our Union, that independence must be preserved or the Irish Protestants must perish or disperse; but we believe there exists no force within the four seas of Britain capable of driving us to the latter alternative; and that here, in the land of our birth, where we are as much Irishmen as any of our Scythian or Belgic or Danish predecessors, we will continue to maintain and propagate these principles of national independence in their ancient freedom.[47]

There is nothing conciliatory in Ferguson's tone; his rhetoric is aggressive and defiant. Where the Hardiman review consisted largely of negative campaigning, willing Irish Protestantism to prove its nationality in the face of Catholic clannishness, the article on Davis has no need of such measures, claiming for Protestantism the key emotional terms – independence, love of Ireland, birthright – which had ironically been the props of anti-Union feeling during the decade. The figure of Thomas Davis thus offered Ferguson a new security and confidence in the stability of a Protestant identity, and a recognisable personality type through which that Protestantism might be given definition. Davis was not only the fulfilment of the prophecy made in Ferguson's article on Burns; he was also the pre-figuration of Congal, whom Ferguson depicted in his 1872 epic poem as the hero of an ancient and threatened people. In particular, Davis's work had set an example to the upper classes, hitherto lacking in national sentiment. Now, the 'stability of the whole social edifice' was encouraged, Davis having laid the groundwork upon which a civil hierarchy might be strengthened and invigorated.

Ferguson's response to Davis on behalf of the *DUM* ensured that his advantages as a symbol of regeneration for a middle-class and professional Protestant community outweighed his drawbacks as a political liability. Through his dead colleague, he was able to produce a manifesto updating and improving the policy

---

Maynooth Grant to £26,000 and thereby put the college on a secure financial basis met with antagonism from both Catholic hierarchy and Protestant extremists. Davis, who was in favour of non-denominational education, clashed with O'Connell on the subject. See Foster, *Modern Ireland*, p. 315. **47** 'Thomas Davis', 192.

for Protestant integration attempted so clumsily in his Hardiman review. The death of the Young Ireland leader thus occasioned an *apologia* for a vibrant, resilient Protestantism in which the operation of virtue would guard against corruption and rebellion in the country. The entire article functions as a necessary gloss to the lament for Davis, and within its matrix of values the poem is confirmed as the credo of a redefined, recharged and defiantly national Irish Protestantism.

THE POLITICS OF PROTESTANT REPEAL

The Protestant Repeal Association was not simply the product of a lone barrister's *volte face* and Young Ireland's successful propaganda. Ferguson's brief but radical change of heart is qualified by the fact that from the outset the Protestant Repeal Association differed intrinsically from the national Repeal movement and from the ideology of the *Nation*. While the latter formulated policy based on positive claims for independent nationhood, the Protestant consortium was forged from negative feelings of disillusionment and disenchantment with the government. Fired by a sense of betrayal, it was reactionary and conditional rather than philosophical and idealistic. For Ferguson, Repeal agitation was an effective means of protest, but did his commitment stretch to a genuine and fundamental wish to see the Union dissolved? Again, any attempt to assess his behaviour must take into account a number of contributory factors rather than isolate any single ideological shift, and must examine in particular the role of the economic and political environment of the late 1840s in his defection.

At the end of 1846 Ferguson returned from a year of convalescence on the Continent. His homecoming was far from joyous. Lady Ferguson writes of his distress at seeing how 'on the country dear to him beyond all others a fearful calamity had fallen – the potato disease had destroyed the food of its people'.[48] It was the beginning of a crisis which epitomized for him the failure of the British government to comprehend the nature of its responsibility to Ireland, and the event shocked him, along with many members of the professional classes, into action. In 1847 he and fellow barrister Sir Colman O'Loghlen became honorary secretaries to the Irish Council, a body of concerned individuals who sought to advise the government on the management and distribution of resources. The advice of the committee was largely ignored, and Ferguson's anger at this snub was exacerbated by the further decline of Ireland's situation with the failure of the potato crop the following year.[49]

The Famine thus accelerated Ferguson's move into political discourse, and much of his writing became embroiled in the controversy over administrative

---

48 *SSFID*, vol. 1, p. 179.   49 See *SSFID*, vol. 1, p. 245, and Duffy, *My life*, vol. 1, p. 202.

reliance on the abstract rules of political economy. Ireland provided visible evidence of the shortcomings of the new science and the condition of the country gave rise to widespread debate on the matter. In 1847, Isaac Butt discussed the issue at length in his study, *A voice for Ireland*, while in the same year W. Neilson Hancock, professor of Political Economy at Trinity College, attempted in a series of lectures to defend the subject, arguing for its effectiveness in ordinary circumstances but admitting that Ireland's situation had now exceeded the boundaries of normality.[50] Ferguson too entered the fray, publishing early in 1847 a pamphlet entitled 'On the expediency of taking stock'. This took the form of an open letter to James Pim, who had recently proposed a plan to suspend the operation of the distilleries in a move to conserve grain resources. Prefacing economic calculation with an impassioned complaint that Ireland was 'starving on account of a formula of the economists', Ferguson laid out his suggestions for the proper assessments of the country's grain supply and an end to *laissez-faire*. 'Political Economy is probably quite true, so far as it goes in matters of this kind' he wrote. 'But Political Economy is a science which deals with value, and when food comes to be human life, and cannot be priced, the subject goes beyond the cognizance of any rule of value.' The Famine had once again shown up the British administration's ignorance of Ireland, and the pamphlet concluded with a plea for proper research on the state of the country.[51]

The pamphlet reveals the depth of engagement with which Ferguson, as a member of an aspirant intelligentsia, was prepared to act as proxy for Ireland's deficient political leadership, following the example he had seen at work in Scotland. His disillusionment and frustration with Westminster are visible in his recourse to satire: in May 1849 he published in the *DUM* a mock-Augustan dialogue, written in heroic couplets and entitled 'Inheritor and Economist'. The poem consists of the debate between Economist, apologist for government Free Trade policy based on political economy and *laissez-faire* philosophy, and Inheritor, the representative of Ireland's vulnerable land-owning classes, who falls victim to Economist's financial and legislative schemes. Inheritor also speaks for various subsidiary allegorical characters – Mortgagee, Pauper, and Tenant – who have likewise suffered as a result of fashionable economic doctrine. Against the backdrop of misery, starvation and penury, the scientific rational-

50 W.N. Hancock, *Three lectures on political economy* (1847). Isaac Butt was professor of Political Economy at Trinity College Dublin from 1836 to 1840. 51 'On the expediency of taking stock' (1847), p. 10. Ferguson suggested that 'a man like Captain Larcom' would be suitable for the task of gathering proper documentation on the current economic state of Ireland. See also Ferguson's speech to the Protestant Repeal Association, in which he decried the efforts of Lord Rosse to apply the principles of political economy to the distressed population. 'To tell a people, agitated as we are, suffering as we are, that we ought to devote our minds to the study of political economy seems to me a sad mockery. Lord Rosse is well aware that, as yet, political economy has no pretensions to be considered a science': *Nation* (1 July 1848), 423.

ism of Economist is presented as abstract mathematical formulation, irrelevant to social need. When Inheritor expresses his anxiety over falling rents, for example, his interlocutor offers him consolation in a litany of figures:

> 'Fear not for that', Economist replies,
> 'Repeal the corn-laws, and your rents will rise:
> Doubt you the fact? by rule of algebra
> I'll prove it plainly in a formula.
> For, say our present export cotton trade
> Is minus y, and call our imports z:
> The minus y plus z, divided by
> X squared (our increased exports), equal y,
> Minus x squared by z divided – thus
> Our minus export has become a plus'.[52]

The darker side to this cynical and lively attack on the political economists is the sobering portrait of the diseased landscape of Ireland; 'the green potato ridges, black/And all the air, as with a sick man's breath, / Stunk o'er a waste of vegetable death'. The tragedy underlying the satirical bite of the work was confirmed for Ferguson when he visited Killarney with his wife and some friends that summer, and witnessed the devastated terrain. During a solitary mountain-climbing expedition, he found himself in the midst of the starving inhabitants of the county, with whom he shared the food he had brought with him. The visit to Killarney would have been perfect, Lady Ferguson recalled, had it not been for the effects of famine all around.[53] For her husband, the scenes can only have exacerbated the despair and frustration of the Irish intelligentsia at the plight of the country, and their anger at parliament's inability to manage the crisis.

Exasperation with the government now started to permeate other aspects of Ferguson's life, and increasingly, he began to involve himself in protests against its apparent indifference to Ireland. Once again it emerges that his antagonism was not based on any ideological thrust towards independent nationhood but derived from a circumstantial disillusionment with policy. His feelings were sanctioned by a special meeting of the Irish Council in March 1848, at which Ferguson, acting as honorary secretary in the absence of Colman O'Loghlen, signed a resolution complaining of Westminster's failure to launch

---

52 C. Morash reprints an annotated abridged version of the poem in *The hungry voice* (1989), pp. 106–20. Originally published in the *DUM* 33 (May 1849), 638–49. For a general discussion of political economy or the 'dismal science', in the period, see Eagleton, *Scholars and rebels*, chapter 4.   53 *SSFID*, vol. 1, pp. 224–6.

a proper enquiry into the operation of the poor law, and expressing deep dissatisfaction at the 'determination on the part of the Government and Legislature to rule this country without regard to the will of the Irish People, as expressed through their Representatives'.[54] Increasingly, the formation of the 'scientific state' in England was seen to be at Ireland's expense, in undermining the integrity of her citizens and their leaders through policy that consistently overlooked the economic needs and social condition of the country.[55]

Ferguson's sense of alienation was exacerbated, finally, when his own profession was directly affected by the threat of centralization. In an address to a public meeting at the Rotunda in Dublin, in the presence of the lord mayor of the city, he expressed his feelings on the subject in terms which began to probe the conditions of a working relationship with London. The resolution he put before the meeting advised resistance to further centralization, condemning the process as unjust, offensive, and economically foolhardy:

> [I]t costs the State more to repress the discontents caused by past metropolitan plunder of local institutions than would support all our civil authorities in dignity and peace; and that a prudent economy, while it would find ample occasion for its exercise in other branches of the public expenditure, would respect those institutions through which the Irish people have, since beyond the time of legal memory, participated in the splendour and emoluments of the State, and which cannot be wrested from them without the perpetuation of a deep and just sense of national wrong.[56]

Expanding on this point, he moved from financial considerations to an insistence that Irish society was under siege; that English absorption of Irish civil institutions would result in the continued impoverishment of the social hierarchy. Playing on the language of political economy he described how, if the 'pernicious system of centralisation' were allowed to continue, the country would be stripped bare of a vital social element:

> Political economists define wealth to be that which has an exchangeable value. Refined society, intelligence, virtue, patriotism – all these bear an exchangeable value – all these are wealth, even on the low ground they put it on. It is not a mere annual sum of money of which they would deprive us, but of our higher, richer, social privileges. It is not

---

54 *Nation* (4 Mar. 1848), 152.   55 See J.C. Brady, 'Legal developments 1801–79', p. 476.   56 M.C. Ferguson, *SSFID*, vol. 1, p. 227.

> because the Viceregal Court sets the fashion in taste or in manners –
> the best taste and the most amiable manners are found in circles not
> within its immediate influence. It is not on that account that we reckon
> it among our social commodities bearing a high exchangeable value,
> and of which we cannot be deprived without deep and lasting injury,
> but because it brings under one head and into one focus all whose posi-
> tion in society affords *prima facie* presumption of social worth, and gives
> us the opportunity of making our social selections from the whole
> body of the rich and educated classes.

An impoverished social élite would be incapable of holding together the social stability of the country. But centralization was not simply a threat to the *haute-monde* of the Castle, for in its potential degradation of the professional classes it also challenged the intellectual leadership at last beginning to show promise in figures such as Thomas Davis. The community of professional and national interest in which Ferguson invested throughout the early 1840s was dependent on an institutional as well as cultural independence, and the growing self-assertiveness and coherence of the legal fraternity in Dublin was evidence of this fact. The issue rankled with him for some time. 'We would be all right here, if we could put an end to this infernal system of centralisation', he wrote to Robert Blackwood in December of 1850.[57]

The very public and highly politicized output of the late 1840s reveals Ferguson's increasingly aggravated response to provocation, but additionally it illustrates the tenacity with which he was prepared to support the Union even in its inadequacy. In the end his conversion lasted no longer than a few months. Given that his statements in defence of the Union over a longer period of three years are more frequent than his pleas for its abolition, it might seem appropriate to conclude that the Protestant Repeal Association never amounted to anything more that the logical extension of the Irish Council – a protest body railing against centralization, maladministration and neglect, even against the perceived insults of Thackeray and the London caricaturists. Ferguson's apostasy is understandable at this level as a culmination of his disillusion-ment with Britain and his simultaneous enchantment with the potent imagi-native force of Young Ireland, which offered him a reading public and a cul-tural context.

While the sum of these temporary circumstances is sufficient explanation for his brief defection in 1848, the basis upon which the Protestant Repeal Association was founded suggests that he hoped it would represent something

---

57 7 Dec. 1850, NLS MS 4088 f222.

more; in short, that it would underwrite his long-term incentive towards the expression of Irish Protestantism as a culturally determined identity. Ireland's Protestants had not, of course, been invisible; the Orange Order and the Brunswick clubs maintained a vociferous anti-Catholic rhetoric, while the Dublin Protestant Operative Association, led by the Reverend Tresham Gregg, successfully promoted a hard-line anti-Repeal policy among the working classes.[58] But none of these outlets were suited to a man in Ferguson's position. The Protestant Repeal Association, on the other hand, held the promise of a platform for moderate, culturally motivated parties committed to the expression of an assertive but non-extremist Protestant identity, fuelled by professional middle-class participation. Protestant Ireland was now given the chance to produce a corporate voice – an ego – integral to a modern Irish political and cultural machine and compatible with the moral and civic vision Ferguson had articulated through the icon of Thomas Davis.

From its inception the Association was concerned with the defence of Protestant identity, prioritizing the necessary preservation and protection of the Protestant religion in the case of Repeal. As Desmond Bowen has noted, the established church in the south was poorly administered and wasteful of its resources, while the further erosion of its authority in some areas as a result of the Famine – largely through the loss of the landlord class – contributed to the general belief that the demoralized Protestant community would have difficulty maintaining itself in a predominantly Catholic culture. Bowen cites from Daniel O'Connell's 1842 letter to Paul Cullen, then papal delegate in Rome, the firm belief that if the Union were repealed 'the great mass of the Protestant community would with little delay melt into the overwhelming majority of the nation'.[59] In the *Nation* six years later, this insecurity revealed itself in the conditions which Protestants repeatedly attached to their tentative expressions of interest in Repeal: a letter from 'an Irish Protestant' to the editor in January 1848, pledging support for Repeal but railing against the domination and abuses of the Roman Catholic clergy, typified the doubts of the would-be converted.[60]

When notice of the formation of a Protestant Repeal Association was published, it sought primarily to allay such fears and to emphasize the promise of religious freedom in the event of the abolition of the Union. The movement's advertisement in the *Nation* highlights rather than conceals anxiety:

> A Protestant organisation for Repeal is being founded at this hour. It will share the glory of the battle and the fruits of the victory. It

---

58 R.F. Foster, *Modern Ireland*, pp. 303–5. 59 *The Protestant crusade in Ireland* (1978), p. 46, p. 263. 60 *Nation* (15 Jan. 1848). Many similar letters were published throughout the year.

will be exclusively Protestant, in order to exhibit the strength of nationality among Protestants. But we rejoice in its exclusiveness on another ground. That section of Irishmen are entitled to negotiate for the full and unquestioned possession of all their civil and religious rights. Never in all the world had a party fallen from ascendancy more just or generous antagonists. The Irish Confederation will guarantee and maintain with their lives the absolute civil and religious equality of all Irishmen.[61]

The appearance of this announcement on the first of April was followed by a more extensive agenda outlining the policy of the Association and again seeking to allay Protestant suspicions. The manifesto stated as its first principle that the movement had 'no intention to revive those religious differences which have unhappily so long divided the national feeling in this country, but their sole object is to demonstrate to the Government that the great body of the Protestant middle classes in Ireland are as ardently desirous of legislative independence as the Roman Catholics themselves'. Its signalled concerns were clearly and essentially legislative, in favour of administrative independence but still supportive of the monarch. The separatist trajectory of the movement could not be overlooked, however, and the subtext reads as a preparation for siege. Those who feared the consequences of Repeal for their religious or political rights must face up to their situation. They must 'look the objection boldly in the face' and ask the Protestants of Ireland 'if they are strong enough to become the English Garrison of this country, are they not strong enough to defend themselves in any emergency?'[62]

This manifesto was reprinted regularly throughout the month of May and was therefore surrounded by reports of recent activities in France, together with pledges of Irish sympathy and support for the French rebels. While events in Europe were doubtless alarming to Protestants (and indeed many middle-class Catholics) the interest shown in them by Young Ireland may have encouraged the initial success of the Protestant movement, in that many began to see Repeal as the last ditch before full-scale rebellion, and thus urged it on the government as a preventative measure. By the end of the month Edward Evans, secretary to the Protestant Repeal Association, pleaded that 'concessions be not delayed, till dignified concession be no longer possible; that the claims of justice upon its own merits may be regarded ere yet it be too late, and while agitation has not yet darkened into revolution'.[63] The manifesto had included a pledge of unimpaired loyalty to the queen, and a

61 *Nation* (1 Apr. 1848), 217.   62 *Nation* (8 Apr. 1848), 232.   63 *Nation* (6 May 1848), 302–3.

statement in defence of the rights of property and against the principles of Republicanism.

At the same time, there was a distinct move within the *Nation* to capitalize on a history of Protestant initiative, but within a carefully defined set of parameters. Desmond Bowen suggests that 'the idealists from Trinity College wanted to have Catholic and Protestant, Milesian and Cromwellian Irish unite in a kind of nationalism like that of the liberal radicalism of Wolfe Tone', but as far as the Protestant movement was concerned the emotional appeal initially skirted such associations, concentrating instead on a pedigree of respectable independence rather than radical dissent.[64] The reprinted version of Davis's lecture to 'The young Irishmen of the middle classes' included the exhortation to 'look back on those who have been the mind chieftains of Ireland – Swift, Lucas, Grattan', while a later article, 'A parley with Irish Protestants', called upon its readers to follow 'the steps which led Grattan to immortality', doubtless hoping to attract moderate Protestant interest.[65]

Ferguson was to pledge his support for the Association in the company of numerous professional colleagues. Well-known barristers such as the MP William Sharman Crawford, John Ireland and George Washington Vance were prominent among the original protagonists of the movement, and when the first meeting was held in May in the Music Hall on Dublin's Lower Abbey Street the attendance included a large representation from the Bar.[66] It was noted that no members of the aristocracy were visible. 'We should say it was a meeting of the middle and trading classes of our citizens', reported the *Nation*; 'in fact, a fair representation of the professional and industrial classes of Dublin'.[67] The assembly was therefore dominated by the very stratum which Duffy and Young Ireland had been eager to incorporate into the Repeal programme, and reflected the specific agenda and insecurities therefore, of a distinctly middle-class urban interest group.

Ferguson's speech to this initial meeting is quoted in full in his wife's biography. His opening line summarized his case. 'Mr Chairman and gentlemen, I am a Protestant and an inhabitant of Dublin, and I desire the restoration of a domestic Legislature.' He continued by addressing key grievances of the meeting; the attempted eradication of the gentry from Ireland, the use of the country as a 'draw-farm' for England, and the repeated moves

---

64 *The Protestant crusade*, p. 137. 65 *Nation* (22 Jan. 1848), 59; *Nation* (8 April 1848), 232. 66 William Sharman Crawford, a northern barrister, was elected Member of Parliament for Dundalk in 1835. He was in favour of Catholic Emancipation but opposed to O'Connell. On the subject of his promotion of repeal, see Brian Kennedy, 'Sharman Crawford on the repeal question', in which Crawford's letter of 1847 to William Smith O'Brien is reprinted. 67 *Nation* (13 May 1848), 306. See also Duffy's comments on the need for a middle-class Protestant contingent within the Repeal movement, *My life*, vol. 1, p. 61.

to centralize in London 'all the wealth, refinement, and social attractions of the Empire'. This erosion of social confidence could no longer be accepted, Ferguson claimed. Ireland's material prosperity and her advancement in arts and civilization had failed to thrive under the Union. Subsequent confusion and class antagonism, together with the contempt and hostility shown to Ireland by parliament, had combined to create an intolerable situation. The failure of the imperial legislature to cope with the country's domestic difficulties and the continuing relegation of Irishmen to low office further obliged the speaker to reject the terms of this 'humiliating allegiance', and to pledge his support for Repeal.[68]

The speech was given a rapturous response but in fact it amounted to little more than a list of general ills with which his audience identified. Ferguson made it clear that his attack on the Union was due to its failure in practice rather than principle, and again confirmed that he had no quarrel with the English people, finishing his address with a stanza of the national anthem. Emotionally, the speech relied on deprivation and loss: in short, there was very little in the way of positive imagery and symbol – other than the touchstone of Grattan – to which he could appeal. Compared to the inclusive fecundity of Young Ireland's combined resources of ballad, history, and myth, Protestant Repeal was politically pertinent but imaginatively barren, and over the ensuing weeks the Association appeared to become increasingly self-conscious of this fact. A letter printed in the *Nation* and addressed to George Washington Vance, the chairman of the Association, reflects the problem, as the writer struggles to locate the heroes of the movement somewhere between Shakespeare and scripture. The meeting, he writes, has 'filled with joy and confidence the souls of your countrymen – Ferguson, Ireland, Daly, Burkett – "oh saviour names, and full of happy omen" – how shall your country requite you? Shall we not feel thrice grateful? Unborn generations shall bless you – our common foe has endeavoured to cast dust in your eyes, but you were not blinded.'[69] At the next meeting, held in early June, the speeches were increasingly bombastic and littered with biblical allusions. The search for symbols was clearly complicated by the Association's contact with various Protestant subcultures, particularly in the north of the country. Four hundred Orangemen included in the membership list had promised to be present in uniform at the next meeting, while at the July convention one individual appeared in United Irishmen costume, declaring himself to be the son of an 'eighty-two Volunteer' and vehemently attacking the Union for the decimation of his linen business.[70]

68 *Nation* (13 May 1848), 306.   69 *Nation* (27 May 1848), 346.   70 *Nation* (15 July 1848), 452.

Clearly, at this stage, the Association was acting as little more than a front for a series of disparate groups, and any sense of a corporate identity was chimerical. Whereas the national Repeal movement could build both upon O'Connell's mass appeal and on the unity provided by Roman Catholicism, the Protestant offshoot was attempting to cement together fragmented parties without recourse to any core identity. For this reason Ferguson's second speech to the Repeal Association, given on 27 June and not reported by his wife, is more significant than its predecessor, in that he begins to forge for the movement a corporate self-image. Speaking before a crowded assembly, Ferguson begins by reminding his audience that the people of Ireland were not yet unanimously behind Repeal, before summarizing in dramatic terms, his own personal road to Damascus. It is a rare glimpse of Ferguson speaking on his own behalf, released from the largely representative register which characterizes his *DUM* contributions. His plea now is for patience:

> for when I recollect how much of my own feelings of indignation were excited when as yet I was a friend of the legislative Union, and while still I had not seen the reasons which induced me to desire the restoration of our domestic legislature, by a large body of my countrymen – forgetful of their duty to me, and others who differed from them, marching past my door with drum and trumpet, as if they could coerce me into opinions which could only be brought to my conviction by force of reason – when I recollect the feelings of indignation which then fired my breast, I see how essential it is to respect the opinions of our neighbours, and to abstain from offering insult to them because they differ from us in their judgement.[71]

The appeal for tolerance takes the moral high ground, but inevitably it highlights Ferguson's concern that the movement would alienate itself from the landed gentry. He continues with an attack on the government's resort to the formulae of political economy in a time of crisis, and appears to be on the point of repeating the basic elements of his previous address when suddenly the speech is opened up by a quotation from Macaulay: '[d]o you not know that danger to the state is to be estimated not by what breaks out from the public mind, but by what remains in it?' This hint at the threat to the security of the state is Ferguson's cue to raise the stakes. Relinquishing completely his reliance on a litany of grievances and ills, he produces instead an evocative image of Ireland as a country habitually treated as a child and a lunatic:

---

[71] *Nation* (1 July 1848), 422.

> It is hardly possible to imagine any condition more deplorable than that of a man in his sound mind who has the misfortune to be placed in a lunatic asylum. He must bear the officiousness and impertinence of caretakers – the attendance of spies – the importunity of moral and intellectual exhorters – and, being a person in his natural senses, must submit to have all the functions of memory, judgement, and understanding performed for him by the minds of others. The misery of such a man is multiplied in an almost endless ratio when his case becomes that of a whole people, whose neighbours, powerful enough to assume the office of their committees and guardians, declare that they are nationally of unsound mind, and incapable of managing their own affairs.[72]

The issue of imprisonment was an emotive one. In March, the arrest and incarceration of John Mitchel had shaken the Repeal movement considerably, despite his recent split from the *Nation*. Pledging support for Mitchel during the speech, Ferguson appears to accept the implications of his chosen metaphor, and rouses his audience with the reminder that 'a people treated so long like lunatics may some day act the part of madmen'.[73]

The use of such an inflammatory image was uncharacteristic of Ferguson. The speech reveals his ability to take Protestant Repeal beyond the passive terms of the indignant and aggrieved to a new pitch of assertiveness and aggression, with a rhetoric sharpened and focussed by his immersion in the political maelstrom and infected with a revolutionary zeal. For a brief moment, his full political potential is visible. But from this point on, Ferguson retreats. He denies the position of influence some parties have ascribed to him, and though he reaffirms the reasons for his change of opinion on the subject of Repeal, he reminds his listeners that he has no quarrel with England, that he wishes 'to hear no crash of any falling Empire'. He claims to have no desire to take part in politics, and that his tastes, habits and avocations render his involvement impossible. In declaring his beliefs, he has merely done his duty, and now his intention is to step down from centre-stage.

It was a timely withdrawal: the subsequent arrest in July of the Young Ireland leaders, including Duffy and Smith O'Brien, and the failure of the rising, signalled the end of the Repeal movement in its current incarnation, and Ferguson had no stomach for the land agitation through which anti-Union sentiments were later to find expression. In August he married Mary Catherine

---

72 *Nation* (1 July 1848), 423. 73 Ferguson's personification of Ireland as the incarcerated individual deprived of autonomy anticipates the manner in which Mitchel's own *Jail journal*, as David Lloyd has illustrated, sought to integrate the identity of the individual with that of the nation, *Nationalism and minor literature*, pp. 49–51.

Guinness, and it is likely that his apparent loss of nerve had much to do with the unsuitability of his activities within the upper ranks of Dublin society. His wife records that her father did not altogether welcome Ferguson's request for her hand. He had read the speech given by Ferguson at the May meeting of the Association, 'differed from his views, and considered his means inadequate'. She also cites a personal letter written to her by Ferguson immediately after his June address, which reveals his awareness of disapproval from his new associates, and attempts a self-vindication, reducing his role from Protestant activist to moderate arbitrator.[74] His wife's prudent editing of his Repeal interests in his biography, moreover, clearly indicates her own views on the subject. Here, the text of his initial Repeal speech is immediately followed by a disclaimer from Ferguson, offered some forty years later in response to a question on his attitudes to Home Rule:

> I sympathised with the Young Ireland poets and patriots while their aims were directed to a restoration of Grattan's Parliament in which all the estates of the realm should have their old places. But I have quite ceased to sympathise with their successors who have converted their high aspirations to a sordid social war of classes carried on by the vilest methods. I was comrade in that sense of Davis, and possibly, but with far less sympathy, of some of his companions. But it was in sympathy only. I never wrote in the 'Nation'. To say that I have upborne their banner, therefore, is more than I would like to vouch.[75]

The summer of 1848 did not quite mark the end of his attacks on the Union, however. That autumn he made a speech in defence of the proprietor of the *Tribune* newspaper, Richard D'Alton Williams, who was tried on a charge of felony in late October. Ferguson's argument centred on his definition of the Union as a legal contract breached by one party. He reminded the court of the fundamental basis of the agreement; 'that in this United Kingdom of Great Britain and Ireland each part is governed by the whole, and neither by the other'. Just as no Irishman could claim supremacy within England, no English garrison had the right to impose itself by force upon Ireland. 'I repeat it again and again', cried Ferguson,

> and I shout it into the ears of the servile traitors who are not ashamed to call themselves an English garrison in their own country, that to assert any authority in any part or section of the United Kingdom less

---

74 M.C. Ferguson, *SSFID*, vol. 1, p. 181, pp. 183–4. 75 M.C. Ferguson, *SSFID*, vol. 1, p. 254.

than the whole, to make laws to bind any other section of the realm, is unconstitutional, unlawful, and not to be whispered in a court of justice. We are part and parcel with them of one Imperial body, their friends and fellow-labourers for the general good; assuming no jurisdiction over them, suffering no jurisdiction of them over us, their equals in the eye of the law, members with them while the Union lasts of one United Kingdom; but their slaves never![76]

The vehemence of Ferguson's rhetoric is striking. His language remains coloured by his immersion in Repeal politics, with his phrase 'while the Union lasts' underlining his continuing sense of the precariousness of the constitutional treaty. But ultimately, he accepts the bond, and by the end of 1848 his flirtation with rebellion was over.

Any final assessment of the implications of the Protestant Repeal Association and the steps leading to its formation must take into account a sense of failure. Throughout the 1840s, Ferguson had been swept up by the cultural promise exuded by Young Ireland and propelled towards protest and defiance. Circumstances in 1848 had offered, briefly, a space within which Protestant participation and legitimacy in Ireland might be secured, but in the end the endeavour came to nothing and reasons for its collapse, in addition to the suppression of the national movement, are not difficult to find. The lack of a common identity was, claims Roy Foster, a permanent feature of Protestant activity. 'Protestant nationalists always called for pluralism – as they had to. But they were never representative of a consistent strain, rather representing a series of reactions against a governing syndrome.'[77] For Desmond Bowen the demise was due largely to the religious divide: 'The Protestant Repeal Association led by Samuel Ferguson failed to win support from either the Protestant people who distrusted the Catholic masses, or from those Catholics who wanted the Repeal movement to be sectarian in expression.'[78] Both explanations are partial but plausible, and thus amidst paranoia and fragmentation, Ferguson's vision of Irish Protestantism in the image of Thomas Davis failed to be realized.

As far as Ferguson's literary career was concerned, the wake of the 1848 Repeal movement was highly problematic, and in this respect Charles Gavan Duffy's version of events is particularly damning. 'Ferguson's confidence in some immediate help from the gentry outlasted that of his companions', he wrote. 'It was pathetic to witness his continual and quite hopeless efforts to inflame their patriotism, like a man labouring to kindle a vesta by rubbing the end where

[76] M.C. Ferguson, *SSFID*, vol. 1, pp. 207–8. [77] *Modern Ireland*, p. 317. [78] *The Protestant crusade*, p. 137.

there was no phosphorus.'[79] The remark suggests the persistence of a schism in Irish society which Ferguson had yet to repair, and the remainder of his career was dominated by his continued recourse to the social bonding agents which he identified in history, antiquity and literature. While the Protestant Repeal movement was short-lived, therefore, and while the vigour of 1840s optimism quickly faded, the decade had a pertinent legacy, manifest in this continued quest for cultural unity, and Ferguson's desire to find credible images for a civic-minded, Protestant Ireland.

79 Duffy, *My life*, vol. 1, p. 203.

CHAPTER FIVE

Ireland's architecture

On a visit to Dublin the philosopher Wittgenstein was taken to view Trinity College. 'Now I understand what was meant by the phrase "the Protestant Ascendancy"' he remarked to his companions, on seeing the college's front square. 'These buildings have the appearance of a fortress. But now the gypsies inhabit the castle.'[1] The architecture of the Irish capital lends itself readily to such interpretation, providing a narrative of wealth and status brought low by change and decay. Dublin's stately town houses and Palladian frontages were central to the discursive relationship between an aesthetic order and a ruling power grounded in the securities of the eighteenth century. In the volatile public arena of nineteenth-century Ireland, challenges to that orthodoxy were manifest in the stylistic shifts which undermined the architectural hegemony of the Ascendancy and reinforced the claims of municipal bureaucracy. Coinciding, in many instances, with the linked aesthetic, political and theological controversies of mid-century Britain, transitions in Irish architecture saw Georgian splendour give way to Victorian utilitarianism, and the authority of the Established Church collide with the demands of a newly-emancipated Catholic body.

The bearing of Dublin's architecture, past and present, on public perceptions of how the city functioned as a social, civic and political space, offers a general context for Samuel Ferguson's knowledgeable, though frequently peevish, opinions of Victorian design. His interest in the architecture of Europe was based on a broad historical and technical knowledge of the field. Notebooks of sketches he made during a year on the continent in 1846 are filled with architectural detail and description, while several of his letters allude to his architectural observations and preferences. His writings in this area consist of three extensive review articles published in the *DUM* between 1847 and 1851; the first on the newly published biography of the eighteenth-century architect James Gandon, and the second and third on major works by the contemporary art theorist and critic John Ruskin. Many of the ideas expressed in these articles were summarized in an 1864 lecture 'Our public and domestic architecture',

---

[1] M.C. O'Drury, 'Some notes on conversations with Wittgenstein', in R. Rhees (ed.), *Recollections of Wittgenstein* (1984), p. 137.

reported by the *Dublin Builder* and later published as 'Our architecture' in a series entitled *Afternoon lectures*. While they cover a range of subjects, the pieces are dominated by the vast divergence in opinion between Ferguson, a self-professed champion of architectural classicism, and John Ruskin, the century's foremost advocate of Gothic. Indeed, Ferguson's treatment of Ruskin was much harsher in many respects than of James Hardiman in 1834. The opposition crystallized, of course, contemporary dialectics in Victorian society: deep-rooted social and political concerns were filtered through the antagonism which greeted the mid-century Gothic revival and its prophets, with architectural form providing a complex metaphor in the debate between aristocratic traditionalism and democratic utilitarianism, or between reactionary Augustan values and revolutionary Romanticism. But what, precisely, did Ferguson's engagement with the contradiction between classical and Gothic style signify in a domestic context, and in a period of sustained social and civic uncertainty?

The matter was partly one of personal taste, and Ferguson's intense dislike of a style at odds with his innate conservatism. In a letter to his mother, written in Paris in early 1846, he described a visit to Amiens to see the cathedral, supposedly the finest specimen of Gothic architecture in France. 'It, as well as all other Gothic edifices I have seen, disappointed me', he wrote.

> The way in which they construct these buildings is this: there is a great lofty vault in the centre, and arcades of less height at the sides, and the beauty of the buildings is thought to consist in making the supports which sustain the roof of this vault as slight as possible, so as to leave the upper part of the hall a sort of lantern of stained glass. If the walls alone had to sustain this weight, they would have to be made of great thickness and solidity, and the light effect could not be obtained. The plan they resort to, therefore, is this: they prop up these walls on the outside with what are called flying buttresses, or arches of stone spanning the external galleries on either side, so that in fact the roof is upheld not by the columns which one sees inside, but by these external props which are hidden from the sight by the stained glass of the windows. Thus an effect is produced on the mind which, being the result of a trick, is displeasing to me; for I like in architecture, as in everything else, to see what the result (whether it be a conclusion in an argument or an architectural effect in building) is supported by; and therefore I have conceived a degree of contempt for Gothic architecture, as not expressing the sincere sentiment which reasonable men ought to embody in their works, as well as cherish in their breasts.[2]

2 Cited M.C. Ferguson, *SSFID*, vol. 1, p. 165.

The passage is self-dramatizing, the writer's aversion to Gothic with its irregularity, individualism and hints of iconoclasm a means of expressing his own will to integrity and strength of character. The language reaffirms, essentially, what Denman terms the 'Presbyterian Ferguson', the poet who would later write of his preference for the simplicity and sincerity of worship in his native Donegore chapel over the elaborate pomp and ceremony of Westminster Abbey.[3] For such a temperament, as Ferguson states baldly later in the letter, 'Gothic architecture is not the style of civilization'.

Nonetheless, Ferguson's criticisms of architectural Gothic have a pointed theological subtext. The implied juxtaposition of solid Protestant worship with the insecurity of Roman Catholic dogma was a conceit to which he would return frequently in his attack on Ruskin, and it suggests two connected preoccupations. The first of these was the writer's concern with England's so-called 'national apostasy' in the mid-nineteenth century. The wave of conversions to Roman Catholicism which affected – and as Ferguson would see it, effeminized – the upper echelons of British society, was symbolized for many by the Gothic revival and related ecclesiological retrogressions. Secondly, and closer to home, the style was implicitly linked to Protestant insecurities, for the most visible sign of Catholic self-assertion in Dublin and throughout the country, following the trajectory of O'Connellite mobilization, was a prolific and successful programme of church building. Leading the field of construction was James Joseph McCarthy, disciple of Pugin and skilful promoter of an Irish ecclesiastical Gothic expressly allied to Gaelic revivalism and a popular nationalist agenda.

If Ferguson's aversion to Gothic and its mid-century revival was shaped in part by these factors, his corresponding retreat to the secure traditions of classical form, and his adulation of the Dublin elevations of James Gandon, were similarly motivated. As previous chapters have shown, underlying his temporary diversions into Repeal, on the one hand, or into a hard-line *DUM* unionism on the other, was an enduring affiliation to traditions of civic virtue and patriotism, qualities embodied and still symbolized, for many of his generation, by Ireland's pre-Union Grattanite parliament.[4] While accepting that any actual return to this kind of order – and the leadership of an 'unpaid, natural gentry', as he termed it – was by and large impossible, he needed to retain a sense of its legacy, particularly through the architectural and institutional symbols of that era.[5] By the second half of the nineteenth century, the architecture of an Irish Ascendancy was already in decline: over ensuing decades, the former

---

3 *Samuel Ferguson*, p. 100; see Ferguson's 'Westminster Abbey: on hearing weekday service there, September 1858', *Lays of the western Gael* (1864). 4 For a particularly useful discussion of this political tendency amongst Ferguson's peers and colleagues, see D.G. Boyce, 'Trembling solicitude: Irish conservatism, nationality and public opinion, 1833–86' (1993). 5 'Architecture in Ireland', *DUM* 29 (June 1847), 695.

Parliament buildings became a bank, great houses were transformed into hotels and hospitals, and elegant Georgian streets were turned into shopping arcades.[6] At a political level, meanwhile, the effective replacement of a native leadership by English administrators and bureaucrats lacking any genuine commitment or connection to the country continued, as part of the process of centralization and rationalization which Ferguson decried in his speeches to the Protestant Repeal Association. Government legislation in this area was seen as a ploy to degrade the city as a national capital, to erode its native institutions and to reduce it to a condition of deteriorated provincialism. The architectural debate was bound up therefore, with issues of leadership and tradition, but also with Ferguson's commitment to Dublin as a credible civic space that might draw authority from its Athenian and Roman allusions.[7] Threatened by centralization, municipal reform and, ultimately, fashion, classical Dublin was under siege from barbarianism on several fronts.

JAMES GANDON'S DUBLIN

Ferguson used his critical encounter with Ruskin to emphasize what he saw as the implicit connection between a society and its visual forms of expression. Architecture, he claimed 'is as much an exponent of the intellectual condition of the immediate period as literature'.[8] His analogy between sound architectural design and a reliable political infrastructure is illustrated by a piece of doggerel he composed on the subject of the mansion of Down Hill, 'one of the grand old mansions of the epoch of Irish independence' as he described it, built in the north of Ireland in the eighteenth century:

> Yes, Down Hill was founded
> When builders were grounded
> (Let Ruskin go lecture!)
> In good architecture;
> Ere aesthetic refiners
> And penny-a-liners,
> With hectoring phrases
> Had made us change places

---

6 On specific changes to classical Dublin following 1841 and the Municipal Reform Acts, see N. McCullough, *Dublin: an urban history* (1989). 7 Classical architectural style became pre-eminent in urban areas generally following the publication of the first volume of Stuart and Revett's *Antiquities of Athens*, in 1762. See K. Hill, '"Thoroughly imbued with the spirit of ancient Greece": symbolism and space in Victorian civic culture'. 8 'Architecture In Ireland', 296.

> With medieval centuries
> And their petty inventories,
>
> . . .
>
> And the men who were able
> From state-room to stable
> To roof and to wall so
> Could build a state also.[9]

Architectural regularity thus implied civic stability, as part of a wider system of reference within which 'taste' stood for both aesthetic and social cultivation, 'barbarism' for both artistic deviance and a new, heterogenous social order.

Such usage was characteristic of contemporary critical practice. Indeed, the belief that the social health of the nation was indicated by the quality of its art gained increasing emphasis from the 1830s onwards, when the combination of a Romantic legacy together with the work of theorists such as Ruskin and Pugin produced a heightened public sensitivity to the values encoded in art and style. It was accepted and indeed expected in critical discourse that an architectural feature was simultaneously a moral text awaiting interpretation, a visual expression of society's ethical or political condition.[10] Thus, Ferguson's aversion to the Gothic style is self-consciously loaded with meaning, his response to architectural form in general serving as an alternative medium of socio-political critique. And if Dublin's buildings spoke a distinct language, those of the previous century, characterized by 'fitness, strength and dignity' were particularly eloquent, for, Ferguson explained, 'all our works of that period are of an intellectually advanced and intellectually consistent people'.[11] The eighteenth century was a repository of independence and stability derived from property ownership and patronage, and symbolized by the architectural achievements of the era: the elegant Ascendancy townhouses, the great public buildings, the opulence and grandeur of ornate plasterwork and Palladian pillars and above all the newly rebuilt Parliament House.

The spate of architectural activity in the nation's capital was dominated by the figure of James Gandon, whose work represented for Ferguson the glori-

---

9 PRONI MS D2473/3/5. M.C. Ferguson cites a fragment, *SSFID*, vol. 2, p. 272. 10 R. Williams, *Culture and society* (1987), p. 130. Victorian aesthetic philosophy drew heavily on the concept of 'associationism', derived from classical doctrine and adopted in the eighteenth-century by the French school of Jacques Blondel. This was in turn transmitted to nineteenth-century criticism through the writings of Archibald Alison, whose *Essays on the nature and principles of taste* (1790) were reprinted and reviewed regularly throughout the following century, setting the standard principles on which popular aesthetics were based. Alison made significant additions to Blondel's critical foundations in his assertion that the process of association was the prerogative not of the architect but the viewer, who, upon observing a work of art, brought to it an individual sensitivity together with associations from history, literature or personal experience. 11 'Our public and domestic architecture', *Dublin Builder* 6 (May 1864), 80.

ous epoch, with its unity of vision and political coherence. Gandon came to Ireland in 1781 under the auspices of Lord Beresford, who commissioned him to design the new Custom House on the river Liffey. During the next two decades he was responsible for completing the east-front extensions to the Parliament House, in 1789, embellishing the Rotunda in 1786 and, from 1786 to 1802, finishing the impressive frontage of the Four Courts.[12] His edifices, rooted in the regularity and purity of the sixteenth-century Italian architect Andreo Palladio, were monuments to authority and affluence in the city. Ferguson's respect for Gandon was based not only on his external, visual achievements, however, but also on the fundamental coherence of art and society he represented. In 1846 Gandon's writings were incorporated in a biography, which formed the basis of Ferguson's extensive review article 'Architecture in Ireland', published in the *DUM* a year later. While much of the review is concerned with technical appreciations of Gandon's designs, and with general questions of architectural form and fitness in the country, it also explores the elements in Gandon's life and work that sustained architecture as a highly evocative symbolic resource.

Three facts regarding the architect were of particular relevance. First, it had been James Gandon who, together with John Woolfe, had undertaken the task of updating and completing Colen Campbell's *Vitruvius Brittanicus* of 1725. Derived from the Roman architect Pollio Vitruvius's original treatise on classical rules of construction, *De Architectura*, this text listed the rudiments of design in British classical architecture.[13] In Ferguson's writings the work is frequently cited, both as the primary practical authority on architecture and as the authoritative source of doctrine on the value of historical precedence; the precept that architecture is based not on the stylistic whims of an age but on established patterns, permanent rules and procedures derived from classical civilization. Its consolidation of an aesthetic orthodoxy which prioritized conformity and historical longevity served to reinforce Ferguson's own social ideals, and he praises Gandon for having extracted from Vitruvius the recognition that 'all the monuments of our grandfathers' and great grandfathers' civilization, both here and in Great Britain, are designed on classic models adapted to the requisites of a northern climate and to the wants of modern life'.[14]

Secondly, Gandon consistently asserted that architecture, and indeed all art in society, was dependent upon patronage, in a two-way system through which a secure aristocracy might be seen to preserve the 'flame of taste' within soci-

---

12 M. Craig evaluates Gandon's architectural contributions from 1781 to 1791 in *Dublin, 1660–1860* (1980), pp. 242–58. 13 The fourth and fifth volumes of Colen Campbell's *Vitruvius Britannicus or The British architect* (1717–71), were completed by Gandon and Woolfe: see J. Gandon Jr and T. Mulvaney, *The life of James Gandon* (1846), pp. 17–22. 14 'Architecture in Ireland', 696.

ety. The arts, he claimed, 'do honour to our nation, immortalising also their patrons, among the foremost of whom we must consider such gentlemen as have embellished their country with monuments of their taste, and thereby favoured many modern architects with opportunities of acquiring lasting reputation'.[15] Such sentiments obviously served as thinly-veiled homage to the architect's own patron, the often unpopular Beresford, but Ferguson's enthusiastic response to them a century later indicates the extent to which he relied on an Irish social élite to provide for the nation's aesthetic well being.

Ferguson expands upon this theme in the opening of his review of the *Life of Gandon*. Under the present system of public administration, he explains, the role of the native gentry had been usurped by philistine businessmen, a group insensitive to fitness and beauty, and unable to maintain the nation's architectural standards. Moreover, this is the fault of the British government in stationing English administrators in Irish civil posts. Such men, Ferguson continues, lack any degree of attachment to the country for which they are responsible, and the repercussions are deeply serious. 'It is true that the distribution of office in this country among men who come hither aliens in feeling, and bring aliens in their train, is a grievance and an affront', he complains, 'entertaining the idea that whatever reminds the Irish of their former existence is a nuisance, and ought to be abated.'[16] The sense of historical continuity, which every nation should treasure, has been ruptured in Ireland, fractured by the intrusion of a new and essentially barbarian force.

In a changed economic environment the role of the aristocracy must be vindicated, if only in aesthetic terms. Ferguson's argument resounds with his atavistic intolerance of the new bureaucratic and utilitarian mode of government. 'Paid commissioners are largely to blame' he insists, 'for the poor, tasteless and anti-historical state of the nation's architecture'. The reality of a civilization threatened and in decline is again confronted as he stakes a claim on behalf of a class which, through its unfailing patronage, ensured a national self-respect now lacking in Ireland. What Gandon teaches above all is 'a lesson of tolerance no less needful towards the memory of the Irish gentry of that day, than towards their successors', for, whatever the political merits of these men may have been, 'they unquestionably made the country in which they lived home, for the time being, of much of the best talent of the age, and have bequeathed to us a noble example of the uses to which a national aristocracy can be turned'.[17] Taste, as Ferguson defines it, is therefore an elemental and hierarchical principle upon which the gentry of the island may be justified and perpetuated, regardless of the vicissitudes of their political role.

15 Cited Gandon and Mulvaney, p. 236, pp. 19–20. 16 'Architecture in Ireland', 693. 17 'Architecture in Ireland', 695, 708.

Thirdly, Gandon offered Ferguson an authority for his denigration of the Gothic style. Gothic Revival architecture, with its irregular, ornate characteristics, was interpreted in the nineteenth century in various ways, often in relation to imperialist expansion and the exploration of exotic countries, but equally with reference to its basis in German Romanticism and the fad for ecclesiastical medievalism in Britain. The origins of Gothic remained a source of constant speculation, however, and Gandon added his own contribution to the numerous eighteenth-century hypotheses in his writings for the *Vitruvius Brittanicus*.[18] Though hesitant on the exact origins of the style, he alludes here to the most popular version of the birth of Gothic, which defined it as the form created by the Goths and Lombards from the broken fragments of classical architecture after the fall of Rome. This is described not in the architect's own words, but in the passage he quotes from the sixteenth-century Italian art critic and historian Giorgio Vasari:

> Vasari, more than two centuries ago, has given the result of every enquiry that can be made into the origins of the Gothic style. 'There is' he says, 'another species of architecture, which, in its ornaments and proportions, is very different from the antique and from the modern; nor is it used at present by good architects, but avoided as being barbarous and monstrous, being entirely deficient in order, so that it may be called disorder and confusion. It was introduced by the Goths, who, after they had destroyed the ancient fabrics, and the architects were slain in war, introduced arches of the fourth point, and filled Italy with this monstrous style of building.'[19]

The pervasive epic overtones were appropriate for a generation brought up on Gibbon's *Decline and fall*, and the potential for analogy with the nineteenth century is self-evident: in the challenge of the barbarian Goths to the noble and civil order of Rome Ferguson was to find a succinct allegory for what he perceived as the assault on his own idealized society from a vulgar and intrusive element. Terms such as 'barbarous' and 'monstrous' were appropriated as his own idiom in the war against Gothic revival. Gandon's great elevations were the epitome of eighteenth-century power and patronage, of an Augustan age which itself looked back to a golden age of classical order, but that era was now in the last stages of a melancholy decline, falling victim to a new barbarianism associated so rigidly in Samuel Ferguson's mind with the Victorian Gothic Revival that the style itself became complete as a symbol of social destruction.

18 K. Clark discusses the history of the Gothic controversy in *The Gothic revival* (1962), pp. 73–5. 19 'On the progress of architecture in Ireland'; in Gandon and Mulvaney, appendix, p. 252. The quotation is taken from Vasari's *Lives of the artists*.

ENGLAND: ARCHITECTURE AND APOSTASY

Much of Ferguson's response to the architectural style-war of the mid-nineteenth century related in the first instance to what he perceived to be insurgent problems in English society, problems magnified to Irish eyes by the effects of the Union. The disillusionment which had begun to characterize his attitudes to England during the Famine and which deeply affected his political activities in 1848 increased his desire for Irish cultural independence and self-assertion. 'The more I see of our neighbours', he wrote to Charles Gavan Duffy, 'the better pleased I am with our own poor people. I think we have the elements of an intellectual supremacy among us.'[20]

Most significantly in matters of taste, England's inferiority had become visible to Ferguson in her loss of artistic standards and her artistic plunder of 'past barbarous epochs'. Nothing provided him with a clearer example of this national dissipation than the new Houses of Parliament in London. His distaste for these buildings is registered frequently throughout his architectural writings, but particularly in his 1864 public lecture on architecture, where they provide the basis for a virulent attack on Gothic as an iconoclastic force. The former Houses of Parliament had been destroyed by fire in October 1834, and the plans for the process of rebuilding initiated a major controversy. For almost the first time, the design of a public edifice was not limited to private commission but opened to competition, with the stipulation that the winning proposal must be Gothic or Elizabethan in style rather than Greek or Roman – the accepted norm for official buildings. There were two reasons for this specification. On one hand it was an attempt to elicit a design compatible with the only surviving remnants of the original structure, St Stephen's Chapel and Westminster Hall. On the other, the decision pandered to the fashionable and popular conception that Gothic, as opposed to classical or Italianate architecture, was the nation's indigenous style, and was therefore appropriate to the constitutional function of the parliament.[21]

The new buildings, which were eventually opened incomplete in 1852, symbolized for Ferguson a series of defects present in British political, social and religious life, and his disparaging allusions to them as the worst example of the revived style, with their 'mystical niches and illuminated frescoes', indicate the strength of his reaction.[22] The medieval style had been mistakenly chosen, he claimed, first, because the feudal middle-ages as depicted by Walter Scott had been misappropriated by the popular imagination as an idyllic heritage, and

---

20 Cited Duffy, *Four years*, p. 158.   21 Clark, *The Gothic revival*, pp. 108–14. The designs eventually selected for the new structure in 1836 were those of Charles Barry, though Pugin, excluded from the competition because of his Catholicism, is generally credited with the internal design.   22 'Architecture in Ireland', 699.

secondly, because the Cambridge Camden Society had succeeded in encouraging the wealthy classes towards the research of English ecclesiastical remains, in which they found gratifying evidence of their ancestral roots in Gothic. On this, Ferguson is terse and dismissive:

> The considerations may to many seem sentimental, and in opposition to the supposed utilitarian and strong common sense character of the nation; and it will long remain a subject for philosophic reflection that a people so practical should have chosen as the embodiment of its aesthetic feeling a style of structure so elaborate in the fripperies of decoration, that its grandeur with difficulty emerges through its littleness.[23]

Finally, Ferguson blames a racial element in the Northern European character, specifically 'a strain of Asiatic sentiment delighting in a barbaric profusion of carved ornament'. The fact that Gothic is found repugnant by the Greek or Italian mentality should act as a warning that it has little or no inherent merit. In language echoing Vasari's description of Gothic as form of violence, he identifies the style of the new Houses of Parliament with the barbarian destruction of Rome, and the invasion of a taste which possessed 'the exuberant life of a new faculty, covering with monsters and grotesques of its own creation everything it received from the civilization it overthrew'.[24] Through his use of the epic parallel Ferguson revealed his reaction not simply to discrete social changes but to transition on a major scale. In this respect, the medieval eye-sore of the new British Parliament represented a hideous fusion of two disruptive tendencies to which he proved particularly sensitive; one, an emergent money-mindedness and commercialism in public life, the other a corrosive sentimentalism amongst the English upper-classes.

Both aspects illuminate the density of the architectural metaphor in the period. In the case of the first, Ferguson's objection to the buildings was by no means an unusual response: as an architectural phenomenon they had dispensed not only with the authoritative precedent of Palladianism but also with the tradition of private patronage, and the resultant design was understood in some circles to manifest an energetic but unattractive spirit of independent commercial self-interest. The Houses of Parliament were symbolic of a new social order of political econ-

23 'Our architecture', p. 56. The Cambridge Camden Society, later the Ecclesiological Society, was founded in 1839 for the historical study of church ritual and architecture. It began publication of its journal, the *Ecclesiologist*, in 1841. See Clark, *The Gothic revival*, p. 155.   24 'Our architecture'. p. 57. The use of the Roman Gothic allegory was not unprecedented: compare the sentiments expressed in the *DUM*'s opening editorial. 'Age cannot command respect or utility ensure protection, while the time-honoured buttresses of our social system are to be given up to the rude assaults of the Goths and Vandals of modern days, that our vain and self-confident speculators in novelties may erect an edifice of their own upon its ruins.' 'New year's day, or our first number', *DUM* 1 (Jan. 1833), 87.

omy and regulatory public administration, dependent upon *nouveau-riche* industrialists and philistine civil servants. They embodied, suggests R.F. Jordan, a discernible shift in an aesthetic hegemony. 'Although the Victorian aristocracy might, in a limited way, still patronize the arts, they no longer dictated taste. The real patrons were now the industrialists, magnates, brokers and so on, or – which came to much the same thing, Boards and City Councils composed of such men.'[25]

Ferguson's aversion to Gothic as employed in the Parliament buildings was clearly related therefore, to his misgivings about the changing nature of government in the wake of Reform. An industrialized manufacturing society, which emphasized the value of created rather than inherited wealth, would breed only indolence, he suggested, through the easy distribution of profit. Its fallacy was 'not the accumulation of great wealth in the hands of a few, but the accumulation of great wealth – that is to say, of the right to live idly on the toil of the producer – in the hands of a great and excessive number'.[26] The abstract rule of economic theory would replace that of class deference and patriarchal control, while society at large would slump into ignorance and brutality. England had already slipped into this vortex, and as his 1849 satire 'Inheritor and Economist' illustrated, Ferguson agonized over the extension of similar social and economic traits to Ireland, where the transferral of the guardianship of taste into the hands of 'economist' was symptomatic of how Irish society would now follow its neighbour into aesthetic and moral decline.[27]

More acutely, the Gothic revival was indicative of the religious dissipation of the English aristocracy. Ferguson had become greatly disenchanted with the character and condition of this class, which had been weakened, he claimed in 1848, by its 'external attachments' or virulent tendency towards Ultramontanism.[28] It had fallen into 'sentimentalism', not only in its literary tastes but, as was manifest in its indulgence in the follies of the Gothic revival, in its religious faith, having succumbed to the damaging influence of Romanism and the Tractarians. National apostasy in England was considered by Ferguson as a major threat to the stabilizing properties of the Protestant church and a gross symptom of widespread social decline. In a letter to William Allingham he described how what he termed the 'barrier' afforded by established religion had become increasingly vulnerable. 'I suppose it will all be swept away', he complained, 'and the field left open for the forces of Newman and Bradlaugh within the present century'.[29] While Tractarianism failed to find a strong foothold in

25 *Victorian architecture* (1966), p. 74, p. 140. 26 'Ruskin's *Seven lamps of architecture*', *DUM* 34 (July 1849), 13. 27 'Inheritor and Economist', *DUM* 33 (May 1849), 638–49. 28 'The *Annals of the Four Masters*: second article', *DUM* 31 (Mar. 1848), 571. 29 Cited M.C. Ferguson, *SSFID*, vol. 1, p. 352. The Tractarians were so designated after the publication of 'Tracts for the times' (1833–41), in which Newman, Pusey, Keble and others promulgated the authority of High Anglicanism and provided the basis for the Oxford Movement.

Ireland, Ferguson was well aware of the large number of secessions to the Roman Catholic faith which followed John Henry Newman's apostasy in 1845, and was doubtless aware, too, of the further damaging wave of conversions in 1850 inspired by Nicholas Wiseman's articles in the *Dublin Review*, attacking ecclesiastical contradictions in Anglicanism.[30] Irish converts included Ferguson's acquaintance and fellow-poet Aubrey de Vere, who had fallen under Newman's spell, as he later described the experience, on a visit to Oxford. In 1850 de Vere attended Newman's influential 'Lectures on Anglican difficulties' and in November of the following year converted to the Roman Catholic faith.[31]

There are indications of the effect of this state of affairs on Ferguson in his review of Ruskin's *Stones of Venice* in September of 1851. Commenting on the subject of wall-friezes, he denounces the grotesque decorations in coloured marble which were beloved of Ruskin and which featured in such churches as San Michele at Lucca. To such excesses, Ferguson stated, 'we shall never be reconciled'. He continues:

> When we speak of being reconciled we mean the reconciliation to these ideas of the people at large of the British islands. For the aristocracy of Great Britain we do not pretend to vouch. Transalpine sympathies have so far alienated many of them from the religious and social principles of the age in which they were born, that it would be rash to speculate on their adhesion to any forms of faith, or any canons of taste.[32]

The disgust expressed here towards the aristocratic class in England is profound. Where others acclaimed a spirit of liberalism or progress, Ferguson saw only weakness and effeminacy, represented architecturally in the delicate curves and hidden intricacies of Gothic, which undermined the strength and authority of Classical style. 'Everything has to be straightened, stiffened, symmetrised', he postulated. England had now lost her muscular aristocratic leadership, and her aesthetic standards bore witness to this impoverishment as 'capricious dilettantism supplies the place of that manly and consistent appreciation of architecture which distinguished the nobility and gentry of the last century'.[33] The class as a whole had been corrupted, and must be condemned for the irresponsibility it had shown towards the aesthetic and moral well being of the nation.

---

30 D. Bowen suggests that the Tractarians failed in Ireland because of the steadfast opposition of James O'Brien, bishop of Ossory. 'His first charge of 1842, his last of 1866, and many statements during his long episcopal rule were directed against the Tractarians, the later Ritualists, and any churchmen who showed the least spirit of conciliation on the Roman Catholic question.' *The Protestant crusade*, p. 77. On the influence of Newman and Wiseman see pp. 230–1.   31 Aubrey de Vere describes his enchantment with Newman and his own conversion to Catholicism in his *Recollections* (1897), p. 263.   32 'Ruskin's *Stones of Venice*, volume 1: the foundations', *DUM* 38 (Sept. 1851), 268.   33 'Ruskin's Seven lamps of architecture', 3.

RUSKIN AND RELIGIOUS CONTROVERSY

The Oxford Movement clearly unsettled Ferguson. Alarmed by its tendency towards increased ritualism in the High Anglican church and its theological shift towards compatibility with Roman Catholic doctrine, he appears to have devoted a considerable amount of thought to exposing what he believed to be the ecclesiological errors of the renegade Oxford divines. In 1843 he had written to Robert Blackwood asking his opinion on Puseyism and suggesting an article on the subject. 'I know a good deal of religious archaeology', he wrote, 'and could easily show that many of the points on which the Puseyites are most urgent are not merely Popish but Pagan; and not merely Pagan but obviously abominable in their origin. I could, if it were deemed expedient, write a series of "Facts for the Times" that would be startling enough.'[34] His concern with the theological and ecclesiastical implications of architectural design, meanwhile, emerges in his criticism as a consistent derogation of Roman Catholicism, which he characterized in terms of medievalism, superstition and duplicity. In this context his praise for Gandon highlights what is absent from the architect's work as much as what is present: Gandon's mind, he claimed, 'had no disposition to middle-age ideas, either abstract or symbolised. The age in which he lived was one eminently averse to mysticism.' Throughout his work would be seen 'neither crockets, nor finials, nor the affectation of monastic seclusion, or feudal rudeness; but an elegant simplicity and fitness everywhere united with forms of stability and grandeur.'[35]

Ferguson's attack on the esotericism of ecclesiastical medievalism was sustained and consistent. A year later in his review of William Reeves' study of Irish ecclesiastical remains, he suggested that the church relics of a former age should be shown up as fraudulent and coercive in the rational light of Protestantism:

> Minds which penetrate the mysticism acquire an increased contempt for all that symbolic apparatus, and rise from the wholesome discovery with clearer views of the divine economy, and a stronger reliance on the simple truths of God. Other minds, and these again the greater number, unable to extricate themselves from the charm of a half-revealed mystery, pleased with the continual development of analogies, and captivated by the formal beauties of the objects themselves, fall from one degree of fascination to another, until, from having been the dupes of mysticism, they become the instruments of religious intrigue and social warfare.[36]

[34] 17 Mar. 1843, NLS MS 4064 f245. Edward Pusey, professor at Hebrew at Oxford, had given his name to the early adherents of what was to become the Oxford Movement. [35] 'Architecture in Ireland', 696. [36] 'Reeves'

The same insistence that medievalism in art was inextricable from medievalism in religious belief was to underwrite the text of his *DUM* reviews of John Ruskin's *Stones of Venice* and *Seven lamps of architecture*. These articles, in which Ferguson comments at length on the subject of ecclesiastical architecture, provided a forum for full expansion of the dichotomy between classicism and Gothic, and served to expose the major philosophical discrepancies between the English art theorist and his Irish reviewer. Throughout, Ruskin's Romantic sensibility finds its antithesis in Ferguson's senatorial, Augustan temperament, while the liberalism and egalitarianism of the former is consistently contradicted by the authoritarian conservatism of the latter. The defender of the pre-Raphaelites and the century's leading advocate of medieval Gothic is treated as an upstart by Ferguson who, manipulating Ruskin's text to his own advantage, uses the occasion to produce a crude polemical system in which Gothic, Roman Catholicism and delusion are weighed against Classicism, Protestantism and enlightenment.

A divergence in aesthetic sensibility between the two men provides a background to the clash. Ruskin's pursuit of Romantic naturalism contravenes Ferguson's respect for conventional, regular form, while his tendency towards religiosity contrasts with Ferguson's emotional restraint. Where Ruskin takes the imitation of Nature to a point of sublimity, Ferguson rejects it completely. Commenting on the reproduction in marble of fruit and flowers as ornamentation, for example, he states: 'we should prefer forms less natural and more conventional in the main lines of our cornices, architraves, and other substantive parts of our dwellings. These, we severally feel, ought to remind us that they are artificial.'[37] Similarly, on the subject of pillaring, Ferguson is anxious to dismiss the naturalistic associations of the form in which the shaft of the pillar descends into a swollen base, and regards the outline as pleasing only in its exposition of the physical laws of pressure.[38] At each stage his obdurate practicality and objectivity serve to deflate Ruskin's subliminal interpretations, prioritizing a cold formalism over naturalistic representation.

Underlying this superficial opposition however, is a deeper ideological contradiction. The severity and constraint of Regular or classical architecture was frequently challenged by Ruskin as exhibiting 'the accuracy of apathy', and as promoting a servile art form in which the craftsman found no means of liberation or self-expression. Gothic, on the other hand, was a 'revolutionary' mode, which released the artist from tradition and authority, 'delighting in the infringement of every servile principle'. Gothic represented an organic phenomenon, which, in contrast to classical perfectionism, celebrated imperfection as a desirable and organic stage in the natural process of development:

Ecclesiastical antiquities', *DUM* 31 (Feb. 1848), 223.   37 'Ruskin's *Stones of Venice*', 270.   38 Ibid., 256.

> It is a sign of life in a mortal body, that is to say, of a state of progress and change. Nothing that lives is, or can be rigidly perfect; part of it is decaying, part nascent. The foxglove blossom – a third part bud, a third part past, a third part in full bloom, it is a type of the life of this world. And in all things that live there are certain irregularities and deficiencies which are not only signs of life, but sources of beauty. All admit irregularity as they imply change; and to banish imperfection is to destroy expression, to check exertion, to paralyze vitality.[39]

Throughout his writings Ruskin sustained a spirited attack on conformity and regularity, rebelling against 'the spacious pomp [...] adopted by the luxurious aristocracies', and defying the principles of servility and stagnating tradition which he saw as characteristic of classical architecture. Gothic architecture, on the other hand, exhibited 'strength of will, independence of character, resoluteness of purpose, impatience of undue control, and a general tendency to set the individual reason against authority'.[40]

Ferguson's comments on same subject however, amount to a total refutation of Ruskin's beliefs, and to a demand for subjugation and compliance. 'To be original is a privilege, but one rarely vouchsafed to the architect', he wrote. 'If he can impress with a sense of majesty, if he can elevate and at the same time expand the soul; if he can communicate a perception of elegance, grandeur and harmony, these will be his triumphs; but in proportion as he rises towards these heights of his art, he will leave individual peculiarities behind, and in the attainment of perfection pass far beyond the reach of any influence of egotism.'[41] Where Ruskin's language is revolutionary and decorative, Ferguson's is biblical and judgmental: architecture demands that the architect 'shall mortify the egotistical sentiment, so there is none in which the temptation is greater or the way more easy to mannerism'.[42] Ruskin's Romantic cultivation of the individual as an organ of change and development in art is challenged by the aesthetics of constraint and conformity advocated by Ferguson; his promotion of Gothic as a 'living architecture' undermined by his opponent's insistence on the orthodoxy and uniformity of classical construction.

The artistic dialectic thus established was immediately susceptible to the imposition of a theological gloss, and Ferguson seized the opportunity without due respect for Ruskin's complex position. Ruskin's advocacy of Gothic in ecclesiastical art and architecture, together with his defence of the Pre-Raphaelites in the second volume of *Modern painters* in 1846, had already given rise to widespread allegations of his Romanist sympathies – allegations which he attempted to refute,

39 'The nature of Gothic', *Stones of Venice* (1981), p. 121.   40 Ibid., p. 131.   41 'Our architecture', p. 52.   42 Ibid., p. 53.

first in an open letter to the *Times* and subsequently in an article denouncing Catholic Emancipation, which he appended to the first volume of *Stones of Venice*. In the same work he launched a ferocious attack on the excesses of the Catholic architect Pugin, with whom he had frequently been associated.[43] Ferguson was not impressed by such measures. Ruskin's apparent alarm at the progress of 'popish ideas' in England was at best unconvincing, he asserted, while a reading of his works suggested nothing less than that the author had succumbed to the influence of Tractarianism. 'We cannot help remarking' Ferguson continued, 'that architectural Puseyism has had no more efficient promoter in England than John Ruskin', and 'no-one not honoured with his personal acquaintance could have supposed him to be the decided Protestant that he now appears'.[44]

This outright condemnation of Ruskin was the basis for Ferguson's review in 1849 of *The seven lamps of architecture*, Ruskin's treatise on the fundamental principles of design and construction. Ferguson's objections begin with the use in the title of a 'mystical' number, suggesting 'a mysterious binding of medieval knots, symbolic monsters, and black letter epigraphs'. This is preliminary evidence of Ruskin's attraction to the esoteric and grotesque; attributes immediately associated with Roman Catholic dogma. The section entitled 'The lamp of sacrifice' sounds to the reviewer 'as if the most important part of the edifice consisted in the arrangements for celebrating mass', while in 'The lamp of power' Ruskin is deemed better off for having 'laid aside his surplus and mysterious looks'. Such jibes are frequent, and their intrusion into the critical text effectively realigns Ruskin's aesthetic position.

> His love of the delicate, the picturesque, and the mysterious, here gratifies itself in congenial forms of fretwork, of irregular arcades, and half-discovered vistas. The solemn roof, suspended from its unseen external props, fills him with a pleasing awe; the inlaid patterns and variegated courses and diamonds of different coloured masonry, delight his sense of colour, and the venerable air of the twelfth century inspires him with a dreamy sentiment of Anglican Catholicity.

Immersing Ruskin in the paraphernalia of medieval ecclesiology, Ferguson succeeds in obscuring his moral and social affiliations to Gothic. He brashly presents his own preferences, meanwhile, as practical, enlightened and honest. 'For our part, we discard sentiments and associations of the medieval kind', he wrote. 'We desire light and distinctness. We wish to see the roof over our heads supported by walls or pillars evidently adequate to the burthen. We admire stateli-

43 See Clark, *The Gothic revival*, pp. 195–6.   44 'Ruskin's *Stones of Venice*', 261.

ness, regularity and spaciousness [...] the lessons of Greek and Roman wisdom.'[45] And so it continues, with Ferguson promoting in his review an antonymous system which pits light against dark; clarity against mystery; classical against medieval; Trinity College in Dublin against the colleges of Cambridge; St George's Spire against the San Zeno campanile; and the Place de la Concorde against the Verona market place. In all, Ruskin's Gothic credo is consistently derided as mawkish, puerile and misguided in its tendencies towards Rome.

Ferguson pursued his attack on Ruskin two years later in his review of the first volume of *Stones of Venice*. Ruskin, who travelled to Venice in 1849 to sketch its unique facades and porticos, found the city in a pitiful state of decay. Still suffering from the long-term effects of the Napoleonic Wars and the more recent rebellious assaults of 1848, its degenerate buildings confirmed his vision of the regrettable decline in Italian architecture, from the true Christianity of medieval Gothic to the decadence and worldliness of Renaissance neo-classicism. *Stones of Venice* portrayed the city accordingly in terms of a moral allegory, in which the integrity of the fourteenth-century virgin had been exchanged for the corruption of the sixteenth-century whore.[46] His thesis of architectural and historical transition was thus diametrically opposed to Ferguson's understanding of the progress of Protestant enlightenment. For Ferguson the sixteenth century represented on one hand, the Reformation, and liberation from medieval obscurity, and on the other, the glorious age of the Renaissance which ushered in the resplendent talent of Palladio. This key difference in perspective increased his antagonism to Ruskin, and his review of the first volume of *Stones of Venice*, 'The foundations', is consequently charged with hostility. Even in his discussions of structural and ornamental technicalities, theological implications, which had previously formed a pervasive undercurrent to the text, begin to surface and predominate.[47]

---

45 'Ruskin's *Seven lamps of architecture*', 1-3. 46 See R. Ellmann's essay on Ruskin, 'Biographical speculations', in *Golden codgers* (1973), for development of this interpretation of *Stones of Venice*. 47 This is perhaps most evident in Ferguson's response to the feature of flying buttresses, the external wall or roof supports characteristic of Gothic design. As his 1846 letter to his mother has illustrated, Ferguson was unhappy with the hidden and deceptive aspects of the structure: Ruskin by contrast found it exciting and defended it as a legitimate appeal to the imagination. Mystery in architecture was not in this respect Ferguson's 'medieval knot' of superstition and dishonesty but a product of the Romantic imagination inspired by natural phenomena. In the face of reality, Ruskin argued in *Modern painters*, we contemplate the clouds as mountains or the sky as a blue vault. Nature, as he had elsewhere explained, 'is always mysterious and secret in her means, and art is most like her when it is most inexplicable' (*Works*, vol. 1, Part 1, Section 2, chapter 2, p. 1). Ferguson, in complete contrast, ignores this wider metaphysical challenge in favour of a limited theological interpretation. His aversion to flying buttresses is exaggerated and his personal antipathy transformed into an opportunistic expression of enlightened Protestant self-righteousness. Of the Gothic roof and its external supports, he writes acidly, '[w]e cannot but think that a sense of insecurity enters into the awful feeling inspired by such interiors [...] However suitable they may be for edifices designed for the purposes of imposing on weak minds by awe-inspiring accessories, they are, in our judgement, inconsistent with the sincerity alike of Protestant worship and of good architecture.' ('Ruskin's *Stones of Venice*', 259).

The theological dialectic is most pointedly marked however, in the conclusion to the review, where Ferguson draws an extended contrast between two church buildings: St Peter's in Rome and Westminster Abbey in London. Perversely it is the former he upholds as the ideal symbol of Protestant faith, while the latter with its picturesque Gothic detail is taken to represent a devious Catholicism:

> The one is open, spacious, self-sustained and simple; the other narrow, gloomy, intricate and mysterious. The one, while expanding, exhilarates the mind, the other, while uplifting, confines and overawes it. The one stands openly and avowedly on evident foundations; the other hangs its masses of stone overhead from props that are unseen and adventitious. The one is all art; the other, half-artifice. We prefer the building, as we do the creed, which appeals to the private judgement of the man of ordinary intelligence, asking no blind confidence in the skill with which a subtle system of compensations and counterpoises may be arranged outside, but presenting its provisions for protection and shelter on the strength of its own visible and tangible means of support.[48]

The passage expresses forcibly the crucial substantive and procedural distinctions which Ferguson identified between Roman Catholicism and Protestantism, or, as he had termed it in his portrait of Thomas Davis, between 'dogmas of abstract faith and the precepts of morality and social duty'.[49] Ruskin, he concluded, was supposedly Protestant and English, and should therefore show a greater degree of responsibility in selecting a style which favoured neither mysticism nor idolatry.

J.J. McCARTHY AND IRELAND'S GOTHIC REVIVAL

The vitriol in Ferguson's treatment of Ruskin conveys his profound abhorrence of Gothic and its ecclesiastical significance. On one level this reflects his wish to make a public contribution to the debate surrounding the proclivities of an influential body of English theologians, and to disparage simultaneously Tractarian supporters among the English aristocracy. On another level however, Ferguson's challenge to Ruskin highlights domestic issues, and a background of increasing Catholic self-assertiveness manifesting itself in ecclesiastical construction. His architectural prepossessions were undoubtedly aggravated

---

[48] 'Ruskin's *Stones of Venice*', 260.   [49] 'Our portrait gallery: Thomas Davis', *DUM* 29 (Feb. 1847), 192.

by a prevailing sense of Irish Protestant insecurity, a scenario in which John Ruskin features less as a representative of English corruption and more as a stooge for the exposition of conflicts closer to home.

The reach of the Roman Catholic hierarchy in Ireland was certainly expanding in the period. In 1850, the year of the so-called 'papal aggression' in Europe under Pius IX, the Irish clergy was significantly reorganized at the synod of Thurles, and given effective leadership in its newly appointed papal delegate Paul Cullen. Cullen was a force to be reckoned with; 'a papal general intent upon saving the souls of the Irish people by establishing in Ireland a Catholic cultural ascendancy which could protect them.'[50] Rebellions by Catholic majorities in Belgium and Poland in the 1830s, meanwhile, together with the emergence of Irish Catholic nationalist incentives under O'Connell and the Repeal agitation had already given the Protestant community cause for disquiet, while the post-Famine activities of a Catholic church counter-reformation against Protestant Evangelicalism and souperism increased a feverish enmity between the two creeds.[51] In conjunction with its clerical restructuring, the Catholic church embarked on a series of building projects which embodied its newly-liberated status:

> In the short run at least, the true beneficiary of Catholic emancipation was not the peasantry hovering perpetually on the brink of starvation, nor even O'Connell's own followers, manoeuvring anxiously and amateurishly between English parties at Westminster, but the Catholic Church itself. The outward and visible signs of emancipation were already apparent long before the Famine. They took the form of churches, schools, seminaries, monasteries and convents, provided for the most part by legacies from the more prosperous sons and daughters of the Church, and by subscription and dues from all classes of the community.[52]

If the financial investment was substantial, the psychological benefits were likewise considerable, as a Catholic social ethos gained in confidence and scope. Simultaneously, the Church of Ireland was losing its grip as its credibility began to diminish and its congregations decline. 'It was clear to every liberal or radical of the age' observes Bowen, 'that the Irish Protestant establishment was an anomaly surviving from another age, and had to be reformed'.[53] Between a fos-

---

[50] Bowen, *The Protestant crusade*, p. 266. [51] See Bowen, *The Protestant crusade*, chapter 1. [52] F.S.L. Lyons, *Ireland since the Famine*, p. 7. Lyons estimates that some £30 million were spent on church building and clergy maintenance in Ireland between 1817 and 1847. See also E. Larkin, 'Economic growth, capital investment and the Roman Catholic church in nineteenth-century Ireland', *American historical review*, 72 (April 1967), 856–8. Following his Irish tour the novelist Thackeray wrote of observing the newly built continental style Catholic Cathedral in Carlow, which he described as 'overloaded with ornaments, nor were its innumerable spires and pinnacles the more pleasing to the eye because some of them were out of the perpendicular'. He continued, '[t]he Catholics point to the structure

silized Protestantism and a revitalized Roman Catholicism, a power struggle for supremacy was taking place.

In architectural terms, the emergence of an assertive Catholic ideology rapidly became identifiable with Gothic; a conceptual relationship between style and creed cemented by the architect Augustus Welby Pugin. Like Ferguson, Pugin visited the cathedrals of Europe during the 1840s but came to quite different conclusions with respect to the stylistic supremacy of classical design. 'I have now seen Rome, and what Italian architecture can do, and I do not hesitate to say that it is the imperative duty of every Catholic to defend Christian architecture with his whole energy', he wrote. 'The modern churches here are frightful. St. Peter's is far more ugly than I expected, and vilely constructed – a mass of imposition – bad taste of every kind seems to have run riot in this place.'[54]

Pugin, who was born in 1812, converted to Catholicism at the age of twenty-three. He dedicated a major part of his prolific and often idiosyncratic career to the design and construction of Gothic church architecture and to the publication of his aesthetic doctrine. In his *True principles of pointed or Christian architecture* (1841), he sought to link the Gothic style with the tenets of religious belief in its pre-Reformation state, while in his 1846 *Contrasts*, he attempted to expose the corruption of modern architecture in comparison with the glorious edifices of the Middle Ages. A devoted medievalist, he was a leading light of the Victorian ecclesiologists in advocating the revival and re-accommodation of traditional church rituals and practice.[55]

In addition to his theoretical influence, Pugin was largely responsible for the physical extension of the Gothic Revival to Ireland, designing first the Loreto convent, Wexford, in 1839, and subsequently Killarney and Enniscorthy cathedrals in 1842 and 1843. In 1845 he received a commission to work on the new buildings of the Catholic seminary at Maynooth, which together with the Queen's Colleges in Galway, Cork and Belfast, had been awarded an increased endowment in that year.[56] The grant was controversial and Maynooth was already considered by many to be a hot-bed of 'papist' agitation, but despite widespread opposition and severe financial handicaps Pugin's designs were executed, and by 1850 the commissioner's report stated that the new buildings would be fit for occupation in the following summer.[57]

---

with considerable pride; it was the first, I believe, of the many handsome cathedrals for their worship which have been built of late years in this country by the novel contributions of the poor man's penury and by the untiring energies and sacrifices of the clergy': *Irish sketch book*, pp. 39–40.   53 *The Protestant crusade*, p. 175.   54 Cited by D. Gwynn, 'Pugin and Maynooth' (1952), 173.   55 See Clark, *The Gothic revival*, pp. 127–8 and 145–7.   56 D.S. Richardson lists and evaluates Pugin's contributions to Irish church architecture in 'Gothic revival architecture in Ireland' (1970), vol. 1, pp. 254–95. See also M. McDermott, *Ireland's architectural history*, chapter 17.   57 Gwynn, 'Pugin and Maynooth', 172. D.S. Richardson also comments in detail on the Maynooth controversy and Pugin's designs, vol. 1, pp. 315–22.

Ireland's architecture

Ferguson was aware of the architect's plans for Maynooth and was suitably unimpressed. 'Pugin's buildings are disagreeable', he stated in 1851, 'but we suppose that he has had monkish and medieval warrant for them'.[58] The architect's legacy was not easily dismissed however, and by the time of Pugin's death in 1852 his philosophy and influence had taken root in Ireland through the figure of James Joseph McCarthy, a Dublin-born Catholic nationalist who was to become the leading exponent of Pugin's ecclesiological Gothic in Ireland. Having studied his mentor's writings and designs, McCarthy became strongly attracted to his architectural medievalism and sought to execute similar principles in his own work.[59] In 1846, at a ceremony attended by several thousand people, the foundation stone of his first major achievement in Gothic, the church of St Kevin's at Glendalough, was laid. Built in the early pointed style, St Kevin's established for the architect a significant link with Catholic antiquity, encapsulating a spirit which he claimed was both pious and patriotic, as 'a revival of the venerable architecture of our Catholic forefathers'.[60]

Over the next five years McCarthy consolidated upon this venture with similar Gothic designs, including the church at Kilskyre in County Meath, the high-Gothic chapel and collegiate buildings of All Hallows at Drumcondra and the Star of the Sea church in Irishtown. Simultaneously, he sought to capitalize on the specific implications of his adopted style, as Jeanne Sheehy explains:

> The very idea of religious revival in the Catholic church was very much bound up, in the forties, with the idea of a return to a more perfect Celtic past. If Pugin and the Ecclesiologists saw the return to the medieval period as a golden age, the temptation to do so was even greater among Irish Catholics, who looked back to a hazy era of religious and political freedom, when Ireland was an 'island of Saints and Scholars'.[61]

Ecclesiastical Gothic was in this respect a vast symbolic resource, through which the architect might express both his dissent from the established creed and his affiliation to the true, pre-Reformation church. The stylistic nostalgia was a means to register in architecture the sentiments of Catholic national feeling in the country, with McCarthy, as Charles Gavan Duffy would later describe him, 'studding Ireland with noble Gothic churches on which the genius of native art was stamped'.[62]

---

58 'Ruskin's *Stones of Venice*', 261. 59 See J. Sheehy, *J.J. McCarthy and the Gothic revival in Ireland* (1977), p. 9, p. 26; and D.S. Richardson, vol. 1, pp. 488–92. 60 Cited Sheehy, *J.J. McCarthy*, p. 7. The foundation stone was laid by the so-called 'temperance priest', Father Mathew. 61 *J.J. McCarthy*, pp. 13–14. 62 *My life* (1898), vol. 2, p. 117. McCarthy was a close friend of Duffy and an avid reader of the *Nation*.

Unlike Pugin, McCarthy was not working in isolation. First, he publicized his various projects and their underlying principles in a series of contributions to Duffy's *Irish Catholic Magazine* in 1847, in which he attacked classical architectural orthodoxy from a Catholic perspective.[63] Secondly, he drew significant support from the membership of the Irish Ecclesiological Society. Founded in late 1840s by a group of Catholic clerics and intellectuals, this organization was based on its English counterpart, the 1839 Camden Society, a Cambridge-based unit which sought to re-accommodate high church ritual and to revive structural features of ecclesiastical architecture required by the ancient rubrics. The Irish Ecclesiological Society, which was largely responsible for securing McCarthy's commissions, comprised a number of influential figures, listing among its patrons in 1849 the archbishop of Dublin, the earl of Shrewsbury and the Reverend Nicholas Wiseman, and among its council, Charles Gavan Duffy and Thomas O'Hagan.[64]

At a general meeting of the Society in February of 1851 McCarthy delivered a paper entitled 'Suggestions on the arrangement and characteristics of parish churches'. The text of this lecture, which was later published in pamphlet form, gives some insight into the workings of the architect's mind, and reveals the presence of a new discipline within the Catholic church. The formal precepts advocated by McCarthy were indicative of rejuvenated ecclesiastical authority and status, while his concentration on ecclesiological specifics – the measurements and purposes of bells, the function of spires and chancels or the revival of the rood-screen between the choir and the nave – provided the creed with a new visual legitimacy. On one hand, McCarthy promoted the true principles of church architecture and on the other denounced the paganism of the classical style which, he claimed, quoting Newman, made 'naked cupids stand for angels and sprawling women for the cardinal virtues'.[65] The paper was not entirely concerned with architectural detail, however. McCarthy composed a preface in which he attempted to bring new bearings to ecclesiastical antiquarianism in the nineteenth century, engaging in a forceful revisionism of post-Reformation history. The architecture of 'enlightened' times should finally be exposed as defective and insincere, he suggested, and the religious edifices of the so-called 'dark ages' re-evaluated. Indeed, the medieval age should be researched and held up as exemplary to modern society, while the church should be replenished with her ancient rites and ceremonies, for 'our safest course at present is to study those remains of Catholic antiquity which have escaped the devastations of faithless times'.[66]

63 Sheehy, *J.J. McCarthy*, p. 8. The source is Duffy's *Irish Catholic Magazine* (May 1847), pp. 112–13. 64 Sheehy, *J.J. McCarthy*, pp. 9–12. 65 *Suggestions on the arrangement and characteristics of parish churches* (1851), p. 32. 66 *Suggestions*, preface, v. Consider R. Kearney's view of a native resistance to classical regularity and orthodoxy in Ireland. 'From the earliest times, the Irish mind remained free, in significant measure, of the linear, centralising logic of the

Neglect of the true requirements for Catholic worship had resulted in centuries of obscurity, but now a welcome process of ecclesiological restoration had been set in motion through which the church would regain her former integrity.

McCarthy's formidable industry and ecclesiological evangelism were influential across a wide social spectrum. His talent was highly acclaimed and in 1853 he was accepted as a member of the Royal Irish Academy. Meanwhile, the ideological premise of his architecture was attractive to a Catholic populace for which he provided, claims Sheehy, 'the affirmation of resurgent strength implicit in building strong Gothic stone churches with tall spires in towns and villages where medieval buildings were either in ruins or had been taken over by the Established church.'[67] In his reading of history he legitimized medievalism, challenged the authority and worth of the Reformation and provided Irish Catholicism with evocative structural metaphors for a strident and re-animated identity.

Ferguson was undoubtedly familiar with McCarthy, if only through his own acquaintance with members of the Irish Ecclesiological Society. The prominent activities of the Irish architect, together with the religious aesthetic fostered by Pugin during the middle years of the century, contribute therefore, to the context in which the upsurge of Protestant atavism in his reading of John Ruskin may be understood. The visibility of Rome in architectural form and furthermore, in the defiant form of Gothic, suggests itself as a partial reason for the undercurrent of anxiety and hostility in his critical writings on the subject, which the high political temperature of the late 1840s and early 1850s served to exacerbate. While the corruption which Ruskin's work represented in England was the major point of contention, the simultaneous emergence of confident Roman Catholic self-expression at home was nonetheless a significant side issue.

The defensiveness and conservatism of Ferguson's architectural review writing is difficult to deal with, particularly in the light of his own political apostasy in the late 1840s. It could be suggested of course, that the publication context of his reviews was an important factor, and that his criticisms were merely another extension of *DUM* editorial policy. Beyond this however, his antipathy to Gothicism appears as a personal conviction. The Gothic Revival in Ireland impinged upon his consciousness so that even in the North of Ireland, with its 'Presbyterian taste for the solidly classical', evidence of its presence disturbed him, and he complained of how, recently in Belfast 'in the midst of factories, shipyards and railway termini, a bastard Gothic chapel was erected by certain silly Protestants'.[68]

Graeco-Roman culture which dominated most of western Europe [...] This would not mean, as the colonial prejudice presumed, that the Irish abandoned order for disorder or reneged on conceptual rigour to embrace formless chaos [...] We have here not meaninglessness but another kind of meaning, not confusion but another kind of coherence': 'An Irish intellectual tradition', in R. Kearney (ed.), *The Irish mind* (1985), p. 9. 67 *J.J. McCarthy*, pp. 5–6. 68 C.E.B. Brett, *Buildings of Belfast* (1968) p. 20; Ferguson, 'Ruskin's *Stones of Venice*', 268.

It seems therefore that a religious antagonism was inextricable from Ferguson's aesthetic preferences, and the resultant sectarianism of his views must be taken on board as part of his complex ideological make-up in the late 1840s and 1850s. While his targets were on one level external, and concerned the theological waywardness of an English aristocracy, they included at another, what he appeared to regard as a threat to domestic well-being, in the form of an overbearing Roman Catholic doctrine, economic ascendancy and hierarchy. Though his quarrel was not with Ireland's Catholic congregation *per se*, his perspective was nonetheless limited in view of his ambitions for an inclusive national heritage. For all his cross-bench activism, he would ultimately fail to accommodate certain aspects of Irish culture and tradition within that inheritance. The handicaps he imposed upon himself as a result are evident in his decision, in 1848, to abandon his research project on the missionary saints of the early Irish church, having been discouraged, his wife claims, by the 'accretions of superstition and puerile legend which overshadowed their fame'.[69]

There is much to be learnt however, from the side of Ferguson's personality which emerges in the confrontation with Ruskin. In complete contrast to the exuberant and seductive prose of the English writer his manner is imperious, dogmatic and utterly reactionary, his temperament stubborn and intransigent. His unwillingness to explore his subject with any kind of imaginative liberty is an indication of his insecurity in the face of such a disruption, and these tendencies serve to expose the depth of his anxiety concerning what he saw as the fragility and vulnerability of art and architecture in Ireland. The clash with Gothic was in effect, a confrontation with the Other, one which forced him to consider – albeit metaphorically – the long-term ideological resistance to his own cultural blue-print for the country. How might it be protected, in the future, from the full and disastrous effects of stylistic and moral aberration? 'It is only by the control of educated judgements' Ferguson wrote in 1864, 'that the public taste, in such a period of irresolute and tentative selection, can be restrained from caprices which might otherwise constitute a permanent reproach to our century'.[70] Again, the issue underscored the need for a responsible cultural and civic leadership, free from the vagaries of fashion, but detached at the same time from the problematic grip of the popular religion.

69 *SSFID*, vol. 1, p. 188.   70 'Our public and domestic architecture', 78.

CHAPTER SIX

Culture, antiquarianism and the Royal Irish Academy

By the early 1850s Ferguson had little more to offer in the way of critical prose, but poetry became increasingly important to him. Expressly cutting his ties with prose romance, which he now saw as an ineffective medium for presenting Irish historical events, he confirmed his faith in the poet as the interpreter of the past:

> His materials are pre-eminently the face of nature and the emotions of the human heart; and he can present these at any point of time backward, with less of the apparatus of costume and manners, than any other realizer of scenes to the imagination. For him there is abundant material from century to century, back as far as tradition reaches, and capable, every particle of it, to be turned to the loftiest national purposes, so as to be only taken up in a generous spirit, passed through the fire of a free genius, and enunciated with frankness and simplicity.[1]

In this spirit he embarked on his long poem *Congal*, the work which he hoped would live on after him, he told Blackwood, and in which he turned, as Yeats later observed, 'to the great poets of the world for his style', in order to produce national material for a Victorian readership.[2]

The past was also to become a retreat for Ferguson in his professional capacity. On taking up a post as deputy keeper of the newly established Department of Public Records, in 1867, Ferguson would become part of a comprehensive and influential government initiative, which produced 'a nascent class of professional record scholars', employed as full-time civil servants.[3] The appointment was one he openly solicited, writing to Thomas Larcom – by then head of the Civil Service in Ireland – to ask for information on the establishment of the new office. 'I believe I could do substantial public service if I were at the head of such a department', he insisted, 'and would be willing to retire from professional life if I could obtain a position so congenial to my tastes and inclinations'.[4] The career change was fortuitous too in view of his declining phys-

---

1 'The *Annals of the Four Masters*', *DUM* 31 (Mar. 1848), 376. 2 30 Nov. 1859, NLS MS 4138 f 139; W.B.Yeats, editorial introduction to *A book of Irish verse* (1895), p. 19. 3 P. Levine, *The amateur and the professional*, p. 124. 4 5 Apr. 1867, NLI

ical stamina: the work was demanding but less strenuous than the Bar. He informed John Blackwood that his new duties were amenable and that he was quite content, 'as when I was in the way of higher advancements my health broke down, and I am convinced I acted wisely in taking the hint'.[5]

The work in the Records office consolidated Ferguson's passion for antiquarianism, a pursuit which dominated the latter decades of his life. He became a specialist on the subject of Ogham inscriptions, and dedicated himself to the task of recording and deciphering Ogham markings around the country.[6] He travelled extensively on the Continent, developing close ties with Brittany, where he found, on his 1863 visit, a welcoming network of *aficionados* including the Celtic antiquarian Hérsart de la Villemarqué.[7] He also toured in Ireland, visiting the north-west in 1864 in the company of fellow antiquarians George Petrie, Whitley Stokes, and the Reverends J.H. Todd and H.H. Dickinson. In Dublin he was a keen activist, involved in several antiquarian and archaeological societies, and a founder member of the *Celtic Athenaeum*. He contributed some thirty papers on antiquarian subjects to the published *Transactions and Proceedings of the Royal Irish Academy*, and headed the reorganization of the Academy museum collection, for which he made various purchases and wrote an official guide and catalogue.[8]

Ferguson was not content however, to leave the past to speak for itself. Repeatedly, he sought to shape it into a public property, promoting a culture of history designed to form an integral part of a national literary inheritance. The failure of government made manifest by the Famine, the continuing inadequacy of the Union and the weakness of an Irish aristocracy had combined, he believed, to render Irish society traumatized and leaderless. But recourse to the past provided stability in the face of change: self-knowledge, the foundation of 'just national feeling' offered a guard against anarchic tendencies and social alienation. 'Society has, it is true, been almost shaken to pieces', he wrote in March 1848, in a *DUM* review of John O'Donovan's three-volume annotated text and English translation of the *Annals of the Four Masters*. 'We have indeed

---

MS 7591. See G. Ó Dúill's account of Ferguson's career in the Public Record Office; 'Samuel Ferguson, administrator and archivist' (1986). 5 3 Dec. 1877, NLS MS 4358 f197. 6 Lady Ferguson describes the process by which Ferguson learned to make paper casts of Ogham inscriptions, *SSFID*, vol. 2, p. 48. The first two chapters of this volume give a full picture of Ferguson's activities as an antiquarian and archaeologist. For an account of Ferguson's antiquarian and archaeological pursuits, see P. Ní Chatháin, 'Sir Samuel Ferguson and the Ogham inscriptions' (1986). 7 The Viscomte Hérsart de la Villemarqué, author of *La Légende celtique*, was the addressee of Ferguson's poem 'Adieu to Brittany', in which he recorded his impressions of his antiquarian tour of Brittany in 1863. This was later included in his *Lays of the Western Gael*. 8 One of the interests of the *Celtic Athenaeum* was to record the existence of manuscripts and private antiquarian collections. For its founder members, including Aubrey de Vere, as President, Isaac Butt as vice president, and Charles Gavan Duffy, Sheridan Le Fanu, John Mitchel and Thomas O'Hagan as council members, see the *Nation*, 7 Mar. 1846, 330. Ferguson's antiquarian contributions to the *Proceedings and transactions of the Royal Irish Academy* are listed in the *Proceedings of the Royal Irish Academy* xv (second series), 'Polite literature and antiquities', vi. Denman provides a complete list in *Samuel Ferguson*, pp. 203-6.

been involved in a sea of troubles, but in the midst of that confusion and repulsion, the reconciling power of mind has been at work.' The country could be proud of her solid cultural achievements, which stood out against the 'frivolous and hurried essays' currently being produced in England. There, literature had been exploited to weaken national attachments, to overthrow educational principles and to disturb settled habits of thought. In Ireland cultural endeavour had had the opposite design and effect: 'all our labours in antiquity and history going to the one point – the propagation, namely, of self-knowledge, self-respect, and attachment to the country in which our lot is cast'.[9]

Was this patriotic war cry of Gaelic antiquarianism simply part of a general British response to social fragmentation? Inevitably Ferguson's cultural nationalism resembles the project of Matthew Arnold's *Culture and anarchy* (1869). Cultivation could not be taken for granted; it had to be promoted as an agreed means of defence against mechanism and utilitarianism, and as the ultimate court of appeal 'by which a society construing its relationships in terms of the cash-nexus might be condemned'.[10] Ferguson, ultimately a believer in progress, railed against what he saw as its concomitant evils; the lapse in standards of taste, the callous rule of political economy and the transfer of power to a mercantile order. This antipathy, compounded by his belief in a cultural means of social salvation, is encapsulated in a verse-epistle addressed to his fellow antiquarian Dr Quarry, following his discovery of some Ogham inscriptions in County Cork. In the poem Ferguson flatters Quarry as a man of deep learning, and urges him to take paper casts of the stones – a request he feels able to make in view of their mutual love of scholarship, for

> wheresoe'er the old humanities
> Of intellectual culture still survive
> The shock of Church Acts and the loathly qualms
> Of learned disgust bred by the changing time
> That shifts the charge of letters, now to hands
> Of Mr Editor, and now to those
> Of Mr Auditor or other Jack
> Of lecture-platform or the altar-step,
> There will petition for scholastic alms
> Not fall on ears unheeding.[11]

Ferguson took particular pride in the Academy museum and was unenthusiastic about Government plans to reconstitute it into what was to become the National Museum. He was responsible for a number of important additions to the collection, including St Patrick's Bell Shrine and the Lough Gur bronze shield. In 1875 he published *A brief handbook of the Museum* in which the extent of his re-organization was made apparent. See T. Ó'Raifeartaigh (ed.), *The Royal Irish Academy* (1985), p. 130. 9 'The Annals of the Four Masters', *DUM* 31 (Mar. 1848), 359–60. 10 R. Williams, *Culture and society*, pp. 62–3. 11 Cited M.C. Ferguson, *SSFID*, vol. 2, pp. 65–6.

The piece conveys the tension the poet identified between the diminishing world of 'intellectual culture' and an increasingly philistine environment controlled by the twin hierarchies of political economy and the press. If such a response had become commonplace among older Victorians perplexed by the *zeitgeist*, then so too had Ferguson's resort to the comforts of scholarly solidarity in the face of dissolute social tendencies. His vision of establishing for the Irish a school of arts and letters, and his continuing attempts to foster historical and literary cultivation against the grain of a prevailing ignorance, were inflected by the specific political difficulties of Irish society, but conformed at the same time to an entrenched philosophy of cultural redemption on the neighbouring island.

There are of course key differences between Matthew Arnold's policies of 'sweetness and light' and Ferguson's cultural nationalism. Arnold's scheme to diffuse culture throughout all classes as a humanizing element within society developed as a quasi-religious response to existing societal tendencies and was based on an extensive set of moral, egalitarian, and pedagogic principles.[12] Ferguson's sphere of activity was limited by comparison, and his formulation and manipulation of an inclusive national inheritance more specific in its pointed use of Gaelic cultural resources. But he shared both Arnold's faith in the defensive function of culture as a guard against insurrection, and his concern at the increasing diffidence of the aristocracy, supposedly the leadership of contemporary society. These pressures coalesce in his review of John O'Donovan's *Annals of the Four Masters*, where he exhorts the Irish gentry to attend to their national heritage:

> For it is the manifest truth, that the loss of the affections of the people wherever and to whatever extent they have been lost to their legitimate heads and protectors, has been mainly owing to the mistake of the latter in thinking that a contemptuous neglect of native feelings, usages and traditions would induce the Irish people ever to forget their own attachments, or ever to be a new and nameless colony, tilling the land for men whose boast it was that they were strangers, however greater might be

---

12 In *Culture and anarchy*, Arnold aimed to establish through a series of evangelistic abstractions a social blueprint for a modern democracy in which high idealism might be maintained. Fearing that the disintegration of former strategies for social order based on feudalism and habits of deference would result in wide-scale anarchy and that a blind worship of machinery would prevail over society, he sought to develop a counter-measure in the form of a non-denominational dogma of national cultural allegiance. 'Culture', he claimed, 'looks beyond machinery, culture hates hatred; culture has one great passion, the passion for sweetness and light.' It should operate not as a separate phenomenon but as an organic part of social activity. Culture would alleviate disaffiliation in society by exalting the 'best self'" in all aspects of life and, in directing the individual towards a respect for authority and the common interest, would negate the anarchic potential of the liberal credo, 'doing as one likes'. Through its nourishment of society's hopes and designs for the State it would lead not only to perfection but also to safety. See *Culture and anarchy* (1964), pp. 76–7; p. 204.

the present power and prosperity, or the past historic renown of any external land or people with which, in preference, they might identify themselves. The effects of that mistake are now seen, in the readiness with which the people lend themselves to anti-social and anarchical projects from which, if the gentlemen of honour and spirit in the country were, as they ought to be, their instructors and advisers, they would recoil with feelings of abhorrence.[13]

Similarly, Ferguson's emphasis on the duty of social leaders to adopt cultural and not simply political responsibility for the country gains a wider context through Arnold and his predecessors. His waning confidence in the aristocracy as the arbiters of taste, together with his resultant impulse to establish in Ireland an accountable hierarchy which would exercise incentive in matters of national culture, blurs with more familiar Victorian philosophies of cultural authority. The blueprint established by Coleridge, in his 1830 treatise *On the constitution of church and state*, envisaged a responsible intellectual élite or 'clerisy' which, comprising activists from the liberal arts and sciences, would provide a civilizing or refining element in the population at large. Such an agency would function to preserve and protect the treasures of past civilization, 'and thus to connect the present with the future'.[14] A version of Edmund Burke's 'virtual aristocracy', the Coleridgean clerisy was to be integral to the dynamics and coherence of state, church and civil law, as a constitutionally ordained cultural bureaucracy.[15] In similar terms, Thomas Carlyle lamented the failings of an existing aristocracy and, famously, idealized the 'hero as man-of-letters', who would sustain culture as part of an 'organic literary class' in society.[16] Matthew Arnold, meanwhile, despairing at the inadequacy of the 'barbarian' aristocracy and the 'Philistine' middle classes, recognized the need for a transcending authority; the 'aliens', or disinterested individuals who, in their devotion to education, poetry and criticism, would form a fraternity of cultural leadership, and the basis of the State.[17]

Though less abstract, Ferguson's consistent endorsement of a scholarly community in Ireland shares in this impetus. His inability to divorce the idea of scholarship from the existence of a dynamic and scholarly congress in Irish society is everywhere apparent: through 'manly works of learning which form the minds of ages and generations of men', he wrote, 'our writers do at present, as

---

13 'The *Annals of the Four Masters*', 360. 14 *On the constitution of church and state*, p. 34. For Coleridge's definition of the composition of the clerisy see p. 36. 15 S. Deane draws useful connections between Coleridge and Burke in this respect in *The French Revolution and enlightenment* (1988), p. 70. See also comments by R. Williams on the relationship, *Culture and society*, p. 63; pp. 127–8, and B. Knights, *The idea of the clerisy* (1978). 16 T. Carlyle, 'On heroes and hero-worship and the heroic in history', *Works*, vol. 7, pp. 147 and 156. 17 'The great men of culture are those who have a passion for diffusing, for making prevail, for carrying from one end of society to the other, the best knowledge, the best ideas of their time': *Culture and anarchy*, pp. 101–5, 109 and 70.

they have done for several years back, here in Dublin, take their place side by side with the best scholars of the age".[18] In his 1848 reviews of O'Donovan's *Annals*, and its companion piece, a review of William Reeves' annotated and illustrated *Ecclesiastical antiquities of Down, Connor and Dromore*, he voiced his approval of the authors' 'manly learning' in terms which subjugated the content of the actual texts to what they signified – the combination of intellect, scholarship and maturity as a fortifying element in Irish society. 'We never can despair of a country', he wrote, 'in which works like these succeed one another in rapid and regular succession, showing, as they do, a systematic application of calm and cultivated minds to the pursuit of that self-knowledge which will be found, after all, to lie at the foundation of whatever just national feeling, and of whatever permanent and wholesome public opinion, can be looked for or desired in this country.'[19] His confidence in figures such as Reeves, O'Donovan and Petrie was based partly on their individual scholarship, but partly too on their collective role as civic ballast. An engagement with history – like the pursuit of literature – was inextricable from the community of scholarship it fostered and defined.

In these terms, Ferguson's participation in the 'golden age' of the Royal Irish Academy, of which he was elected President in 1881, and indeed the existence and rationale of the Academy itself, may be understood as the fulfilment of his long-term vision of cultural fraternity and civic virtue; a vision which had its origins in his early experiences of post-Enlightenment Belfast and Edinburgh. Despite its largely Protestant membership profile, the Academy managed to maintain 'a distinctive "national" ambience', and certainly represented more than a clubbable retreat for an Irish gentry bereft of political power and social context.[20] In fact, as shall be seen, it maintained a highly contemporary, independent profile alongside other European academies of the sciences, antiquities and *belles lettres*. By the closing decades of the century, furthermore, it stood at a critical point of intersection between private patronage and government sequestration, and between the local interests of the civic-minded amateur and the state-sponsored agenda of the professional archivist. During Ferguson's period of office as president, the question of the Academy's government grant and the transfer of its antiquities collection to the newly-established national museum were key issues on which the position of the institution was tested, and its aspiration towards independence, civic virtue and national responsibility reaffirmed.

18 'The *Annals of the Four Masters*', 360. 19 'The *Annals of the Four Masters*', 359. 20 T. Eagleton, *Scholars and rebels*, p. 13. On the 'pluralist' religious and political profile of the RIA, and the role of its various 'non-standard' members, see N. Whyte's valuable study, *Science, colonialism and Ireland* (1999), chapter 6. E. Crooke discusses the alliance of nationalist and unionist incentives within the organization in *Politics, archaeology and the creation of a national museum*, chapter 4.

For Dublin's antiquarian researchers, meanwhile, the study of Gaelic antiquity was a manifest link to the refined, secure world of genteel Ascendancy scholarship. But at the same time the pursuit of the past – in local history, genealogy or the collection of artefacts – was widely practised as a fashionable leisure activity by the Victorian middle-classes throughout Britain. Phillipa Levine's study of the social patterns of Victorian life reveals that the antiquarian community, like those established through the pursuit of history and archaeology, can be seen to represent an 'invisible college', within which individuals disaffiliated from the conventional class determinants of wealth or heritage sought to establish and define themselves within exclusive élites of amateur enthusiasts.[21] For an educated, professional and clerical social stratum, this was also part of a process of *civic* self-definition, a means for the regional town or city to assert its history and identity and, most importantly, defy the label of provincialism. It was significant too that antiquarianism – and Celtic antiquity in particular – provided access to a European network of interest and scholarship through which those involved might bypass London as a centre of authority, in favour of cities such as Edinburgh or Copenhagen, where antiquarian societies were well established. In this respect it offered a basis for an alternative international hierarchy, which overlooked imperial relations and prioritized instead, relationships between those cultures which appeared to possess parallel historical profiles. Antiquarian and local studies thus provided a means of resisting, if only symbolically, the pull of centralization and identification with the modernizing, rationalizing agenda of the metropolitan government, a factor which explains their appeal outside the confines of institutions such as the Royal Irish Academy, and across a broad spectrum of popular and nationalist interest.[22]

In the second half of his life, after his marriage and his retreat from a political vanguard, Ferguson evolved a mature strategy for cultural nationality and historical self-knowledge. In his 1848 reviews of Reeves and O'Donovan, he began to outline the terms in which he might elucidate what Burke had distinguished as 'an interior History of Ireland, the genuine voice of its records and monuments', and through which he might cultivate amongst his contemporaries

21 *The amateur and the professional*, p. 36. The concept is adopted from D.J. de Solla Price and D. de Beaver, 'Collaboration in an invisible college', *American Psychologist* 21 (1966), 1011–18. 22 Consider K. Trumpener's discussion of the function of antiquarianism as part of a resistance to modernity, disguised as national interest: 'In watching the effects of imperialism and modernization on the traditional societies within their purview, segments of both Anglo-Irish and lowland society become convinced of the need to preserve indigenous antiquities and traditionary customs, and even to decelerate the course of modernization altogether, by reseparating the national governments of the peripheries from the central government in London and from a British economy. The new, middle-class cultural nationalism and antiquarianism that these concerns engender are thus based at once – and this cannot be stressed enough – on a new degree of imaginative sympathy with countrymen more directly oppressed and affected, and at the same time on a rhetorical appropriation of their situation and customs as if they in fact constituted a shared tradition': *Bardic nationalism* p. 32.

a spirit of *amor patriae* and an instinct for civic leadership.[23] From this point on, however, though his pursuit of the past remained a vital component of a coherent civic agenda, his understanding of history also began to manifest the increasingly conservative tendencies of his political outlook, together with his deep-seated anxieties about Ireland's direction. These latter aspects of his cultural agenda would become increasingly ingrained, and would predominate, finally, in his 1882 presidential address to the Royal Irish Academy, a consummate *apologia* for the latter half of his career.

ANTIQUARIANISM VERSUS HISTORY: THE USES OF THE PAST

Historiography had undergone a revolution since the introduction in the eighteenth century of a secular and non-partisan methodology as a replacement for the chronicles of the Reformation. The major historians; Gibbon in *Decline and fall* (1776), Hume in his *History of England* (1754) and William Robertson in his *History of Scotland* (1759) established a historical ethos which sought to be both philosophical and instructive. Collectively they laid the foundations for the 'new' history of the nineteenth century, synthesized by Scott and revitalized by Romanticism.[24] In the transition from an Enlightenment to a Romantic ideology, suggests Hayden White, historians were able to abandon concepts which were reductive and mechanistic, and to develop an integrative and organic sense of the past. With a heightened degree of theoretical self-consciousness, historians after 1830 'were inspired by the hope of creating a perspective on the historical process that would be as "objective" as that from which the scientists viewed the processes of nature and as "realistic" as that from which the statesmen of the period directed the fortunes of nations'.[25]

The shift to a distinctive Victorian historiography had a marked effect both on public consciousness of the past and on the professional representation of it. Commenting on the flowering of English narrative history which characterized the decades between 1848 and 1878, J.W. Burrow describes how in their elaboration of the three great crises of Britain's history – the Norman Conquest, the Reformation, and the 1688 Revolution – Victorian historians, including Froude, Freeman and Macaulay, sought to produce a definitive statement of English constitutional development, forging from discrete events a thesis of

---

23 'Tracts on the popery laws', *Works* (1955), vol. 6, p. 45. See W.J. McCormack's chapter, 'Edmund Burke and the imagination of history', in which he cites this extract and comments on Burke as a 'pre-romantic philosopher of the sublime' in relation to the Irish past and mid-eighteenth century antiquarianism, *Ascendancy and tradition*, p. 65. 24 See J.R. Hale, *The evolution of British historiography* (1967), pp. 30–42. For a theoretical analysis of the emergence of the 'new' history see S. Bann's introductory chapter to *The clothing of Clio* (1984). 25 *Metahistory* (1973), pp. 38–48.

organic continuity.[26] The progressive emphasis was particularly prevalent in Macaulay, whose *History of England*, published between 1848 and 1855, constituted what Herbert Butterfield would later define, in 1931, as the 'Whig interpretation of history'. For the liberal historian, wrote Butterfield, historical narrative was no longer simply the study of origins or causes but the systematic evaluation of civilization's development; 'the analysis of all the mediations by which the past was turned into our present.'[27]

To what extent did Ferguson's response to the past run self-consciously against this grain? Certainly, he was aware of trends in historiography, and aware too of the scope and effect of broad national histories such as those furnished by Gibbon and Macaulay. In the 1830s, his response to Scott and the writers of the Scottish Enlightenment suggested his openness to philosophical progressivism, and throughout his career he held opinions on a range of British and Irish historians, most notably Gibbon whom he esteemed as 'that great historian'.[28] He was familiar too with chroniclers of the Irish past ranging from Geoffrey Keating to Charles O'Conor, and may have been the *DUM*'s favourable reviewer of Thomas Moore's somewhat incoherent *History of Ireland*, in 1835.[29] Increasingly however, his preference was for history to be accumulative and for the most part, non-judgmental, offering no context for predictions on the political trajectory of the country. Even in his early writings, he had underlined the importance of regional antiquarian research as a means of reinforcing local attachments, but by 1848 his protestations against any overarching and teleological history had acquired an added stress and urgency. In his review of O'Donovan he stated:

> A general history of Ireland is not at present what we require. Such a work cannot be undertaken with advantage, until after long additional accumulations; and even when perfected, will probably lead only to feelings of regret and despondency. These indeed, are the broad results of almost all general histories. One cannot rise from the perusal of Gibbon, of Hume, or even of Livy, without deploring the madness of mankind.[30]

Instead, Ferguson proposed that research into the past should remain both intimate and disconnected from any overarching perspective. 'The histories we now

26 *A liberal descent* (1981), chapter 1. 27 *The Whig interpretation of history* (1951), pp 4 and 47. 28 In his review of *Ecclesiastical antiquities* Ferguson attacks Reeves for referring to Gibbon as 'a flippant writer', p. 223. Lady Ferguson reports that her husband admired Lecky but resented Froude (*SSFID*, vol. 2, p. 207), while Denman claims that Ferguson was heavily influenced by Macaulay, despite the latter's whiggish disposition, with Macaulay's popular *Lays of ancient Rome* providing the model for Ferguson's *Lays of the Western Gael* (*Samuel Ferguson*, p. 78). 29 See Denman on Ferguson's use of Keating as a source, *Samuel Ferguson* pp. 121–2. Ferguson considered Charles O'Conor's Latin translation of pre-Norman Irish annals, the *Rerum Hibernicarum scriptores veteres*, as a national treasure: see his comments in 'The *Annals of the Four Masters*', 362. J.P. McBride makes this suggestion regarding Moore, vol. 1, p. 137n. 30 'The *Annals of the Four Masters*', 361.

require are particular and local, such as would furnish no material for large philosophic inductions', he insisted, 'but such as will enable us to know one another and the land we live in, and every spot of it, that such confidence may beget mutual confidence and united labour'.[31] His aim was a historical culture which would stabilize and preserve, not agitate, and which would therefore be confined to individual and regional associations rather than stretching to national perspectives.[32] In his review of Reeves, he stressed that the importance of history was not to judge, but

> to preserve the landmarks of chronology, to record the origins and progresses of tribes and families, and, in all old-inhabited countries, to increase the love and veneration of the people for the place assigned to them in the world, by investing each locality with its own associations and connecting all by the record of events of common interest – that men may feel they are not come into the world strangers but members of a family long-planted in the land before them, owing reverence to the place and institutions of their forefathers, and by that common sentiment strengthening the social bond among one another.[33]

As evidence of the power of such explorations he cited his own connections to Ireland, using Reeves' details of lowland Antrim and the moat of Donegore to prove his personal relationship to a historical landscape. 'We linger along this valley with affectionate delay' he mused on reading the respective passage, for 'here were the dwellings of friends and kindred; and in the grave-yard, overlooking the scene of all these strange vicissitudes, repose the bones of our forefathers.'[34]

---

[31] 'The *Annals of the Four Masters*', 361. Ferguson's apparent distrust of abstraction and philosophy in general is indicated in his comments to the RIA in 1882: 'Philosophical inquiry into the higher functions of our nature, and the moral and social crystallizations to which they give rise, may proceed by ostensibly scientific methods of definition an axiom; but, seeing that we can take out of a definition no more breadth of view and accuracy of generalization; and considering the many circumstances which may modify these, it seems to me that the Academy has acted wisely in leaving that class of subjects to the Chairs and Scrinia of learning elsewhere.' 'Address delivered before the Academy, by Sir Samuel Ferguson LL.D., Q.C., President': 30 November 1882. *Proceedings of the Royal Irish Academy* 16 (1879–1888), 185–201 at 187. This speech will henceforth be referred to as 'Academy address'. [32] The de-limiting role of 'antiquarian' history – as opposed to 'monumental' or 'critical' history – is described by Nietzsche in 1873. 'All that is small and limited, mouldy and obsolete, gains a worth and inviolability of its own from the soul of the antiquary migrating into it and building a secret nest there. The history of his town becomes the history of himself; he looks on the walls, on the turretted gate, the town council, the fair, as an illustrated diary of his youth, and sees himself in it all – his strength, industry, desire, reason, faults and follies. "Here one could live", he says "as one will go on living; for we are tough folk and will not be uprooted in the night".' *On the use and abuse of history* (1957) pp. 17–20. [33] 'Reeves' *Ecclesiastical antiquities*', *DUM* 31 (Feb. 1848), 207. [34] 'Reeves' *Ecclesiastical antiquities*', 213. Ferguson also draws attention to Reeves' depiction of the valley of Moyra, later the setting for *Congal*, which he describes in the review as 'the scene of the greatest battle, whether we regard the numbers engaged the duration of the combat or the stake at issue, ever fought within the bounds of Ireland', 210.

Over the thirty years that followed, Ferguson maintained this opinion, consolidating upon his position both in the nature of his own research and writing and in his advice to others. In his presidential address to the Royal Irish Academy in 1882 he spoke with regret of the *lacunae* in the country's cultural identity. 'That this country should be without an adequate history and without a characteristic literature rising above the conventional buffooneries, has been a source of pain and humiliation to educated Irishmen for generations', he stated. This reflection alone provided an incentive towards literary achievement in the present day, he continued, but there were serious reservations with regard to the restoration of the country's past:

> So far as concerns a general History of the country, we must, probably, be content to let the work for the present rest in preparation and material. If the time had arrived when Ireland could be said to have taken one or the other definite position from which her past could be contemplated in distinct, unshifting perspective, we might be more impatient of delay. But it seems to me that no great History of any country has ever been written from any but a fixed point of contemplation, not attainable in transitional times, such as ours for so great a length of time unhappily have been.[35]

In the meantime the annals, parish and ecclesiastical records and local antiquities as explored by men such as Reeves and O'Donovan would suffice, and would, in the necessary absence of a general history, provide 'a new store of agencies for the creation and propagation of just national feeling'.[36]

As Géaroid Ó Tuathaigh has argued, Ferguson's distinction between local and national in this respect is strategic. 'A "national history" is instinct with political connotation; the celebration of local identity may be indulged without any political scruple.'[37] And it is difficult to avoid the conclusion that Ferguson's attitude amounts, at the very least, to prevarication. The accumulation of diffuse historical material, not as a supplement but as an alternative to the production of a narrative overview, and the prioritizing of bardic and medieval antiquity over more recent, politically sensitive events in Ireland, was ultimately a means of evading decision. Of course, he was by no means alone in adopting such a stance.[38] But his protestations serve to highlight a series of anxieties which increased from the mid century onwards. On one hand, as we

---

35 'Academy address', 195. 36 'Reeves' *Ecclesiastical antiquities*', 207. 37 'Sir Samuel Ferguson – poet and ideologue', p. 14. 38 The full context of Victorian historiography is beyond the scope of this chapter, but in relation to French romanticist, revolutionary and antiquarian modes in Ireland, see D. McCartney, 'The writing of history in Ireland' (1957), and R. Kelly, 'History's muse: the prose writings of Thomas Moore' (2001), chapter 5.

have seen, he was perturbed by social changes and the transformation of life under a flourishing Victorian industrial regime, which he saw as having brought about the ruthless erosion of a civilized, hierarchical order. Ferguson was no Luddite: his interests in engineering, science and industry are evident in his 1836 articles on the topography and economic capabilities of Ireland. But he despised the commercialization and petty bureaucracy accompanying technological and industrial development. Contemplating the process of decay in 1848, he lamented the fall of a previous age. 'The nation without head or counsel has been delivered over to vile empirical politicians, to train it up into a new state of society', he complained. Everything noble, dignified and refined was being eliminated; nothing remained but 'the mere material of economic equations.'[39]

At the same time he began to reveal with growing frequency his doubts with regard to the possibility of political stability in Ireland under the existing administration. The spirit of disillusionment in which he had joined and addressed the Protestant Repeal Association in 1848 failed to subside after his retreat from active commitment, and the more he immersed himself in antiquarianism and poetry over the ensuing decades, the more his insecurities emerged. In 1875 he wrote to fellow poet Aubrey de Vere concerning the unveiling of O'Connell's statue, an occasion which Ferguson viewed as deeply portentous:

> I fear that the event will greatly shake the confidence of those who thought civil and religious liberty meant freedom of opinion and believed the phrase would always convey their present ideas who used it forty years ago. You may find me unamenable. I really believe my present mood in almost every line reflects and is in sympathy with the minds of the great mass of educated men in Ireland. God grant that it may not be prophetic of coming troubles, which I fear, I fear.[40]

His worries were not of course, without foundation: Fenian activities during the 1860s, the disestablishment of the Church of Ireland in 1869 and Gladstone's first Land Act in 1870 combined to produce an unsettled atmosphere in the country. In February 1882, amidst mounting public pressure for Home Rule, Ferguson summarized his feelings in a letter to Blackwood, writing dejectedly of the growing tendency towards Irish independence, and of how the obstinacy of the Irish race prevented any inclination towards contentment and industry. 'If I am right, the question will be between a continued military occupation and a concession to the Irish of self-government', he stated. In view of the

---

[39] 'The *Annals of the Four Masters*: second article', *DUM* 31 (May 1848), 584. [40] 24 July 1875, NLI MS 13,122–13,128.

prevalence of English democracy: 'I think the concession the more likely. I shall be truly glad to find myself mistaken, for I am sure great troubles would follow and still worse times for the unhappy possessors of Irish property.'[41]

Much of Ferguson's problem lay in his ironic alienation from the country he had struggled to make familiar, an alienation which increased as political agitation escalated during the last few years of his life. The urgency of his need to comprehend these realities is apparent in his late poems, 'At the polo ground' and 'In Carey's footsteps', which deal with the assassination of Lord Frederick Cavendish, the new viceroy, and the under-secretary, T.H. Burke, in Phoenix Park in 1882. Denman has described the poems, in which Ferguson effects an imaginative leap first into the mind of the Fenian assassin, James Carey, and subsequently into that of a Catholic priest reflecting on the murder, as 'meditative excursions into an alien ideology'.[42] In each case the poet traces the thought process of the protagonist through hesitation, doubt and reasoning in order to expose the psychological motivations and implications of the crime. He projects onto Carey's mind a range of grievances in which nationalism is merely a front for the expression of economic inequality and class repression. Carey stands at the polo ground

> Beside the hurdles fencing off the ground
> They've taken from us who have the right to it,
> For these select young gentry and their sport.
> Curse them! I would they all might break their necks!
> Young fops and lordlings of the garrison
> Kept up by England here to keep us down:
> All rich young fellows not content to own
> Their chargers, hacks, and hunters for the field,
> But also special ponies for their game;
> And doubtless, as they dash along, regard
> Us who stand outside as a beggarly crew.[43]

That fact that the poems are so obviously exercises in imitation of Browning's dramatic monologues underlines the desperation in Ferguson's approach: his conversion to this particular form so late in his poetic career was, as his wife observes, a radical stylistic departure, a last resort in his attempts to explicate the motivations of the individual rather than the collective terrorism of the mob.[44] The result is unconvincing and incomplete. Carey is transformed into a villain from

---

41 Ferguson to William Blackwood Jr., 8 Feb. 1882, NLS MS 4431 f150. 42 *Samuel Ferguson*, p. 170. 43 See M.C. Ferguson for the source text, *SSFID*, vol. 1, pp. 258–66. 44 *SSFID*, vol. 1, p. 264.

a Victorian melodrama; the priest, in the companion poem, becomes a haunted Macbeth ruminating on his acquiescence in the crime. In the end the intense individual focus is a distraction: Ferguson fails to confront the full political and ideological circumstances of the event and becomes absorbed instead in the morbid personalities of his subjects. As Denman observes, the poems achieve a breakthrough in moving from retrospection to the contemporary world, and like much of Ferguson's writing attempt to incorporate an unfamiliar cultural tradition, but 'where the earlier work had been exploratory, and prepared to appropriate the material on behalf of an ideally eclectic mainstream of literature in English, here there is only a sad fascination at difference'.[45]

The value of the two dramatic monologues is ultimately in their exposition of Ferguson's continued sense of obligation to his country in the last five years of his life. In the same spirit he pursued with Aubrey de Vere a project to organize some form of proportional representation in Ireland, and by the year before his death was suggesting that a form of home rule based on 'a restoration of the Parliament of 1799' should be adopted for the country.[46] Despite these efforts to adapt however, his final years were marked by disillusionment and frustration. In what she recalls as 'those awful days of shame', Lady Ferguson describes how her husband's confidence in his native country gradually weakened, admitting that 'the close of his long life of patriotic endeavour to raise and elevate his countrymen was saddened by their evil doings'.[47] Events had moved beyond his range of comprehension, as social and political progression in Ireland – a subject he had no difficulty examining from an imaginative distance in *Congal* – proved unmanageable in reality.

THE ROYAL IRISH ACADEMY AND THE SCHOLARLY IDEAL

Ferguson's system of reference to an eighteenth-century cultural and civic template has already been examined in relation to his response to the Victorian architectural debate, and in his espousal of antiquarian scholarship he was similarly dependent upon this idealized social model. He had long held in his mind's eye an image of Irish Augustan scholarly distinction. 'Enter that stately mansion', he invited his reader in 1836, 'the rooms are lined with cabinets of minerals – the towers of yonder castles are mounted not with birthday patararoes but with telescopes and sextants – the assembly round this festive board are not

---

[45] *Samuel Ferguson*, p. 173. [46] See Ferguson's letters to Aubrey de Vere, 3 Nov. 1885 and 18 Feb. 1885, NLI MS 13,122–13,128, in which he outlines his proposals for proportional representation in Ireland. Ferguson's conditions for home rule in Ireland in the wake of Gladstone's Home Rule Bill are listed in a letter cited by M.C. Ferguson, *SSFID*, vol. 1, p. 255. [47] *SSFID*, vol. 1, p. 267.

boon companions but men of science.'[48] His resort to the previous century was based not on nostalgia but on appropriation: the amateur bibliographers, philologists, archaeologists, antiquarians and minerologists who comprised a class of gentlemen scholars in the previous century provided him with a set of values relevant to his own impoverished environment.

In his review of the *Annals of the Four Masters* in 1848, Ferguson sought to supplant popular representations of a dissipated Irish aristocracy with an alternative image of the 'polished men' of the eighteenth-century:

> Base caricaturists have made money and gained a kind of spurious reputation by defaming them; reckless humourists have recommended themselves to the scornful laughter of English readers by exaggerating their peculiarities; and drawing ludicrous pictures of the state of society which prevailed among them; but men who judge them by the legitimate evidences of their acts and monuments – by their mansion houses, their libraries, their collections of paintings and sculpture – by the works written by them, and published amongst them, and for them – and by the testimony of contemporary competent judges know for a fact, that [...] the spurious civilization of little economists and quibbling logicians is not an improvement on the solid and elegant acquirements and constitutional and legal learning of the Irish noblemen and gentlemen of the last century.[49]

The portrait exists in a political vacuum in that Ferguson ignores the hegemonic context of an Ascendancy or ruling class *per se*. He identifies only with the scholarly and cultivated caste that he saw it to have contained, a process of affiliation serving a dual purpose. First, through his depiction of this grouping as a pre-lapsarian generation whose fall has precipitated Ireland's decline, he was able to gesture towards his own scheme for cultural salvation, characteristically couched in biblical terms: 'our first parents fell, and yet mankind have been redeemed.'[50] Secondly, his sustained identification with this eighteenth-century 'imagined community' of gentlemen scholars allowed him to align his historical and literary explorations with an appropriate precedent, by circumventing the post-Napoleonic impetus of romantic nationalism in favour of an eighteenth-century tradition of Protestant patriotism.[51]

From Ferguson's perspective moreover, a patriotic incentive merged conveniently with his attempts to recreate the aura of his eighteenth-century prede-

---

48 'Attractions of Ireland, no. 3 – society', *DUM* 8 (Dec. 1836), 675. 49 'The *Annals of the Four Masters*: second article', 571. 50 'The *Annals of the Four Masters*: second article', 584. 51 J.T. Leerssen has traced the transitional process within which the salvaging of bardic culture through antiquarianism was adopted as the prerogative of an English-

cessors by invoking a sense of intellectual heroism: as W.J. McCormack comments, what was significant about the antiquarians of the 1790s was 'not so much the achievement of the researchers as the trepidation of the "gentlemen"'.[52] Could a nineteenth-century equivalent be found in the membership and values of the Royal Irish Academy? The 1836 articles on Ireland show that Ferguson was quick to resort to the *alumni* of the Academy as competitive evidence of Dublin's academic and scientific prowess, but as the organization itself came to feature more prominently in his career, through his committee appointments and ultimately his presidency, he increased his emphasis on its credibility as a repository of culture which, through its scholarship, erudition and sense of heritage, bore an organic and essential relationship to Irish cultural life. Its scholars were portrayed in the same light of patriotic endeavour, inspired by a kind of academic gallantry in their efforts to assimilate and restore the remnants of former times; 'for, if there was ever a legitimate patriotic hope at the bottom of scholastic effort', he stated, 'it animated the men who brought these things together and put them in their present posture and capacity for use'.[53]

But the Academy *was* more than a gentleman's club, nonetheless, and more than an eighteenth-century Irish hangover. Established in Dublin in 1785 and granted a royal charter the following year, the Royal Irish Academy resembled a number of European intellectual societies founded during the preceding century, including the English Royal Society (1662), the Dublin Society (1731), the Royal Society of Arts (1758), the Society of Antiquities of Scotland (1780) and the Manchester Literary and Philosophical Society (1781). Its closest links in this respect were without doubt, to Scotland and the Scottish Society of Antiquities, which, founded in 1780, maintained a similar social and cultural profile.[54] The Irish institution evolved from a select committee on antiquities

---

orientated Protestant upper-class in Ireland. The phenomenon was largely philological, he suggests, resulting from the proselytising use of the Irish language together with the transmission of native learning to continental linguists, who proved links with Welsh and established the importance of Ireland's 'fringe' vernacular.

The key figure in opening a relatively specialised subject to a wider circle of enthusiasts was the seventeenth-century Celtic philologist Edward Lhuyd, whose research provided a composite basis for the activities of scholars such as Charles O'Conor, Sylvester O'Halloran, Joseph Cooper Walker and Charlotte Brooke. 'The interest generated in Irish antiquity and Gaelic culture was to prove highly significant for the development of an iconography on which a national ideology could draw. The validation of Gaelic antiquarianism through the scientific foundations laid by the philologists was important in that it paved the way for later scholars whose collective desire to be both loyal British subjects and also citizens of the kingdom of Ireland was thereby fulfilled.' By the next generation, Leerssen suggests, 'Protestant patriotism was beginning to appropriate Gaelic culture as a legitimate point of interest': *Mere Irish*, p. 339. 52 *Ascendancy and tradition*, p. 66. 53 'Academy address', 195. 54 Indeed, Scotland's antiquarians looked to their Irish counterparts with admiration largely because of their evident patriotic affiliations: lamenting that the Scottish gentry and nobility preferred to be listed in the membership of fashionable London societies, one celebrated Edinburgh antiquarian noted that in Dublin, as in Copenhagen, 'a keen spirit of nationality and patriotic sympathy' motivated the cause of archaeological science. See *Proceedings of the Society of Antiquities of Scotland*, 1: 4, cited by D. Wilson, 'The archaeology and prehistoric annals of Scotland' (1851).

appointed by the Dublin Society, from which it gradually detached itself in order to draw up an independent constitution. Its stated intention was to facilitate comprehensive enquiry into the three branches of learning – science, antiquities and *belles-lettres* – but the latter quickly became peripheralized as it was agreed that fiction, poetry and criticism should be left to the periodical press. During the nineteenth century, as the Academy grew in stature and reputation, it came to rely on three fundamental elements for continued success; the strength of its acquisitions in manuscripts and museum artefacts, the publication of its official proceedings and lectures and the influential personalities of its members, who ranged from artists and antiquarians to mathematicians, physicists and astronomers.[55]

In his 1864 lecture 'On the literary influence of academies', Matthew Arnold praised the French for their solicitation of national intelligence through the establishment of the French Academy of Letters. Such an agency was a means of promoting what the historian Ernest Renan termed '*civilité*', representing for Arnold 'a force of educated opinion', or 'an intellectual metropolis' which defied the levelling instincts of commercialism and industrialization. It served the interests of the nation in maintaining standards of expression and taste, not simply in language but in national culture as a whole, and in negating the destructive malaise of Arnold's abhorred narrowness of vision or 'provincialism'.[56] It was very much in these terms that the Royal Irish Academy signified, for Ferguson, the essence of 'urbanity'. His approbation of individual activists was extended to the collective phenomenon of the Society, which both signified and centralized Irish cultural achievement in housing the country's guardians of historical, literary and scientific endeavour.

Ferguson was elected to the Academy in 1834 and four years later delivered his first paper to its members. In 1840 he was appointed to the Academy's council to sit on the Committee of Antiquities, and in 1881 became president, following the death of the scientist Sir Robert Kane. His Presidential address of 1882 therefore reflects a period of almost fifty years during which his acquaintance with the organization developed into a sympathetic and philosophical understanding of its internal workings and public function. Opening his speech with an insistence that the encyclopaedic character of the Academy must be sustained, he drew together science, art and antiquarianism within a single vision of scholarly achievement and influence. Science in particular, he suggested, must

---

55 See R.B. McDowell, 'The main narrative', in T. Ó Raifeartaigh (ed.), *The Royal Irish Academy*, pp. 1–10. 56 'Not having the lucidity of a large and centrally placed intelligence, the provincial spirit has not its graciousness; it does not persuade, it makes war; it has not urbanity, the tone of the city, of the centre, the tone which always aims at a spiritual and intellectual effect, and not excluding the use of banter, never disjoins itself from politeness, from felicity.' 'On the literary influence of academies', *Works*, vol. 3, pp. 241–4 and 249.

continue to be valued as the vanguard of exploration and pedagogy.[57] The social relevance of the Academy was underlined and its existence validated through its integral role in both education and civilization. Not only in science but also in history and antiquities, in polite literature and philological study, and in the general interests of what Ferguson termed 'rare learning', the public relevance of the institution was emphasized. And in particular, Ferguson suggested that it be responsible for circulating the fruits of scholarly research into a Gaelic heritage, as a restorative and refining influence, for 'unless the diffusion of these new materials result in something more solid and socially influential than pure criticism, the object which has animated so many minds in accumulating and preserving them will be but imperfectly attained.'[58]

Through their endeavours in this respect, Ferguson insisted, his fellow scholars in the Academy might be considered the true inheritors and preservers of an eighteenth-century patriotism:

> They yield to none of their countrymen in the desire, and they greatly excel the bulk of them in the ability, to make Ireland once again a home of Arts and Letters. The works of this Academy can testify to what they have been able to achieve in that direction during nearly half a century of patriotic endeavour. To their hands mainly has been committed the guardianship of those materials out of which such a literature as I have been contemplating may be evolved; and in their hands, mainly, the work of speeding that development now rests in this Academy.[59]

The organic relationship between the institution and the public was dependent upon these individuals, who were accountable in this context for the cultural and moral health of the nation. Collective responsibility for a national culture was thus transferred from a defective aristocracy, which had failed in its duties, to an Irish Academy circle, representative of a more virtuous, more reliable authority in civic life.

Viewed in isolation, Ferguson's speech of 1882 may appear as little more than a rather self-congratulatory manifesto, but in the light of public events, it becomes significant in registering the ethos of the Academy as an independent

---

57 'These are the excursions into the Unknown or the partially known which justify the existence of Societies like the Academy. They supplement and extend the stock of knowledge communicated by our universities and teaching institutions. Their results, as they take shape, assimilate with the teaching of the future, and add to the supply of those theoretic instruments with which Practice and Invention work in ease of labour, in increasing the goods and diminishing the evils of human existence. The process may be slow, and the steps, as taken, hardly noticeable, but the resulting combinations make themselves felt in the constantly increasing force of civilisation': 'Academy address', 186.   58 'Academy address', 188 and 195.   59 'Academy address', 197.

scholarly institution, against the prevailing context of government intervention in Irish cultural life. As long as it remained autonomous in its sphere of intellectual and aesthetic judgement, it provided an important alternative to government and official administrations, capable of preserving the domain of 'taste' as a free field. But this was not straightforward. The Royal Dublin Society had already moved under government auspices from its existing premises to Dublin's Ballsbridge, and the 'old palace' as it was known. The Academy had come under pressure to make a similar move from its Dawson Street lodgings, and to become the 'gatekeeper' at the new government buildings in Leinster House.[60] But any such move was seen to entail a loss of autonomy, a relinquishing of the 'amateur' and independent status on which, in the view of its president, the Academy was reliant for public credibility. While wishing their sister institution well, Ferguson reinforced this position, stating that 'we desire on our own part to remain self-contained in our lodgings, as we mean to keep ourselves independent in our pursuits.'

At the same time, the Academy was in negotiations with the government over the transfer of its antiquities collection to the newly established National Museum in Dublin. This was undoubtedly a difficult task to face: the collection had been painstakingly accrued through a series of private donations and acquisitions, and included some valuable items, including the Cross of Cong and the Tara torques. Ferguson's spin on the matter is revealing: the collection would be handed over to the Museum as agreed, but this was to be seen as a financial exchange and a means for the government to recoup the estimated £60,000 which the Academy had received in the form of annual grants since the time of the Union. Indeed, the value of the collection was much greater, Ferguson stated, than the total sum received in that period. The matter of the grant was therefore to be seen as one of trade rather than charity, a gloss which again served to reinforce the Academy's aspiration towards self-reliance as an institution, and, significantly, towards national responsibility rather than subservience to London.[61] The visible distinction from government sponsorship or interest was crucial in this respect, in order to distinguish the members of the Academy from the process of creeping centralization which impinged on the management of the Irish past, and to secure their place as the acceptable inher-

---

60 See T. de Vere White, *The story of the RDS*; J. Meenan and D. Clarke (eds), *The Royal Dublin Society* (1981); N. McCullough, *Dublin: an urban history*, pp. 89–90; and E. Crooke, *Politics, archaeology and the creation of a national museum*, chapter 4.   61 In 1890 the museum finally subsumed the antiquities collection: see E. Crooke, *Politics*, chapter 4. Some years earlier Ferguson had written to William Smith O'Brien on the subject of the academy's request for an increase of £100 p.a. in the RIA's government grant, with the comment that the government's likely refusal was no doubt because they wished to secure Irish artefacts for the British museum or else that they feared 'to foster the growing Irish feeling that has lately shown itself here, among other manifestations, in the purchase of a rich collection of Irish antiquities ...', 7 July, 1843, NLI MS 432, 1020.

itors of an eighteenth-century patriot tradition, translated into the viable language of nineteenth-century civic virtue.

ANTIQUARIANS AND ARCHIVISTS

In his unofficial capacity, Ferguson's numerous affiliations ranged from the Kilkenny Archaeological Society to the Society of Antiquaries of Scotland, and the extent of his voluntary engagement with such groups emerges from Lady Ferguson's description of her husband's activities in the second volume of his biography. Here, the scale of his commitment to the exploration of the past becomes evident from reprinted extracts of his correspondence, reviews, reports and scholarly papers, together with accounts of his archaeological tours of Brittany, Sligo and the Aran Islands. The resultant impression is of Ferguson's limitless dedication and enthusiasm, his meticulous attention to intricate technical detail and his boundless capacity for laborious research.[62] But what the biography also illustrates is the extent to which Ferguson's antiquarian and archaeological interests were simultaneously the basis of his social relationships. As has already been established, he cultivated a wide circle of antiquarian devotees, including such figures as William Reeves, James Henthorn Todd, Eugene O'Curry, Sir William Wilde and, until his death in 1866, George Petrie. Ferguson was particularly close to the Stokes family, comprising Whitley Stokes senior, his three sons and his daughter Margaret, all of whom were involved to some extent in similar historical pursuits. Finally, he maintained an extensive network of correspondents throughout Ireland, Scotland and Europe, including the Viscomte de Villemarqué, in Brittany, Henri Martin in France, Professor Rhys in Oxford and Dr Stuart in Edinburgh. Lady Ferguson makes a specific list of over a dozen other names of clergy and lay devotees to Irish antiquities and archaeology, who 'shared in the tastes and pursuits of Ferguson' and whom he counted as his friends.[63]

The existence of this coterie is of significance if Ferguson's social context in the second half of his life is to be fully understood, and in order to qualify Gréagoir O'Dúill's suggestion that 'the mature barrister remained isolated and erratic in Dublin because his personal mixture of social conservatism and cultural nationalism was unusual in all classes except a small clerical and professional circle to which he gained assured entry only by his marriage in 1848'.[64]

---

[62] Denman lists Ferguson's affiliations in his biographical summary, *Samuel Ferguson* pp. 186–94. See also M.C. Ferguson, *SSIFD*, vol. 2, chapters 17–19, which deal with Ferguson's work as an antiquarian and archaeologist. [63] *SSFID*, vol. 2, pp. 76–7. [64] 'Samuel Ferguson: administrator and archivist', p. 121.

This view has its limitations first, in that Ferguson's social circle appears to have been determined as much by his personal fields of interest as by his union with a member of the Guinness family, and secondly in that his social contacts may be considered the result of choice rather than relegation. Far from becoming isolated as a consequence of his cultural activism, he consciously developed through the nature of his research a specific and supportive fraternity.

Again, this might be viewed in the wider context of Victorian middle-class cultural practice, in which the pursuit of the past provided a basis for communal engagement and social networks. The fashion for literary antiquarianism frequently took the form of book clubs and public lectures, while the study of history itself became 'an antiquarian speciality, proliferating in text societies and local historical groups, with less and less critical discrimination towards the masses of uncovered materials.'[65] As the popularity of antiquarianism increased, organizations such as the Surtees and Camden societies, established in the 1830s, together with existing eighteenth-century institutions such as the Royal Society of Antiquities, gave the lead to hundreds of smaller, provincial clubs and associations throughout the country.[66] Antiquarian research thus came to provide the foundation for the emergence of distinct social liaisons and groupings within the population.

Basing her research on historian Noel Annan's thesis of the 'intellectual aristocracy', which emerged through inter-marriage and family links from the ranks of the professional middle classes, Phillipa Levine has identified the distinct communities which evolved in Victorian society from the amateur study of history, archaeology and antiquities. Such groups shared not only a common interest but various characteristics: membership was predominantly male, Oxbridge-educated and Anglican, drawn primarily from the professional sector of middle-class but tending to include a high proportion of clergymen, who were attracted to such subjects as a result of their access to ecclesiastical records. In each case, the intellectual community was governed by homogeneity and a sense of common identity. That those involved shared both educational background and social referents made for a general consensus in the group. 'The organizational impetus which thus surfaced within antiquarianism in the mid nineteenth century suggests this strong sense of community among like-minded scholars', writes Levine. 'The idea of a community based on a code of practice defining exclusion and inclusion suggests a shift within antiquarian circles away from the individual private collector to the more convivial society in which the county museum and county history acted as symbols of shared access.'[67] In their

---

65 R. Wellek, *A history of modern criticism* (1965), vol. 3, p. 89. 66 P. Levine, *The amateur and the professional*, pp. 40–7. See also J. Evans, *A history of the Society of Antiquities* (1956). 67 *The amateur and the professional*, chapter 2, and p. 54.

collective aspirations and communal ego, members of the amateur society network who were motivated by what Levine describes as a sense of corporate duty were able to define themselves as a distinct social caste.

Throughout Victorian Britain the antiquarian society came to function, first and on a general level, as a channel for national or civic idealism, and as a means to express defiance in the face of industrialization and modernity:

> The reconstitution of the past was a means of consolidating and realizing place and identity in a landscape increasingly unfamiliar. A historical landscape, peopled with events, buildings and figures from the past and verified by historical fact was a triumph of possession. Nostalgia provides an insufficient explanation for the popularity of organized antiquarian pursuits. It was rather an alternative cultural force of amazing vigour, an attachment to local identity motivated in many ways by the same sentiments as that civic pride which spurred on the town-hall and sewer-builders of the later nineteenth century. It asserted a sense of provincial dignity and distinctiveness and provided a crucial link between past glories and present triumphs.[68]

In these terms, the acquisition of the past provided a means to counter alienation and disaffection and, most influentially, to foster a sense of social continuity. As such, the general British Victorian model clearly intersects with Ferguson's use of antiquarian studies as a primary element of an Irish cultural nationalism, highlighting once again the extent to which his activities were susceptible to a range of broad ideological impulses unacknowledged by the poet himself.

Secondly, the antiquarian society represented a valuable social signifier, or in other words a means of social demarcation which replaced outmoded determinants of status with a new set of credentials. Antiquarianism was in this respect one of a number of intellectual activities serving as common denominators to define the boundaries of an elite. Marshall Berman has usefully identified similar trends in the non-professional pursuit of science. Through what he classifies as 'the tradition of the wealthy amateur', with its connotations of scholarship and leisure, both ascendant middle-class professionals and gentlemen scholars were able to bypass existing aristocratic structures which remained in place until 1914, and to take precedence within a system of small, informal scientific study groups. For such individuals, Berman explains, the stated rationale of research and enlightenment was frequently a means to an end, for 'this utilitarian purpose was weakened by a more tempting and tangible cultural one;

---

68 *The amateur and the professional*, p. 61.

the acquisition of aristocratic respectability through the pursuit of knowledge, of antiquities, geography and the like'.[69] The amateur tradition was thus a viable route towards self-elevation without reference to traditional class affiliations.

Berman's thesis introduces to the subject of amateur scholarship in general the impulse towards the formation of an ascendancy, and Levine similarly identifies in the nature of social and academic relationships within amateur communities a hegemonic motivation. From the outset, the self-justifying and self-limiting facility of such a group was exercised as a means of control. 'The creation of a closely defined élite, marked more by who was excluded than who was embraced, was a means of limiting access to those deemed acceptable on both social and intellectual grounds', suggests Levine. 'The high degree of social homogeneity amongst those groups, reinforced by the development of a genealogy through marriage and family ties, suggests that a process of selection did indeed exclude the unacceptable.'[70] Internally, the exclusiveness of the community was reinforced by a complex system of support and solidarity, cementing the connections between individuals and marking its boundaries. This ranged from an emphasis on the value of collective work to letters of introduction, favourable reviews and defences of each other's theses, and from active lobbying to the internal 'policing' of plagiarism or poor scholarship, with frequent engagement in academic squabbles and feuds. The antiquarian community operated as a caucus, with its academic interchanges functioning simultaneously as an administrative system.[71]

The above description closely resembles the pattern of Ferguson's involvement in antiquarian pursuits, as evidenced, for example, in his sustained efforts between 1842 and 1845 to attack in print William Betham's ill-judged *Etruria Celtica*, or in his vigorous condemnation of plagiarists of Petrie's 1845 study of Irish round towers.[72] A similar tendency towards antiquarian 'lobbying' was exhibited in his attempts in 1843 to engage the support of the Member of Parliament, William Smith O'Brien, in the campaign to increase the Academy's parliamentary grant by £100 *per annum*, specifically for the purchase of Irish antiquities.[73]

---

69 'Hegemony and the amateur tradition in British science', 30–50.   70 *The amateur and the professional*, p. 38.   71 *The amateur and the professional*, p. 21.   72 Ferguson reviewed William Betham's *Etruria Celtica*, considered by many antiquarians to be a work of poor scholarship, in 1842, and over the ensuing three years pressurized Blackwood into publishing his article, which finally appeared in April 1845. (See Ferguson's letters to Blackwood, 14 Dec. 1842, NLS MS 4061 f20, and 9 April 1845, NLS MS 4070 f238.) Ó Dúill comments on the background to the controversy and with reference to Betham's position as the government's chief archivist suggests that 'Ferguson's repeated shrillness in insisting on the importance of the publication of this review essay (which damaged relations with his main publisher) may have been related to the vacancy expected on Betham's retirement.' 'Samuel Ferguson: administrator and archivist' p. 119. Ferguson promoted Petrie's work on several occasions, suggesting in a letter to Blackwood that his essay on round towers deserved a review notice (1 Mar. 1845, NLS MS 4070 f234) and denouncing the 'plunder and piracy' which both Petrie and O'Donovan had suffered: see for example, his comments in 'The *Annals of the Four Masters*', 359.

It is from a wider perspective however, that the discourse of the 'invisible college' in nineteenth-century British society is of use, in changing the complexion of Ferguson's social and academic relationships. The context which Levine and Berman provide indicates that Ferguson's social status during the latter half of his life was not wholly determined by his marriage, but was dependent upon a system of relations within a specific field composed largely of middle-class intellectuals and clerics, in which antiquarianism was regarded both as a common denominator and a means of access. The concept of the amateur society as a discernible caste within Victorian class society therefore suggests once again that definitions of Ferguson as an 'Ascendancy' writer must be realigned. While there was an inevitable and substantial intersection between an Irish antiquarian fraternity, the members of the Royal Irish Academy and a Protestant ruling élite, these points of fusion should not obscure the particularity of Ferguson's circle nor its recurrence as a distinct sociological phenomenon in Victorian life. Through antiquarianism, Ferguson's intellectual pursuits and social relationships became symbiotic in a manner which was not only supportive of his cultural evangelism, but which effectively reinforced his individual authority.

A study of Ferguson's career as an Irish antiquarian must, in conclusion, take into account the importance of this role in its own right rather than as a subsidiary commitment to his poetry and critical writing. His historical and philological work must be evaluated as a significant and alternative area of enquiry to the writer's literary activities, particularly in view of the fact that antiquarian research was, as one critic has noted 'the field in which Ferguson came closest to achieving parity of recognition for his Irish studies in England'.[74] The writer's affiliation to this aspect of cultural discourse in Ireland emerges finally, as a pertinent means of circumscribing his identity, ideology and achievement.

Undoubtedly, Ferguson's call for an antiquarian, localized history reflected his increasing anxieties about the tendencies of Irish political life, as he turned away from the implications of a national and generalized, or a philosophical and abstract historiography, towards the past in its most discrete and placatory form. His insistence in 1840 that through the disinterment of the country's artefacts the people of Ireland should be able to 'live back in the land they live in', gradually developed over the following decades into what might with some validity be interpreted as a negative response to Ireland's present and future condition, disguised as a positive investment in a national cultural inheritance composed of elements drawn from an edited Irish past.[75] The sense of retreat engen-

---

73 In his attempts to engage William Smith O'Brien's support, Ferguson proudly informed him that 'with the exception of the collection at Copenhagen there is not in the world so rich a cabinet of Celtic remains as this neglected society has now formed': Ferguson to O'Brien, 7 July 1843, NLI MS 432/1020. 74 C. Graham, 'Hibernian knight's assimilation of differences', 139. 75 Ferguson expresses this idea in 'The *Dublin Penny Journal*', *DUM* 15

dered by this policy is perhaps what later provoked Yeats to comment on how for Ferguson, towards the end, 'when he had exchanged poetry for antiquarian studies, his Nationalism (in the political sense) though not his patriotism, became less ardent'.[76] The semantic discrimination here is both accurate and useful however, in exposing the context of a patriotic tradition within which Ferguson constructed his cultural ideals, and which provided him with a precedent for Gaelic scholarship. Emphasizing the extent to which his own endeavours were underwritten by the legacy of an eighteenth-century movement of gentlemanly philological and scientific study, he succeeded in circumventing a problematic nationalism while offering a sanitized version of Irish cultural revivalism to his contemporaries.

Nonetheless it is clear that Ferguson's programme had much in common with a nineteenth-century philosophy of culture. In 1848 he had written to Aubrey de Vere stressing the necessity of alternatives to political action in the country, and presenting his own vision:

> I rely more on the slow but certain effect of a national literature operating among the heads of society and thence downwards than on any instruction or organization of the populace. It has been for many years my great object to promote a literature of this kind, and I have the satisfaction of seeing the foundations laid in our Royal Irish Academy and Museum, and the materials already in part supplied by our native scholars and poets.[77]

The passage embodies the two elements which were to dominate his later comprehension of cultural dynamics: first, the promotion of culture – literary, archaeological or antiquarian – as the cohesive force which would restore social integrity and harmony to the country, and secondly, the identification of the groups and institutions which would assume responsibility for the dissemination of such material. The proximity of this philosophy to a discernible movement in Britain to safeguard and institutionalize a public heritage must be appreciated as an indication of the fact that Ferguson's manifesto was not uniquely applicable to his own country, but was relevant to widespread social and cultural pressures in Victorian life as a whole.

Finally, the emergence once again of the concept of an intellectual or cultural élite, distinct from traditional ideas of Ascendancy and reinforced in the latter decades of his career by a self-delineating antiquarian network, confirms the premise that Ferguson's ideological position was shaped by emergent social

(Jan. 1840), 115–6.   76 'The poetry of Sir Samuel Ferguson'.   77 21 Feb. 1848, NLI MS 13123/10.

structures in Victorian society rather than long-established political and religious allegiances. The secure, scholarly fraternity which he found in the Royal Irish Academy and his antiquarian circle was in this respect no mere adjunct to an overarching hegemonic class, but a recognizable and largely independent circle, through which Ferguson sought to establish a basis for a legitimate national identity, and to fulfil his ambitions for Irish cultural independence and civic virtue.

Conclusion

The last fifteen years of Ferguson's life were marked by failing health and his awareness of impending death. In 1872, the year in which his epic poem *Congal* was finally published, he wrote to John Blackwood of how, in the midst of other friends falling around him, he was conscious of approaching 'the grand climaction'.[1] To the end, he found it difficult to reconcile illness with his desire for activity and engagement, and in a letter to Aubrey de Vere in 1885 described how his wife continually discouraged him from attempts to deal with the complexities of the Irish political scene. '"You", she says, "have no right to intervene in party politics. You are" – I take it very ill – "an old man; you have no right to let angry or indignant thoughts into your mind, which would be better occupied with things of more lasting interest." And she is no doubt right.'[2]

The extended period of the writer's physical decline appears to have accelerated and heightened his sense of closure with regard to his public life, allowing him to evaluate retrospectively his intentions and achievements and even to shape, to a considerable extent, his own reputation as a cultural activist. In his later years, he sought to depict himself as misunderstood and excluded as a consequence of his single-minded pursuit of a virtuous ideal. On one level his efforts had been grossly undervalued. 'Little do these ignorant, turbulent discontented poor Irish know of the labour and learning that have been devoted to the building up for them a School of Arts and Letters', he wrote, in an ironic frame of mind, to Whitley Stokes.[3] On another, his hybrid identity had resulted in isolation, and with a similar pointed humour he informed Blackwood in 1858, 'I have two just satisfactions. I am an Irishman and a Protestant. The one keeps me out of favour with the castle, and the other out of favour with the church.'[4]

These and similar remarks illustrate Ferguson's increasingly self-righteous tone, in presenting himself as the unacknowledged saviour of Irish letters, the heroic campaigner dedicated to a worthy individualist cause. Writing elsewhere in reference to the younger Stokes, he emphasized the sacrifices involved in his endeavours to help such men lay the foundations of what he hoped might yet

---

[1] 17 Jan. 1872, NLS MS 4289 f35. [2] 3 Mar. 1885, NLI MS 13, 122–8. [3] Cited M.C. Ferguson, *SSFID*, vol. 2, p. 99.
[4] Ferguson to John Blackwood, 16 Aug. 1858, NLS MS 4131 f33.

be a national Irish literature. 'With this view', he stated, 'I have published my works here at the cost of being, for the present at least, equally unknown here and in England'. The jocularity disguised a more serious sense of grievance that he had been overlooked, and in private he complained frequently of critical neglect.[5] In fact, his writing was well known in Ireland and had not gone totally unnoticed among the more discerning of his English contemporaries: Ford Madox Brown wrote to the poet William Allingham, 'Sam Ferguson is again very much to be thanked for remaining unknown and causing a new sensation to those who think it a shame not to have read what has been written.'[6] But the contrivance of literary isolation prevailed to the point of becoming an affectation even in the face of the 1878 knighthood, awarded partly in recognition of his literary successes.

More pertinently, Ferguson's contribution to Irish cultural life had rarely been conceived or executed in isolation: his quintessential instinct was communitarian, even if the groups and networks to which he became affiliated were to some extent, compromises or approximations of some ideal intellectual fraternity. The liberal enlightenment ethos which characterized his Antrim origins, his Presbyterian schooling and his early personal and literary contacts, including O'Hagan, Tennant and the *Ulster Magazine* circle, were at odds perhaps with his conservative unionism, but they fired the intellectual and philosophical energies of his youth, and laid the foundations for his distinctive civic perspective. Belfast's proximity to a Scottish tradition of cultural and philosophical engagement, manifest not only in the Tory *Blackwood's* but in Scotland's universities, academies and societies, furnished a sense of a fraternity existing across a political spectrum and pursuing the principles, at least, of cultural self-determination. As for Dublin, if tension and alienation marked a fraught relationship with the Protestant ideologues of the *Dublin University Magazine*, then other circles were available: the welcoming scholars of the Ordnance Survey Memoir, of the Young Irelanders and the *Nation*, or later, of the Royal Irish Academy and a host of Celtic and antiquarian organizations, offered a home for the young writer amidst like-minded *aficionados*. Above all, Ferguson's access to the capital's social circles through the ranks of middle-class professionals, and the 'guild' culture of Dublin's legal fraternity, brought him to the heart of a genteel but intensely pragmatic civic establishment.

The emphasis placed by Ferguson's own interpretation of events on isolation and exclusion must be shifted therefore, to the writer's integration and par-

---

5 Cited M.C. Ferguson, *SSFID*, vol. 2, p. 85. In 1883, Ferguson complained to Blackwood that his *Poems* had received very little critical attention. 'It may be the fact of my being Protestant and a Conservative, on the one hand, and of my publishing in Dublin and taking Irish matter to so great an extent for my text, on the other, may account for this state of affairs', he wrote (2 Jan. 1883, NLS MS 4444 f57). 6 *Allingham's Letters* (1911), 27 Jan. 1860.

ticipation in the varied groups from which he drew his cultural dynamism. The communal nature of his engagement with Ireland and its heritage was characteristically Victorian, in its dependence on the scholarly network rather than the inspired individual, while his success as a cultural activist was similarly rooted in the circulation of popular journalistic, philosophical, literary and antiquarian discourses throughout his society, rather than in any extraneous and unique agenda. It was largely through a *process* of social and professional liaison, therefore, that Ferguson managed to forge definitions of the kind of Ireland in which he wanted to live. The heroic character of his achievement, as Yeats was later to celebrate it, lay in his evangelical ability, and the vocalism and urgency of the challenge he put before his colleagues. We cannot at all sympathize, Ferguson had written in 1848, with those who complain of their lot being cast too late or too early.

> On the contrary, we deem it highly fortunate that we are too far separated from mere Irish times to make the revival of either the language, the laws, or the customs of the old natives, in the remotest degree possible. Scholars are, at the same time, near enough to lay their hands at will on their characteristics, to surround themselves to any extent with their influences, and to use these influences *ad libitum*, in moulding the coming age. It is the very time for men of a large and noble ambition to live in Ireland; all danger of relapse into barbarism past – all risk of denationalisation still before them, and still strong enough nobly to employ all their faculties in countering and overthrowing it. If this generation do its duty, that which follows us will be as far removed from Celtic rudeness on the one hand, as it will from any likeness of Anglican effete refinement on the other.[7]

Set against the social variety of Ferguson's alliances is the consistency of his vision in relation to two predominant factors. The first was the priority of Dublin itself, whether highlighted through the commercial idiom of the tourist's picturesque, or shaped in terms of the obsolete Augustanism of Gandon's classical facades. Dublin – the urban stronghold of an otherwise geographically problematic island – provided points of connection to the broad, sustaining culture of the Victorian city; the resistant and quintessentially sociable *polis* of the civic ideal. Repeatedly, Ferguson's emphasis was on the elevation of the Irish capital towards the status of its continental counterparts, and on the praise due to those Irish scholars, artists and men-of-letters who had made, he claimed,

---

7 'The *Annals of the Four Masters*: second article', *DUM* 31 (May, 1848), 580–1.

huge personal sacrifices to win back the interest of the Irish nobility and gentry, and thus to create 'as great inducements to the cultivation of all the higher arts in Dublin as now exist in most of the capital cities of Europe'.[8] In the city, one gained the initiatives of intellectual discourse amongst like-minded professionals stranded through civic institutions and societies, and one could bypass, crucially, the authority of a land-based hegemony with its awkward political baggage. Celebrated for its progressive industrial and engineering projects, and lauded at the same time, paradoxically, for its retrogressive classical structures and allusions, the city provided the co-ordinates of a viable identity, particularly for those who emerged, like Ferguson, from a composite and complex ideological and social background.

The second element was Ferguson's attempt to project the acceptable face of Irish Protestantism, based largely on the interests of an intellectual, professional middle class, and grounded in the language of civic and patriotic aspiration. It was through *this* need, as much as through their common engagement with the literature of Ireland, that he forged a mutually beneficial alliance with Young Ireland – an alliance much closer than his critics have ever wished to suggest. The relationship with Duffy and the *Nation*, in addition to contacts with William Smith O'Brien, Thomas D'Arcy McGee and John Mitchel, clearly laid the groundwork for Ferguson's engagement with Repeal, when driven too far by a British policy of creeping centralization and catastrophic neglect. And in the iconic figure of fellow-barrister and fellow-poet Thomas Davis, Ferguson located the characteristics he sought; the personality which might stand, synedochically, for a modern self-respecting nation. The version of Ireland he thus projected was masculine, unadorned, and culturally rather religiously defined, but it was an Ireland geared towards defending itself as much against the encroachments and inequities of the imperial relationship as against the internal threats of anarchy and insurrection.

From the late 1840s onwards, Ferguson's personal philosophy was franked by claims for an active scholarly fraternity to provide ballast within the country as a whole. This insistence was seminal to his engagement with the artefacts of a Celtic past; no caste-based colonial appropriation of a foreign culture, but a retrieval of the raw material of the country as the basis for the formation of a stable domestic – and integral – civic leadership. Inevitably, as Seamus Deane points out, such strategy resembles Arnold's Celticism, 'a neo-Burkian version of cultural nationalism as a philosophy designed to act as an alternative to and even a safeguard against revolutionary republicanism'.[9] In similar terms Burke sought out a 'natural aristocracy' as an integral, organic part of society, an ele-

---

8 Cited M.C. Ferguson, *SSFID*, vol. 1, p. 240.   9 *A short history*, p. 85.

ment which would 'stand upon such elevated ground as to be enabled to take a large view of the wide-spread and infinitely diversified combinations of men and affairs in a large society; to have leisure to read, to reflect, to converse; to be enabled to draw the court and attention of the wide and learned, wherever they are to be found.'[10] Inevitably too, Ferguson's vision was shared by contemporaries of more extreme political hue, including his old adversary Isaac Butt and several others from the *DUM* stable, who likewise saw themselves as consolidating 'an idealized Protestant aristocracy of intellect', and maintaining a systematic Burkean inheritance.[11] Investment in 'mental cultivation' was no individual concern but a general Victorian preoccupation, a watchword of the times on both sides of the Irish sea.

Ferguson's take on the process was remarkable, however, partly in the adaptation of his own cultural hinterland – the trickle-down values of Scotland's Enlightenment and Ulster's United Irishmen – to the demands of mid-century Dublin, and partly in his timely appeal to Ireland's nascent urban professionals, a potentially dynamic formation in Irish intellectual and political life. If the former aspect necessitated some awkward splicing of values, the latter involved the splicing of a credible audience. Ferguson's problems in sustaining a coherent agenda were largely to do with the fluid ideological composition of his constituency: while they appear in the simplification of hindsight to have been socially and politically homogenous, his readers, friends and colleagues over the course of his life in fact constituted a fairly diverse grouping, riddled with discrepancies and conflicting desires. To solder together a community of interest, Ferguson repeatedly tried to produce an adequate *nomenclature*. Appropriately, McCormack depicts him as a man literally struggling for words in his attempt to address – and thereby create – a solid phalanx of intellectual, cultural and civic energy in the Ireland of his time.[12] But for all his efforts and investments, a truly central and enduring constituency, harnessed to what he understood to be the country's needs, would ultimately prove elusive.

Who then, did he really represent, if not the nebulous 'Protestant Ascendancy' of his latter-day critics? Certainly it was too early to speak of an Irish 'intelligentsia', which would only properly emerge through the clerics and teachers of a nationalist order. And the reified notion of 'intellectuals' is too abstract to convey the pragmatic and functional quality of the community he envisaged. Charles Gavan Duffy perhaps went some way towards circumscribing a specific group closely allied to but distinct from the Irish gentry, referring in the context of Protestant Repeal to 'the cultivated classes represented

---

10 'An appeal from the new to the old Whigs', *Works* (1899), vol. 4, pp. 174–6.   11 J.P. McBride, vol. 1, p. 84.   12 *From Burke to Beckett*, p. 143.

by Ferguson and [Colman] O'Loghlen, who governed themselves by judgement and conscience, and whose aim was to revive the entire Irish nation'.[13] Ferguson himself only came close when he left behind the supremacist rhetoric of the Hardiman fracas and recognized one of the defining characteristics of his community – its intermediate and *mediatory* role between the rock of an O'Connellite kinesis and the hard place of unsympathetic British administrations. Caught in the middle were the individuals he celebrated in a review article of 1868, those men 'nourished on the principles of civil and religious freedom', who showed most sympathy with a native history and recollection:

> The expediency of encouraging the Irish mind to dwell on the past has often been questioned; but the educated classes amongst whom these tastes prevail have carried the pursuit too far to be arrested, even were that course desirable. They may reconcile themselves to the necessity of being denizens of a land without a philosophic history, but they will not be condemned to the condition of colonists in a new country.[14]

Ultimately however, Ferguson was aware of his cultural contribution – and specifically, the civic incentive in which it was embedded – being eclipsed by more potent forces, increasingly sidelined by an Irish who, as Eagleton suggests, 'were to prefer clergy to clerisy'.[15] Indeed, his complaints of critical neglect translate easily into the reality of his political alienation from a society changing both demographically and democratically, and a culture which was, in spite of traditional and agricultural allegiances, moving towards modernity. That Yeats would strategically if sentimentally *mis*-recognise him as 'the greatest Irish poet', was effectively, a means of laying Ferguson to rest at the same time as laying the groundwork for his own very different elevation. And Ferguson's circle, stamped by Yeats with the worst irrelevancies and excesses of late Victorianism, was simultaneously overlooked by a Revival élite with little interest in its ethics of civic virtue, scholarship and professional service. Thus was Ferguson – the quintessential Irish Victorian at the heart of a discernible cultural strategy – reduced to the worthy but slightly eccentric antiquarian enthusiast possessed of what Frank O'Connor would describe as 'a sense of reality like a pile-driver'.[16]

Ferguson died in 1886, and the essence of his civic vision died with him. Culturally, he had come to embody the hangover of a previous age, a time-locked combination of eighteenth-century Irish patriotism and nineteenth-cen-

---

13 *My life*, vol. 1, p. 243. 14 'Lord Romilly's Irish publications', *Quarterly Review* 124 (Apr. 1868), 423–5. 15 *Scholars and rebels*, p. 25. T.W. Heyck discusses the inapplicability of the term 'intellectuals' to British social life before 1870, suggesting 'men of letters' as a more appropriate denomination, *The transformation of intellectual life in Victorian England* (1982), pp. 15–16. 16 *The backward look* (1967), p. 149.

Conclusion

tury civic pride. The subsequent success of a national literary agenda based on simpler forms and iconography would ironically obscure much of what its acclaimed fore-runner stood for in his retreat to the Irish past: by the latter decades of the nineteenth century, Ferguson's brand of cultural nationalism looked jaded, dessicated by its own virtuous excesses of intricate antiquarian scholarship. His sense of an Irish social leadership, meanwhile, invigorated by scholarly commitment and bonded together by a proprietorial urban responsibility, was redundant in a modern age with little time for such localized, self-limiting concerns. Set against the rise of a forceful, viable nationalist political discourse, the civic ideal became little more a Victorian curiosity; a casualty, in effect, of the path to independence, and another road not taken in the accelerating course of Irish ideological history.

Bibliography

PUBLISHED WRITINGS BY FERGUSON, USED OR CITED

From the *Dublin University Magazine*

'A dialogue between the head and heart of an Irish Protestant', 2 (Nov. 1833), 589–93.
'Inaugural ode for the new year', 3 (Jan. 1834) n.p.
'Hilloa our fancy, flight the first', 3 (Jan. 1834) 25–42.
'Hardiman's *Irish Minstrelsy*, no. 1', 3 (Apr. 1834) 465–78.
'Hardiman's *Irish Minstrelsy*, no. 2', 4 (Aug. 1834) 152–67.
'Hardiman's *Irish Minstrelsy*, no. 3', 4 (Oct. 1834) 447–67.
'Hardiman's *Irish Minstrelsy*, no. 4', 4 (Nov. 1834) 514–42.
'Irish storyists – Lover and Carleton', 4 (Sept. 1834) 298–311.
'The death of the children of Usnach', 4 (Dec. 1834) 674–90.
'The captive of Killeshin', 5 (Jan. 1835) 58–79.
'The rebellion of Silken Thomas: part 1', 5 (Feb. 1835) 193–215.
'The rebellion of Silken Thomas: part 2', 5 (Mar. 1835) 293–312.
'The rebellion of Silken Thomas: part 3', 5 (Apr. 1835) 438–58.
'The rebellion of Silken Thomas: part 4', 5 (June 1835) 705–23.
'The rebellion of Silken Thomas: part 5', 6 (July 1835) 50–71.
'The rebellion of Silken Thomas: part 6', 6 (Aug. 1835) 207–23.
'Corby MacGillmore: part 1', 6 (Sept. 1835) 278–95.
'Corby MacGillmore: part 2', 6 (Nov. 1835) 537–57.
'Corby MacGillmore: part 3', 6 (Dec. 1835) 640–61.
'Rosabel of Ross: part 1', 7 (Jan. 1836) 96–116.
'Rosabel of Ross: part 2', 7 (Mar. 1836) 327–42.
'Rosabel of Ross: part 3', 7 (Apr. 1836) 380–400.
'The black Monday of the glens', 6 (Sept. 1835) 332–44.
'The sketcher foiled', 8 (July 1836) 16.
'The attractions of Ireland, no. 1 – scenery', 8 (July 1836) 112–31.
'The attractions of Ireland, no. 2 – scenery and society', 8 (Sept. 1836) 315–33.
'The attractions of Ireland, no. 3 – society', 8 (Dec. 1836) 658–75.
'The capabilities of Ireland', 9 (Jan. 1837) 46–57.
'Gallery of illustrious Irishmen – George Petrie', 14 (Dec. 1839) 638–42.
'The *Dublin Penny Journal*', 15 (Jan. 1840) 112–28.
'Robert Burns', 25 (Jan. 1845) 66–81.
'Robert Burns: second article', 25 (Mar. 1845) 289–305.

'Petrie's round towers', 25 (Apr. 1845) 379–96.
'O'Connor's *History of the Irish Brigade*', 25 (May 1845) 593–608.
'Our portrait gallery – Thomas Davis', 29 (Feb. 1847) 190–9.
'Architecture in Ireland', 29 (June 1847) 693–708.
'Reeves' *Ecclesiastical antiquities*', 31 (Feb. 1848) 207–27.
'The *Annals of the Four Masters*', 31 (Mar. 1848) 359–76.
'The *Annals of the Four Masters*: second article', 31 (May 1848) 571–84.
'Inheritor and Economist – a poem', 33 (May 1849) 638–49.
'"Dublin": a poem, in imitation of the third satire of Juvenal', 34 (July 1849) 102–9.
'Ruskin's *Seven lamps of architecture*', 34 (July 1849) 1–14.
'Ruskin's *Stones of Venice*', 38 (Sept. 1851) 253–71.

From *Blackwood's Edinburgh Magazine*

'The wet wooing: a narrative of '98', 21 (Apr. 1832) 624–45.
'The return of Claneboy', 34 (Dec. 1833) 928–52.
'Shane O'Neill's last amour', 35 (Feb. 1834) 249–66.
'Father Tom and the Pope; or a night at the Vatican', 43 (May 1838) 607–19.
'Betham's *Etruria Celtica*', 57 (Apr. 1845) 474–88.

Miscellaneous

'On the expediency of taking stock: a letter to James Pim, jun. esq.' (Dublin, 1847).
'Ireland's claims to an adequate parliamentary representative of learning in a letter to James MacCullagh' (Dublin, 1847).
'Our public and domestic architecture', *Dublin Builder* 6 (May 1864) 78–81. Also printed as 'Our architecture', *Afternoon lectures on literature and art: second series* (1864).
'"On the study of Celtic literature" by Matthew Arnold', *Athenaeum Journal of Literature, Science and Fine Arts* 2072 (13 July 1867) 45–6.
'Address delivered before the Academy by Sir Samuel Ferguson, LL.D, Q.C., President. 30 November 1882', *Proceedings of the Royal Irish Academy* 16: *Polite literature and antiquities 1879–1888*, no. 33, 185–201.
Hibernian nights' entertainments, ed. M.C. Ferguson, 3 vols (Dublin, 1887).
Lays of the western Gael and other poems (Dublin, 1865).

NOTE: Peter Denman provides a comprehensive checklist of Ferguson's published works in *Samuel Ferguson*, pp. 195–213. See also Lady Ferguson's bibliographical appendix, *SSFID*, vol. 2, pp. 369–74 and Patrick Curley's manuscript sources in 'William Drennan and the Young Samuel Ferguson', unpublished PhD thesis, QUB, (Belfast, 1987).

JOURNAL SOURCES (NINETEENTH CENTURY)

Athenaeum Journal of Literature, Science and Fine Arts

Blackwood's Edinburgh Magazine
Cox's Law Reports

Dublin Penny Journal
Dublin University Magazine
Dublin University Review
Freeman's Journal
Irish Builder
Irish Quarterly Review

Nation
Proceedings and Transactions of the Royal Irish
    Academy
Ulster Magazine
Tait's Edinburgh Magazine

GENERAL BIBLIOGRAPHY

Abbey, J.R. *Scenery of Great Britain and Ireland in aquatint and lithography, 1770–1880: a bibliographical catalogue* (London: Curwen, 1952).

Abrams, Philip. *The origins of British sociology 1834–1914* (Chicago: Chicago UP, 1969).

Abse, Joan. *John Ruskin: the passionate moralist* (London: Quartet, 1980).

Alison, Archibald. *Essays on the nature and principles of taste*, 5th ed. (London, 1790).

Allan, David. *Virtue, learning and the Scottish Enlightenment: ideas of scholarship in early modern history* (Edinburgh: Edinburgh UP, 1993).

Allingham, H. and D. Radford (eds), *William Allingham: a diary* (London: Penguin, 1985).

Allingham, William. *Allingham's letters* (London, 1911).

Andrews, J.H. *A paper landscape: the Ordnance Survey in nineteenth-century Ireland* (Oxford: Clarendon, 1975).

Annan, Noel. 'The intellectual aristocracy', in J.H. Plumb (ed.), *Studies in social history: a tribute to G.M. Trevelyan* (London: Longmans, 1955).

Armstrong, Isobel. *Victorian scrutinies: reviewers of poetry, 1830–1870* (London: Athlone, 1972).

Arnold, Matthew. 'On the study of Celtic literature' and 'On the literary influence of Academies', in R.H. Super (ed.), *Complete prose works*, vol 3 (Ann Arbor: U of Michigan P, 1962).

———. *Culture and anarchy 1867* (Cambridge: Cambridge UP, 1946).

Ball, F.E. *The judges in Ireland* (London, 1920).

Bann, Stephen. *The clothing of Clio: a study of the representation of history in nineteenth-century Britain and France* (Cambridge: Cambridge UP, 1984).

Bardon, Jonathan. *Belfast: an illustrated history* (Belfast: Blackstaff, 1982).

Barrell, John. *The idea of landscape and the sense of place, 1730–1840* (Cambridge: Cambridge UP, 1972).

———. *The political theory of painting from Reynolds to Hazlitt* (New Haven: Yale UP, 1986).

Barrington, Jonah. *The Ireland of Sir Jonah Barrington: selections from his personal sketches, 1827–1832*, ed. Hugh B. Staples (Seattle: U of Washington P, 1967).

Barthes, Roland. *Criticism and truth* trans. K.P. Keuneman (London: Athlone, 1987).

Bassin, Joan. *Architectural competitions in nineteenth-century England* (Michigan: U.M.I. Research Press, 1984).

Beckett, J.C. and R.E. Glassock (eds), *Belfast: the origin and growth of an industrial city* (London, 1967).

Belfast. *The Belfast Literary Society, 1801–1901: a historical sketch, with memoirs of some distinguished members* (Belfast, 1902).

Bell, Alan (ed.), *Walter Scott: bicentenary essays* (Edinburgh: Scottish Academic, 1987).
Bell, A.S. (ed.), *The Scottish antiquarian tradition* (Edinburgh: John Donald, 1981).
Benn, George. *A history of the town of Belfast from the earliest times to the close of the eighteenth century* (Belfast, 1877).
Berman, M. 'Hegemony and the amateur tradition in British science', *Journal of Social History* 8 (1975) 30–50.
Bermingham, Ann. *Landscape and ideology: the English rustic tradition, 1740–1860* (London: Thames and Hudson, 1987).
Bishop, I.M. 'The Education of Ulster students at Glasgow University during the nineteenth century', unpublished MA thesis, QUB (Belfast, 1987).
Bodkin, Thomas. *Four Irish landscape painters* (Dublin: Talbot Press, 1920).
Booth, M.R. 'Irish landscape and the Victorian theatre', in A. Carpenter (ed.), *Place, personality and the Irish theatre*.
Bowen, Desmond. *The Protestant crusade in Ireland, 1800–1870* (Dublin: Gill and Macmillan, 1978).
Bowler, P. *The invention of progress: the Victorians and the past* (Oxford: Blackwell, 1989).
——. and N. Whyte (eds), *Science and society in Ireland: the social context of science and technology in Ireland, 1800–1950* (Belfast: Institute of Irish Studies, 1997).
Boyce, D.G. 'Trembling solicitude: Irish conservatism, nationality and public opinion, 1833–86', in D.G. Boyce et al. (eds), *Political thought in Ireland*.
——. *Nineteenth-century Ireland: the search for stability* (Dublin: Gill and Macmillan, 1990).
——. *Ireland, 1828–1923: from ascendancy to democracy* (Oxford: Blackwell, 1992).
——, R. Eccleshall and V. Geoghegan (eds), *Political thought in Ireland since the seventeenth century* (London: Routledge, 1993).
Boyle, James. *Ordnance Survey Memoir for Antrim* PRONI F2 (1838–9)
Brady, J.C. 'Legal developments, 1801–79', in W.E. Vaughan (ed.), *A new history of Ireland*.
Brady, J. and A. Simms (eds), *Dublin through space and time* (Dublin: Four Courts, 2001).
Brett, C.E.B. *Buildings of Belfast, 1700–1914* (London: Weidenfeld and Nicolson, 1967).
Brooke, Charlotte. *Reliques of Irish Poetry* (Dublin, 1816).
Brooks, M.W. *John Ruskin and Victorian architecture* (London: Rutgers UP, 1987).
Brown, David. *Walter Scott and the historical imagination* (London: Routledge, 1979).
Brown, Malcolm. *Sir Samuel Ferguson* (Lewisburg: Bucknell UP, 1973).
Brown, Terence. *Northern voices: poets from the north of Ireland* (Dublin: Gill and Macmillan, 1975).
——.*Ireland's literature: selected essays* (Mullingar: Lilliput, 1988).
—— and N. Grene (eds), *Tradition and influence in Anglo-Irish poetry* (London: Macmillan, 1992).
—— and B. Hayley (eds), *Samuel Ferguson: a centenary tribute* (Dublin: Royal Irish Academy, 1987.
Bryson, Gladys. *Man and society: the Scottish enquiry of the eighteenth century* (1945).
Burke, Edmund. *The works of the Right Honourable Edmund Burke*, 8 vols (London, 1881).
Burrow, J.W. *Evolution and society: a study in Victorian social theory* (Cambridge: Cambridge UP, 1966).

Bibliography

——. *A liberal descent: Victorian historians and the English past* (Cambridge: Cambridge UP, 1981).
Butler, Marilyn. *Maria Edgeworth: a literary biography* (Oxford: Oxford UP, 1972).
——. *Romantics, rebels and reactionaries: English literature and its background, 1760–1830* (Oxford: Oxford UP, 1985).
Butterfield, Herbert. *The Whig interpretation of history* 1931 (London, 1951).
Cahalan, James M. *Great hatred; little room: the Irish historical novel* (Dublin: Gill and Macmillan, 1983).
——. *The Irish novel* (Dublin: Gill and Macmillan, 1988).
Cairns, David and Shaun Richards. *Writing Ireland: colonialism, nationalism and culture* (Manchester: Manchester UP, 1988).
Calder, Angus. 'The Enlightenment', in I. Donnachie and C.A. Whately (eds), *The manufacture of Scottish history*.
Caracciolo, Peter L. (ed.), *The Arabian Nights in English literature* (London: Macmillan, 1988).
Carleton, William. *Traits and stories of the Irish peasantry: second series*, 3 vols, 1833 (New York: Garland, 1979).
Carlyle, Thomas. *Reminiscences of my Irish journey in 1849* (London, 1882).
Carpenter, Andrew (ed.), *Place, personality and the Irish writer: Irish literary studies 1* (Gerrards Cross: Colin Smythe, 1977).
Chitnis, A.C. *The Scottish Enlightenment and early Victorian society* (Dover: Croom Helm, 1986).
Clark, Kenneth. *Landscape into art* (London: John Murray, 1949).
——. *The Gothic revival: an essay in the history of taste*, 3rd ed. (London: John Murray, 1962).
Coleridge, S.T. *On the constitution of church and state* 1830 (London: Dent, 1972).
Corbey, R. and J.T. Leerssen (eds), *Alterity, identity and image: selves and others in society and scholarship* (Amsterdam: Rodopi, 1991).
Cosgrove, Denis and Stephen Daniels (eds), *The iconography of landscape* (Cambridge: Cambridge UP, 1988).
Craig, Maurice. *Dublin, 1660–1860* (Dublin: Allen Figgis, 1980).
Croker, John Wilson. *A sketch of the state of Ireland, past and present* (Dublin, 1808).
Croker, Thomas Crofton. *Researches in the south of Ireland* (Dublin: Irish UP, 1968).
Crooke, Elizabeth. 'Archaeology and nationalism in nineteenth-century Ireland', *Museum Ireland* 9, 21–8.
——. *Politics, archaeology and the creation of a national museum in Ireland* (Dublin: Irish Academic, 2000).
Culler, Jonathan. *Framing the sign: criticism and its institutions* (Oxford: Blackwell, 1988).
——. *The pursuit of signs* (London: Routledge, 1981).
Curley, Patrick. 'William Drennan and the young Samuel Ferguson: liberty, patriotism and the Union in Ulster poetry between 1770 and 1848', unpublished PhD thesis, QUB (Belfast, 1987).
Curley, Thomas M. *Samuel Johnson and the age of travel* (Athens: U of Georgia P, 1976).
Curran, W.H. *Sketches of the Irish Bar* 2 vols (London, 1855).
Daly, Mary E. *Dublin: the deposed capital: a social and economic history, 1860–1914* (Cork: Cork UP, 1984).

Davis, Richard. *The Young Ireland movement* (Dublin: Gill and Macmillan, 1987).
Davis, Thomas. *Literary and historical essays*, ed. C.G. Duffy (Dublin, 1846).
Dawe, G. and J.W. Foster (eds), *The poet's place: Ulster literature and society* (Belfast: Institute of Irish Studies, 1991).
Deane, Seamus. 'An example of tradition', *The Crane Bag* 3, no. 1 (1979) 373–9.
——. 'Edmund Burke and the ideology of Irish liberalism', in R. Kearney (ed.), *The Irish mind*.
——. *A short history of Irish literature* (London: Hutchinson, 1985).
——. *The French revolution and enlightenment in England* (Cambridge, Mass: Harvard UP, 1988).
—— et al. (eds), *The Field Day Anthology of Irish Writing*, 3 vols (Derry: Field Day, 1991).
De Certeau, Michel. *Heterologies: discourse on the Other*, trans. B. Massumi (Manchester: Manchester UP, 1986).
De Courcy, Catherine and Ann Maher (eds), *Fifty views of Ireland* (Dublin: National Gallery of Ireland, 1985).
Denman, Peter. 'Ferguson and *Blackwood's*: the formative years', *Irish University Review* (Autumn, 1986) 141–58.
——. *Samuel Ferguson: the literary achievement* (Gerrards Cross: Colin Smythe, 1990).
De Vere, Aubrey. *Recollections* (London: Edward Arnold, 1897).
Devine, T. and D. Dickson (eds), *Ireland and Scotland, 1600–1850: parallels and contrasts in economic and social development* (Edinburgh: John Donald, 1983).
Dewar, Daniel. *Observations on Ireland* (London: 1812).
Donnachie, I. and C.A. Whately (eds), *The manufacture of Scottish history* (London: Polygon, 1992).
Draper, R.P. (ed.), *The literature of region and nation* (London: Macmillan, 1989).
Duffy, Charles Gavan. *Four years of Irish history, 1845–1849* (London, 1883).
—— (ed.) *The ballad poetry of Ireland* (Dublin, 1845).
——. *Young Ireland: a fragment* (Dublin, 1880).
——. *A short life of Thomas Davis, 1840–1846* (London, 1890).
——. *My life in two hemispheres*, 2 vols (London, 1898).
Dwyer, John. *Virtuous discourse: sensibility and community in late eighteenth-century Scotland* (Edinburgh: John Donald, 1987).
—— and Richard B. Sher (eds), *Sociability and society in eighteenth-century Scotland* (Edinburgh: Mercat, 1993).
Eagleton, Terry. 'Ideology and Scholarship', in J. McGann (ed.), *Historical studies and literary criticism* (Wisconsin: U of Wisconsin P, 1985).
——. *Heathcliff and the great hunger: studies in Irish culture* (London: Verso, 1995).
——. *Scholars and rebels in nineteenth-century Ireland* (Oxford: Blackwell, 1999).
Edgeworth, Maria. *Castle Rackrent* 1800. (Oxford: Oxford UP, 1964).
——. *Belinda*, 1801, 2 vols (London, 1833).
——. *The Absentee*, 1812 (London, Everyman 1910).
Elliott, Marianne. *Partners in revolution: the United Irishmen and France* (New Haven: Yale UP, 1982).
——. *Watchmen in Sion: the Protestant idea of liberty* (Derry: Field Day, 1985).

Ellmann, Richard. *Golden codgers: biographical speculations* (Oxford: Oxford UP, 1973).
Emerson, Roger. 'The Enlightenment and social structures', in P. Fritz and D. Williams (eds), *City and society in the eighteenth century* (Toronto: Hakket, 1973).
Engel, E. and M. King. *The Victorian novel before Victoria* (London: Macmillan, 1984).
Evans, Joan (ed.), *The lamp of beauty: writings on art by John Ruskin* (Oxford: Phaidon, 1959).
——. *A history of the society of antiquities* (Oxford, 1956).
Ferguson, Adam. *Essay on the history of civil society*, 1767, 6th ed. (Edinburgh, 1793).
Ferguson, M.C. *Sir Samuel Ferguson in the Ireland of his day*, 2 vols (Edinburgh, 1896).
——. *The life of the right rev. William Reeves* (Dublin, 1893).
Finley, Gerald. *Landscapes of memory: Turner as illustrator to Scott* (London: Scolar 1980).
Fisher, J and J.H. Robb. *The book of the Royal Belfast Academical Institution: centenary volume, 1810–1910* (Belfast, 1913).
Flanagan, Thomas. *The Irish novelists, 1800–1850* (New York: Columbia UP, 1959).
Fleishmann, Avrom. *The English historical novel: Walter Scott to Virginia Woolf* (Baltimore: Johns Hopkins UP, 1971).
Foley, T. and S. Ryder (eds), *Ideology and Ireland in the nineteenth century* (Dublin: Four Courts, 1998).
Forbes, D. 'The rationalism of Walter Scott', *Cambridge Journal* 7 (1953), 20–35.
Foster, John Wilson. *Colonial consequences: essays in Irish literature and culture* (Mullingar: Lilliput, 1991).
——. and H. Chesney (eds), *Nature in Ireland: a scientific and cultural history* (Dublin: Lilliput, 1997).
Foster, R.F. *Modern Ireland, 1600–1972* (London: Penguin, 1989).
——. *Irish story: telling stories and making it up in Ireland* (London: Allen Lane, 2001).
Foucault, Michel. *Power/knowledge: selected interviews and other writings, 1927–1977* ed. Colin Gordon (Brighton: Harvester, 1980).
Freeman, T.W. 'Land and people, c.1841', in W.E. Vaughan (ed.) *A new history of Ireland*.
Fritz, P. and D. Williams (eds), *City and society in the eighteenth century* (Toronto: Hakket, 1973).
Gandon, James Jr. and Thomas Mulvaney. *The life of James Gandon Esq. with original notices of contemporary artists and fragments of essays* (Dublin, 1846).
Gibbons, Luke. *Transformations in Irish culture* (Cork: Cork UP/Field Day, 1996).
Gilpin, William. *Three essays on picturesque beauty, picturesque travel, and sketching landscape*, 2nd ed. (London, 1794).
Graham, Colin. *Ideologies of epic: nation, empire and Victorian epic poetry* (Manchester: Manchester UP, 1998).
——. 'Hibernian knight's assimilation of differences', *Irish Review* 11 (Winter, 1991–2).
Gross, John. *The rise and fall of the man of letters: aspects of English literary life since 1800* (London: Weidenfeld and Nicolson, 1969).
Gunn, Simon. *The public culture of the Victorian middle class: ritual and authority and the English industrial city* (Manchester: Manchester UP, 2000).
Gwynn, Denis. 'Pugin and Maynooth', *Irish Ecclesiastical Record* 77–78 (June 1952).
Habermas, Jurgen. *The structural transformation of the public sphere: an inquiry into a category of bourgeois society*, trans. T. Burger (Cambridge: Polity, 1989).

Hale, J.R. (ed.), *The evolution of British historiography* (London: Macmillan 1967).
Hall, Wayne E. *Dialogues in the margins: a study of the Dublin University Magazine* (Gerrards Cross: Colin Smythe, 2000).
Hancock, W. Neilson. *Three lectures on political economy* (Dublin, 1847).
Harbison, P., H. Potterton and J. Sheehy. *Irish art and architecture: from prehistory to the present* (London: Thames and Hudson, 1978).
Hardiman, James (ed.), *Irish Minstrelsy or Bardic remains of Ireland with English translations 1831*, 2 vols (Shannon: Irish University Press, 1971).
Harley, B. 'Maps, knowledge, power', in D. Cosgrove and S. Daniels (eds), *The iconography of landscape*.
Hayley, Barbara. 'Irish periodicals from the Union to the *Nation*', *Anglo-Irish Studies* 2 (1976), 83–108.
Hechter, Michael. *Internal colonialism: the Celtic fringe in British national development, 1536–1966* (London: Routledge, 1975).
Hersey, George L. *High Victorian Gothic* (Baltimore: Johns Hopkins UP, 1972).
Heyck, T.W. *The transformation of intellectual life in Victorian England* (London: Croom Helm, 1982).
Hill, Jacqueline R. 'The intelligentsia and Irish nationalism in the 1840s', *Studia Hibernica* 20 (1980), 73–109.
——. 'The legal profession and the defence of the *ancien regime* in Ireland, 1790–1840', in D. Hogan and W.N. Osborough (eds), *Brehons, serjeants and attorneys*.
——. *From patriots to unionists: Dublin civil politics and Irish Protestant patriotism, 1660–1840* (Oxford: Clarendon, 1997)
Hill, Kate. '"Thoroughly imbued with the spirit of ancient Greece": symbolism and space in Victorian civic culture', in Alan Kidd and David Nicholls (eds), *Gender, civic culture and consumerism*.
Hobsbawm, Eric and Terence Ranger. *The invention of tradition* (Cambridge: Cambridge UP, 1983).
Hodder, W. 'Ferguson: his literary sources', in T. Brown and B. Hayley (eds), *Samuel Ferguson: a centenary tribute*.
Hogan, Daire. *The legal profession in Ireland, 1789–1922* (Dublin: Incorporated Law Society of Ireland, 1986).
——. and W.N. Osborough (eds), *Brehons, serjeants and attorneys: studies in the history of the Irish legal profession* (Dublin: Irish Academic, 1990).
Holcomb, Adele M. 'Scott and Turner', in Alan Bell (ed.), *Walter Scott*.
Holmes, Robert. *The case of Ireland stated* (1847).
Holmes, R.F.G. *Our Presbyterian heritage* (Belfast: Presbyterian Church in Ireland, 1985).
Hont, I. and M. Ignatieff (eds), *Wealth and virtue: the shaping of political economy in the Scottish Enlightenment* (Cambridge: Cambridge UP, 1983).
Hume, David. *Essays moral and political, 1741–1742* (London, 1904).
Hutchinson, John. *James Arthur O'Connor* (Dublin: National Gallery of Ireland, 1985).
Hutchinson, John. *The dynamics of cultural nationalism* (London: Allen and Unwin, 1987).

Inglis, Henry D. *A journey throughout Ireland 1834* (London, 1836).
Inkster, I and J. Morell (eds), *Metropolis and province: science in British culture, 1780–1850* (London: Hutchinson, 1983).
Johnson, Samuel. *Journey to the Western Isles* 1773 (London, 1971).
Jordan, R. F. *Victorian architecture* (Baltimore: Johns Hopkins UP, 1966).
Kane, Robert. *The industrial resources of Ireland* (Dublin, 1844).
Kearney, R. (ed.), *The Irish mind* (Dublin: Wolfhound, 1985).
Kelly, Gary. *English fiction of the Romantic period, 1789–1830* (London: Longman, 1989).
Kelly, Ronan. 'History's muse: the prose writings of Thomas Moore', unpublished PhD thesis, Trinity College (Dublin, 2001).
Kenny, Colum. *Tristram Kennedy and the revival of Irish legal training, 1835–1885* (Dublin: Irish Academic, 1996).
Kennedy, Brian, 'Sharman Crawford on the repeal question', *Irish Historical Studies* 6 (1948–9), 270–3.
Kennedy, Tom (ed.), *Victorian Dublin* (Dublin: A. Kennedy, 1980).
Kidd, Alan and David Nicholls (eds), *Gender, civic culture and consumerism: middle-class identity in Britain, 1800–1940* (Manchester: Manchester UP, 1999).
Klancher, Jon P. *The making of English reading audiences, 1790–1832* (Wisconsin: U of Wisconsin P, 1987).
Knights, Ben. *The idea of the clerisy in the nineteenth century* (Cambridge: Cambridge UP, 1978).
Lee, Joseph. *The modernisation of Irish society, 1848–1918* (Dublin: Gill and Macmillan, 1973).
Leerssen, J.T. *Mere Irish and Fíor-Ghael: studies in the development of Irish nationality, its development and literary expression prior to the nineteenth century* Utrecht Publications in general and comparative literature 22 (Amsterdam and Philadelphia, 1986).
——. 'On the treatment of Irishness in Romantic Anglo-Irish fiction', *Irish University Review* (Autumn 1990), 251–63.
——. *Remembrance and imagination: patterns in the historical and literary representation of Ireland in the nineteenth century* (Cork: Cork UP/Field Day, 1996).
Lehmann, W.C. *John Millar of Glasgow, 1735–1801* (Cambridge: Cambridge UP, 1960).
Levine, Phillipa. *The amateur and the professional: antiquarianism, historians and archaeologists in Victorian England, 1838–1886* (Cambridge: Cambridge UP, 1986).
Liu, Alan. *Wordsworth: the sense of history* (Stanford: Stanford UP, 1989).
Lloyd, David. 'Arnold, Ferguson, Schiller: aesthetic culture and the politics of aesthetics', *Cultural Critique* 2 (1985/6), 137–69.
——. *Nationalism and minor literature: James Clarence Mangan and the emergence of Irish cultural nationalism* (Berkeley: California UP, 1987).
——. and P. Thomas. *Culture and the State* (London: Routledge, 1998).
——. *Ireland after history* (Cork: Cork UP/Field Day, 1999).
Longley, Edna. 'Including the North', *Text and Context* 3 (Autumn 1988), 17–24.
Low, Donald. 'Periodicals in the age of Scott', in A. Bell (ed.), *Walter Scott.*
Lukacs, Georg. *The historical novel* 1936 trans. H. and S. Mitchell (London: Penguin, 1981).
Lunney, L. 'Ulster attitudes to Scottishness: the eighteenth century and after', in Ian S. Wood (ed.), *Scotland and Ulster.*

Lyons, F.S.L. *Ireland since the Famine* (London: Fontana, 1971).
McBride, Ian. 'The school of virtue: Francis Hutcheson, Irish Presbyterians and the Scottish Enlightenment', in D. George Boyce et al. (eds), *Political thought in Ireland*.
McBride, J.P. 'The Dublin University Magazine: cultural nationalism and Tory ideology in an Irish literary and political journal, 1833–1852', unpublished PhD thesis, TCD (Dublin, 1987).
McCahan, Robert. *Life of Sir Samuel Ferguson* (Coleraine, n.d.).
McCarthy, J.J. *Suggestions on the arrangement and characteristics of parish churches* (Dublin, 1851).
McCarthy, M.F. (ed.) *The poems of J.J. Callanan* (Cork, 1861).
McCartney, Donal. 'The writing of history in Ireland', *Irish Historical Studies* 10: 40 (September, 1957), 347–62.
McCormack, W.J. *Ascendancy and tradition in Anglo-Irish literary history from 1789 to 1939* (Oxford: Clarendon, 1985).
———. *From Burke to Beckett: ascendancy, tradition and betrayal in literary history* (Cork: Cork UP, 1994).
McCorristine, L. *The revolt of Silken Thomas* (Dublin: Wolfhound,1987).
McCullough, N. *Dublin: an urban history* (Dublin: Anne Street, 1989).
McDermott, M. *Ireland's architectural history* (Dublin: Folens, 1975).
———. *Dublin's architectural development, 1800–1925* (Dublin: Tulcamac, 1988).
MacDonagh, Oliver. *Ireland: the Union and its aftermath* (London: Allen and Unwin, 1977).
MacDonagh, Thomas. *Literature in Ireland: studies Irish and Anglo-Irish* (1916).
McDowell R.B. 'The Irish courts of law, 1801–1914', *Irish Historical Studies* 4 (1956–7), 363–391.
———. and D.A. Webb. *Trinity College, Dublin, 1592–1952: an academic history* (Cambridge: Cambridge UP, 1982).
McFarland, Elaine. *Ireland and Scotland in the age of revolution: planting the green bough* (Edinburgh: Edinburgh UP, 1994).
McGann, Jerome (ed.), *Historical studies and literary criticism* (Wisconsin: U of Wisconsin P, 1985).
———. *Social values and poetic acts* (Cambridge, Mass: Harvard UP, 1988).
McIntyre, Alasdair. *After virtue: a study in moral theory* (London: Duckworth, 1981).
———. *Whose justice? which rationality?* (London: Duckworth, 1988).
McMaster, Graham. *Scott and society* (Cambridge: Cambridge UP, 1981).
Mackintosh, James. *The miscellaneous works of the right honourable James Mackintosh*, 3 vols (London, 1846).
MacLeod, Dianne. *Art and the Victorian middle class: money and the making of cultural identity* (Cambridge: Cambridge UP, 1996).
MacSweeney, Patrick. *A group of nation builders* (Dublin, 1913).
Malins, E. and the Knight of Glin. *Lost demesnes: Irish landscape gardening, 1660–1845* (London: Barrie and Jenkins, 1976).
Mangan, James Clarence. *Poems*, ed. D.J. O'Donoghue (Dublin 1910).
Meenan, F.O.C. 'The Georgian squares of Dublin', *Studies* (Winter, 1969), 405-415.
Meenan, J. and D. Clarke (eds), *The Royal Dublin Society, 1721–1981* (Dublin: RDS, 1981).

Mingay, G.E. *The gentry: the rise and fall of a ruling class* (London: Longman, 1976).
Moir, Esther. *The discovery of Britain: English tourists, 1540–1840* (London: Routledge, 1964).
Molloy, Kevin. 'Thomas Davis and the idea of the Irish nation', unpublished PhD thesis, TCD (Dublin, 1988).
Montgomery, H.R. 'An essay towards investigating the causes that have retarded the progress of literature in Ireland' (Belfast, 1840).
Morash, Christopher (ed.), *The hungry voice: poetry of the Irish Famine* (Dublin: Irish Academic Press, 1989).
——. 'Celticism: between race and nation', in T. Foley and S. Ryder (eds), *Ideology and Ireland*.
Morgan, Peter. *Literary critics and reviewers in early nineteenth-century Britain* (London: Croom Helm, 1983).
Murray, K. 'Dublin's first railway', *Dublin Historical Record* 1 (1938-9), 19–40.
Murray, P. 'George Petrie, 1789–1866', unpublished M.Litt. thesis, 3 vols. TCD (Dublin, 1980).
Ní Chatháin, P. 'Sir Samuel Ferguson and the Ogham inscriptions', *Irish University Review*, 16: 1 (Spring, 1986), 159–69.
Nietzsche, Fredric. *The use and abuse of history 1873*, trans. A. Collins (Indianapolis: Library of Liberal Arts, 1957).
Nisbet, R.A. *The sociological tradition* (London: Heinemann, 1966).
Nowlan, Kevin B. *The politics of Repeal* (London: Routledge, 1965).
Ó'Buachalla, Breandán. 'The Gaelic background', in T. Brown and B. Hayley (eds), *Samuel Ferguson*.
O'Connor, Frank. *The backward look: a survey of Irish literature* (London: Macmillan, 1967).
O'Donovan, John (ed.), *Ordnance Survey letters* (Bray, 1928).
O'Dowd, Liam (ed.), *On intellectuals and intellectual life in Ireland* (Belfast: Institute of Irish Studies, 1995).
O'Driscoll, Robert. 'Ferguson and the idea of an Irish national literature', *Éire–Ireland* 6: 1 (Spring 1971), 82–95.
——. *An ascendancy of the heart: Ferguson and the beginnings of modern Irish literature in English* (Dublin: Dolmen, 1976).
O'Dúill, Gréagóir. 'Sir Samuel Ferguson, administrator and archivist', *Irish University Review* 16: 2 (Autumn 1986), 117–40.
——. 'No rootless colonist: Samuel Ferguson and John Hewitt', in G. Dawe and J.W. Foster (eds), *The poet's place*.
O'Flanagan, J.R. *The Irish Bar: comprising anecdotes, bon-mots and biographical sketches of the Bench and Bar of Ireland* (London, 1879).
O'Hagan, John 'The poetry of Sir Samuel Ferguson', (Dublin, 1887).
Oldfield, Adrian. *Citizenship and community: civic republicanism and the modern world* (London: Routledge, 1993).
Ó Raifeartaigh, T. (ed.), *The Royal Irish Academy: a bicentennial history, 1785–1985* (Dublin: Royal Irish Academy, 1985).
Ó Tuathaigh, M.A.G. 'Sir Samuel Ferguson – poet and ideologue', in T. Brown and B. Hayley, (eds), *Samuel Ferguson*.

Pearson, Peter. *The heart of Dublin: the resurgence of a historical city* (Dublin: O'Brien, 2000).
Perkin, H. *The rise of professional society: England since 1880* (London: Routledge, 1989).
——. 'Middle-class education and employment in the nineteenth century: a critical note', *Economic History Review* 14 (1961–2).
Phillopson, Nicholas. 'The Scottish Enlightenment', in R. Porter and M. Teich, (eds), *The Enlightenment*.
Pocock, J.G.A. *Virtue, commerce and history: essays on political thought and history, chiefly in the eighteenth century* (Cambridge: Cambridge UP, 1985).
Porter, Roy and Mikulas Teich (eds), *The Enlightenment in national context* (Cambridge: Cambridge UP, 1981).
—— and ——. *Romanticism in national context* (Cambridge: Cambridge UP, 1988).
Price, Uvedale. *Essays on the picturesque* (London, 1794).
Pugin, A.W. *Contrasts: or a parallel between the noble edifices of the fourteenth and fifteenth centuries, and similar buildings of the present time* (London, 1836).
Purviance, Susan. 'Intersubjectivity and sociable relations in the philosophy of Francis Hutcheson', in John Dwyer and Richard B. Sher (eds), *Sociability and Society*.
Rabinow, P. *The Foucault Reader* (London: Penguin, 1986)
Reader, W.J. *Professional men: the rise of the professional classes in nineteenth-century England* (London: Wiedenfeld and Nicolson, 1966).
Reid, James Seaton. *A history of the Presbyterian Church in Ireland*, 2nd ed., 3 vols (London, 1853).
Rendall, Jane. *The origins of the Scottish Enlightenment* (London: Macmillan, 1978).
Rhees, Rush, ed. *Recollections of Wittgenstein* (Oxford: Oxford UP, 1984).
Richardson, Douglas Scott. 'Gothic revival architecture in Ireland', unpublished PhD thesis, Yale (New Haven, 1970).
Ruskin, John. *Works*, ed. F.T. Cook and A. Wedderburn 39 vols (London: Allen and Unwin 1903–1912).
——. *The nature of Gothic* ed. Jan Morris (London: Faber, 1981).
Said, Edward. *Orientalism* 1978 (London: Penguin, 1991).
Scott, Walter. *Waverley* 1814 (Oxford: Clarendon, 1981).
——. *Rob Roy* 1817 (London: Dryburgh 1930).
——. *The fair maid of Perth* 1828 (London: Dryburgh 1894).
——. *The journal of Walter Scott* ed. W.E.K. Anderson (Oxford: Clarendon, 1972).
Seed, John and Janet Woolff *The culture of capital: art, power and the nineteenth-century middle class* (Manchester: Manchester UP, 1988).
Shattock, J. *Politics and reviewers: the Edinburgh and the Quarterly in the early Victorian age* (London: Leicester UP, 1989).
—— and M. Woolf (eds) *The Victorian periodical press: samplings and soundings* (London: Leicester UP, 1982).
Shaw, Harry E. *The forms of historical fiction* (Ithaca: Cornell UP, 1983).
Sheehy, Jeanne. *J.J. McCarthy and the Gothic Revival in Ireland* (Dublin: Ulster Architectural Heritage Society, 1977).
——. *The rediscovery of Ireland's past: the Celtic revival, 1830–1930* (London, 1980).

Sher, Richard B. *Church and university in the Scottish enlightenment: the moderate literati of Edinburgh* (Edinburgh: Edinburgh UP, 1985).

Sloan, R. *William Smith O'Brien and the Young Irelander rebellion of 1848* (Dublin: Four Courts, 2000).

Small, Ian. *Conditions for criticism: authority, knowledge and literature in the late nineteenth century* (Oxford: Clarendon, 1991).

Smith, Adam. *An enquiry into the nature and causes of the wealth of nations 1776*, 3rd ed., 3 vols (London, 1784).

Smith, Angele. 'Landscapes of power in nineteenth-century Ireland' *Archaeological Dialogues* 5:1 (1998).

Smith, G.H. *The North East Bar: a sketch historical and reminiscent* (1910).

Smyth, G. *Decolonisation and criticism: the construction of Irish literature* (London: Pluto, 1998).

Stewart, A.T.Q. *The narrow ground* (London: Faber, 1977).

Stocking, George W. *Race, culture, and evolution: essays in the history of anthropology* (London: Macmillan, 1968).

Stokes, William. *The life and labours in archaeology of George Petrie* (London, 1868).

Sullivan, Alvin (ed.), *British literary magazines: the Romantic age, 1789–1836* (London, 1983).

Sutherland, Kathryn. 'Fictional economies: Adam Smith, Walter Scott and the eighteenth-century novel', *English Literary History* 54: 1 (Spring, 1987), 97–127.

Thackeray, W.M. *The Irish Sketch Book* (Belfast: Blackstaff, 1985).

Trumpener, Katie. 'National character, nationalist plots: national tale and historical Novel in the age of *Waverley*, 1806–1830', *English Literary History* 60: 3 (Fall, 1993), 691–710.

——. *Bardic nationalism: the Romantic novel and the British empire* (Princeton: Princeton UP, 1997).

Tytler, A. *Essay on the principles of translation* (London, 1790).

Vance, Norman. *Irish literature: a social history* (Oxford: Blackwell, 1990).

Vaughan, W.E. (ed.), *A new history of Ireland, vol. v: Ireland under the Union, 1801–1870* (Oxford: Clarendon, 1989).

Vernon, James. *Politics and the people: a study in English political culture, 1815–1867* (Cambridge: Cambridge UP, 1993).

Walker, Graham. *Intimate strangers: political and cultural interaction between Scotland and Ulster in modern times* (Edinburgh: John Donald, 1995).

Watson, J.R. *Picturesque landscape and English Romantic poetry* (London: Hutchinson, 1970).

Welch, Robert. *A history of verse translation from the Irish, 1789–1987* (Gerrards Cross: Colin Smythe, 1988).

Wellek, René. *A history of modern criticism, 1750–1950: vol. 3: the age of transition* (Cambridge: Cambridge UP, 1965).

White, Hayden. *Metahistory: the historical imagination in nineteenth-century Europe* (Baltimore: Johns Hopkins UP, 1973).

White, Terence de Vere. *The story of the Royal Dublin Society* (Tralee: Kerryman, 1955).

Whyte, Nicholas. *Science, Ireland and colonialism* (Cork: Cork UP, 1999).

Williams, Raymond. *Culture and society: Coleridge to Orwell 1958* (London: Hogarth, 1987).

——. *The country and the city* (London: Chatto, 1973).

Wilson, Arline. 'Liverpool as "the Florence of the North"', in Alan Kidd and David Nicholls (eds), *Gender, civic culture and consumerism.*

Wilson, D. 'The archaeology and prehistorical annals of Scotland, 1851', in Bell, Alan (ed.), *Walter Scott.*

Wood, Ian S. (ed.), *Scotland and Ulster* (Edinburgh: Mercat, 1994).

Wordsworth, William. *A guide through the district of the lakes* in *Prose Works*, vol. 2, ed. W.J.B. Owen and J.W. Smyser (Oxford: Oxford UP, 1974).

——. *Letters* ed. Alan G. Hill (Oxford: Clarendon, 1978).

Wright, G.N. *A guide to the county of Wicklow* (London, 1822).

Yeats, W.B. 'Irish poets and Irish poetry: the poetry of Sir Samuel Ferguson', *Irish Fireside* (9 Oct. 1886), 923–41.

——. 'The poetry of Sir Samuel Ferguson', *Dublin University Review* 2 (Nov. 1886), 81–6.

——. 'Introduction', *A book of Irish verse: selected from modern writers* (London, 1895).

——. *Uncollected prose* ed. John P. Frayne 2 vols (New York, 1970).

——. and Thomas Kinsella. *Davis, Mangan, Ferguson? Tradition and the Irish writer* (Dublin: Dolmen, 1971).

Yeo, E.J. *The contest for social science: relations and the representation of gender and class, 1851–81* (London: Rivers Oram, 1996).

Young, Arthur. *A tour in Ireland: with general observations on the present state of that kingdom, made in the years 1776, 1777, 1778 and 1779* (London, 1780).

Index

Alison, Archibald 89, 135n
Allingham, William 85n, 141, 182
Andrews, J.H. 77n, 80
Annan, Noel 175
antiquarianism 23, 83, 174–7
Aristotle 15n, 34, 56
Arnold, Matthew 10, 15n, 16, Ferguson's review of 'On the study of Celtic literature', 37n, 68–9, Culture and anarchy 157–9, 171, 184
Ascendancy 12, 16, and the DUM 18, 76, 131–3, 178, 185
Ashford, William 87–8
Athenaeum 68n
'Attractions of Ireland' 77, 89–91, 95–8

Ballad Poetry of Ireland 105, 107–8
Banim brothers 17, and Walter Scott, 43, 106
Bar and legal profession 19–21, 99–104, North-Eastern circuit, 102–3
Barrell, John 86
Belfast 16, 35–6, 65
Belfast Academical Institution 37, 50
Belfast Literary Society 36
Berkeley, George 15n
Berman, Marshall 176–7
Betham, William 177
Blackie, John Stuart 24
Blackwood, Alexander 59n, 62, 88
Blackwood, John 60n, 156, 166, 181
Blackwood, Robert 59n, 121, 143, 155
Blackwood, William 16, 23, 46, 52–3, 56, 58
Blackwood's Edinburgh Magazine 16, 56, and house style, 57–8, 77
Bowen, Desmond 122, 124, 129, 142n
Brehon laws 103
Brooke, Charlotte 69
Brown, Ford Maddox 182
Brown, Malcolm 10, 64
Browning, Robert 167

Burke, Edmund 25, 26, 55, 159, 161, 162n, 184–5
Burns, Robert 39, 67, 99, 106–7, Ferguson's articles on, 109, 116
Burrow, John 162
Butler, Marilyn 21
Butt, Isaac 18, 51, Ferguson's row with, 61–2, 65, 185, 101, 103, 118, 156n, 185
Butterfield, Herbert 163
Byron, George 39

Cairns, David 11, 54–5
Callanan, J.J. 69, 106
Camden Society 140
Carleton, William 59n, 62, Traits and stories 66–7, 83, 89n, 90, walking tour with Ferguson, 96, 106, 109
Carlyle, Thomas 14, 85, 104, 110n, 159
Carolan 52, 67
Catholic Emancipation 18, 36, 52,63, 149
catholicism 53, 76, 78, 111, 115, 131, and church building 133, 149, 154
Celtic Athenaeum 156
centralization 20, 79, 99, 104, 120–1, 184
Cicero 14, 15n, 34
civic idealism 14–15, 27, 34–5, 83
Cobbett, William 65n, 89
Colby, Thomas 80
Coleridge, Samuel Taylor 15n, 16, On the constitution of church and state 55–6, 75, 110, on 'clerisy', 159
Colleges' Bill 115, 150
Comparative Method 41
Congal 116, 155, 164n, 168, 181
Cooke, Henry 37, 40
Crawford, William Sharman 124
Croker, Thomas Crofton 44, Researches in the south of Ireland 73–4, 90
Crooke, Emily 23n, 92n, 160n, 173n
Cullen, Paul 122, 149

Culler, Jonathan 97
Curley, Patrick 29n
Curry, William 88–9, 95

Danby, Francis 93
Darwin, Charles 69
Davis, Richard 112
Davis, Thomas 10, 25, 27, 30, 82, 100, 103–117, *Letters of a Protestant on Repeal*, 111; Ferguson's 'Lament for Thomas Davis' 112–17, 121–2, 148, 184
De Vere, Aubrey 100, 114n, conversion to Catholicism 142, 156n, Ferguson's letter on fears for Ireland's future, 166; and plans for proportional representation,168, 179, 181
Deane, Seamus 25, 54, 159n, 184
Denman, Peter 10, 59n, 60n, 61, 65, 77, 113n, 133, 163n, 168
disestablishment 166
'Down Hill' 134
Drennan, William 18, 29, 37, 40, 89n, 103
Dublin Builder 132
Dublin University Magazine 18–19, 53, 55, political ethos 59–65; Ferguson's estrangement from, 62–3, 104, 105, comparisons with the *Nation*, 106, 114, 131, 182, 185
Dublin Penny Journal 48, 93
Dublin Saturday Magazine 93
Duffy, Charles Gavan 20–3, description of Ferguson 29, 30, 85, 99–100, and the *Nation*, 104–12; the *Vindicator*, 105; and Robert Burns, 106, 124, 127–8, on failure of Protestant Repeal association, 129, 139, 151–2, 156n, 184
Dunne, Tom 54
Dwyer, John 35

Eagleton, Terry 11, 13n, 75, 81, 119n, 186
Edgeworth, Maria 17, 31, 48, *The Absentee*, 86–7, 109
Edinburgh 14, 16–7, 30, 32–3, 35, 161
Emmet, Robert 103
Evans, Edward 123

Ferguson, Adam 17, 31–2, 35, *Essay on the history of civil society* 41, 64n, 56, 64, 73
Ferguson, Mary Catherine and *Sir Samuel Ferguson in the Ireland of his day*, 11; editing of Ferguson's writing 45; 53n, 94n, marriage 126–8, 181

Ferguson, Samuel and sub-aqueous tunnelling, 9; and Blackwood family 16; relationship with the *DUM* 18, 57–64; ancestry, 29n; and translation, 53n, 68n; apology to Hardiman 58; 'Father Tom and the Pope', 59n; and Protestant Repeal 20, 99–100, 117–28; Ordnance Survey 21, 81; antiquarianism 23, 83, 156, 160–74; Academy museum, 157n; work in Public Records Office 23, 155–6; *Hibernian nights' entertainments* 45–50; and Belfast Academical Institution 37; *Ulster Magazine* ballads 39; and Walter Scott 43–50; 'Irish Minstrelsy' 52–6, 66–76; 'Inaugural ode for the new year', 63'; 'Dialogue between the head and heart of an Irish Protestant', 64, 72; contributions to tour guides, 88–9; 'The Attractions of Ireland' 89–91; and picturesque travel 94–7; and the North-Eastern legal circuit 102n; condemnation of Thackeray, 105; and Young Ireland 105–8; articles on Robert Burns, 109–10; and Thomas Davis 110–16; 'Inheritor and Economist', 189–9; review of the *Life of Gandon*, 131–9; opinions on the Oxford Movement 141–3; reviews of Ruskin 143–8; *Congal*,116, 155, 181; and Matthew Arnold, 10, 37n, 157–9; and Home Rule, 166; 'At the polo ground' and 'In Carey's footsteps', 167; response to the Famine, 117; Ogham inscriptions, 156–7; and Royal Irish Academy 23, 83, 156, 160, academy address 168–74; views on history and historiography, 163–5
Foster, R.F. 13n, 40, 129
Froude, J.A. 162

Gandon, James 9n, Ferguson's review of the *Life of Gandon* 131–9, and buildings in Dublin 136, 143, 183
Gibbon, Edward 38, *Decline and fall*, 138, 162, Ferguson's opinion of, 163
Gibbons, Luke 70n
Gilpin, William 86–7
Gladstone, William 166, 168n
Glasgow 16, 33, 35, 36
Gordon, Robert 103, 108
Gothic Revival 27, 132–3, 138, in Ireland, 148–54
Graham, Colin 11, 113n, 178n
Grattan, Henry 25, 65n, 101–2, 124, 125, 128
Guinness family 12, 128, 175

Index

Habermas, Jurgen 13n
Hamilton, William Rowan 22, 82–3
Hancock, W. Neilson 118
Hardiman, James 25, 52–6, Ferguson's apology to, 58, 132, 134
Hechter, Michael 92n
Hegel, G.W.F. 15n
Heyck, T.W. 19n, 186n
Hibernian nights' entertainments 29, 32, 45–50, 53, 56, 69, 'natural piety' 72n, 76, 77, and picturesque romance, 94
Hill, Jacqueline 12, 20n, 101n
Hill, Kate 14n, 134n
historiography 162–5
Hodder, William 48n
Holmes, Robert 20, 103
Home Rule 166, 128, 166, 168
Houses of parliament 139–41
Hume, David 21, 32, 35, 38, *Dialogues* 64, 65n, 73, 162
Hutcheson, Francis 17, *Inquiry into our original ideas of beauty and virtue*, 34

Inglis, Henry 90
Ireland, John 124–5
Irish Catholic Magazine 152
Irish Council 117, 121
Irish Ecclesiological Society 152
Irish Minstrelsy 25, Ferguson's review of 52–60 and 67–76, 111
Irish Quarterly Review 20, 101, 102

Jordan R.F. 141

Kane, Robert 171
Kearney, Richard 152–3n
Keating, Geoffrey 163
Kennedy, Tristram 101
Knight's penny cyclopaedia 88

Larcom, Thomas 21–2, 80, 81, 93, 118n, 155
Lays of the western Gael 44, 133n, 156n, 163n
Le Fanu, Sheridan 156n
Lecky, W.E.H. 163n
Leerssen, J.Th. 11, 13n, 24, 30n, 49, 54, 69, 71n, 73n, 76, 169–70n
Lever, Charles 44, Ferguson's disapproval of, 63, 104–5
Levine, Phillipa 23n, 161, 175, 178

Liverpool 14
Lloyd, David 10, 12, 16, 55, 64, 68–9, 75, 79, 106, 107, 127n
Lloyd, Bartholomew 83n
Lloyd, Humphrey 83
Locke, John 17, 34–5
Lockhart, John Gibson 57
Lover, Samuel 62, *Legends and stories* 66, 90, 106
Lyons, F.S.L. 149n

Macaulay, Thomas Babington 126, 162–3
McBride, Ian 17n, 36
McBride J.P. 18n, 59–60, 163n
McCarthy, J.J. 133, 151–3, *Suggestions on the arrangements and characteristics of parish churches'*, 152
McCormack, W.J. 12n, 13, 45n, 56, 87n, 162n, 170, 185
McCracken, Henry Joy 29
MacDonagh, Thomas 107
McFarland, Elaine 16n, 30, 36n, 37n
M'Gee, Thomas D'Arcy 110, 184
McIntyre, Alastair 15n
Mackintosh, James 44n
McNevin, Thomas 65
Macpherson 30, 68n
Maginn, William 57
Mangan, James Clarence 10, and Ordnance Survey, 81, 106, 110
Martin, Henri 174
Maturin, William 17, 34
Meenan, F.O.C. 13n
Millar, John 31
Mitchel, John 20, 23, letter praising Ferguson's poetry, 108, 110, Ferguson pledges support for, 127, 156n, 184
Moir, Esther 88
Molyneux, William 35, 15n
Montesquieu 43
Montgomery, Henry 18, 'An essay towards understanding the causes which have retarded the progress of literature in Ireland, 37–8, 40
Moore, Thomas 39, 89n, 163
Morash, Chris 7on, 119n
Morgan, Lady 43
museum Ferguson's handbook for, 157n; national, 173

Nation newspaper 99, 104, 105–7, Ferguson's negotiations with Duffy 108n, Ferguson denies writing for, 128
'national character' 65–6 and racial typography 67–74
national tale 32, 43
Neilson, William 36
'New Light' Presbyterianism 17, 34, 36, 38n
Newman, Cardinal Henry *Lectures on Anglican difficulties*, 141–2, 152
Nietzsche 164n
Northern Whig 29

O'Brien, William Smith letter from Ferguson, 42n, 65, 108, 124n, 127, 173n, 177, Ferguson lobbies on Academy grant, 178n, 184
Ó'Buachalla, Brendán 16n, 35
O'Connell, Daniel 21, 99, 102, 116n, 122, 126, 166
O'Connor, Frank 186
O'Connor, James Arthur 87, 93, 95
O'Curry, Eugene 81, 53n, 174
O'Donovan, John 21–2, on *Irish Minstrelsy* review, 52–3, 53n, and Ordnance Survey team, 80–3; friendship with Ferguson, 81n; Ferguson's review of *Annals of the four masters*, 156, 158–9, 160, 163, 169, 183n
O'Dowd, Liam 13n
O'Driscoll, Robert 10, 64
O'Dúill, Gréagóir 25, 114, 174, 177n
O'Flanagan, Theophilus 45
Ogham inscriptions 156, 157
O'Hagan, John 103
O'Hagan, Thomas 23, Address to Belfast historical society, 38–40, 50, 60, 156n, 182, 103, 152
Oldfield, A. 15n
O'Loghlen, Colman 103, 117, 119, 186
O'Loghlen, Michael 103
'Orange Young Ireland' 65
Ordnance Survey 21, 29, 78–9, and Topographical department 80–2, 98, 110
O'Sullivan brothers 18, 61, Samuel 58n, 60; Mortimer, condemnation of Catholicism 62
Ó Tuathaigh, Géaroid 50, 165
Oxford Movement 27

Paine, Tom 17, 34–5
Petrie, George 21–2, 53n, and Ordnance Survey 80–3, 88, and Irish picturesque 91–5, 97, 156, 160, 174, Ferguson's defence of against plagiarism, 177
Phoenix park murders 167
picturesque 78, 85–91, 94–7
Pim, James 22, 93, 118
political economy 118–20
Polybius 34
presbyterianism 16, 36–7, and 'New Light' presbyterianism 17, 37, 60, use of Psalms, 114n, 133, 153, 182
professional classes 13, 15, 19, 20, 101, 111–12, 116, 178, 182–4
Protestant Ascendancy 11–13, 12n, 54, 64, 133, 185
Protestant Repeal Association 26, 99, 100, 117, Ferguson's speeches to, 121–30, 134, 166, 185
Public Records Office 155–6
Pugin, Augustus Welby 133, 135, 146, *True principles of Christian architecture* and *Contrasts*, 150; and Ireland's Gothic revival, 150–1
Pusey, Edward 143

Quarry, Dr Ferguson's verse-epistle to, 157

railway, Dublin-Kingstown 96
Reader, W.J. 19
Reform bill 65
Reeves, William Ferguson's review of *Ecclesiastical antiquities*, 143, 160, 164, 174
Renan, Ernest 15n, 171
Richards, Shaun 11, 54–5
Robertson, William 21, 31, 41, 71n, 162
Royal Irish Academy 9, 21, membership of 23, 30, 62n, Ferguson's praise for, 83, 98, 110, 153, national profile, 160–1; history and ethos, 170–1; Ferguson's presidential address 171–3; government grant controversy, 173–4, 182
Royal Dublin Society 173
Ruskin, John 27, 131–5, Ferguson's review of *Stones of Venice*, 142, 147–8; *Seven lamps of architecture*, 144–5; *Modern painters*, 145

Saunders Magazine 110
Scotland and Ulster 30–5
Scott, Walter 32, 42–50, influence on Irish writers, 43; *Waverley*, 42; *Rob Roy*, 47; *The betrothed*, 46n; *The fortunes of Nigel*, 46n, 78n; *The fair maid of Perth*, 46n, 48–9; *Ivanhoe* 71, 74, 94, 107, 139, and the 'new' history, 162
Scottish Enlightenment 17, 31–4, 40–2

Index

Seed, John 14n
Sheehy, Jean 152n, 153
Smith, Adam 17, 21, 31–2, and *Wealth of nations*, 34, Ferguson's familiarity with, 42n; *Theory of moral sentiments*, 34–5; *Lectures on jurisprudence* 41–2, 48–9, 75
Smollett, Tobias 42
Smyth, Gerry 10n, 57n
Southey, Robert 107
Spenser, Edmund 90
Stanford, Charles Stuart 61, 63
Stepan, Nancy 69
Stewart, Dugald 21, 31, and William Drennan, 37n, 39, 41; influence on Scott, 42n, 49
Stocking, G.W. 70n
Stokes, Whitley 181
Stokes, William 22, 83, 93, 156, family, 174
Swift, Jonathan 35, 124

Tacitus 34
Teeling, Charles 18, 39–40, 60
Tennant, R.J. Ferguson's letters to regarding *DUM*, 61–2, 65, 89n, 182
Thackeray, William 63, 105, 121, on church architecture 149n
Tractarians 141–2, 148
Tone, Wolfe 101, 124
Trinity College, Dublin 19; exclusion of dissenters 36; 100, 110; and Wittgenstein, 131
Trumpener, Katie 32, 43, 161n
Turner, William 94

Ulster Magazine 29, 39–40, 50, 182
United Irishmen 16, 18, 20, 26, legacy in Belfast 29; and Robert Holmes, 103; and Protestant Repeal 125; 185

Vance, George Washington 125
Vance, Norman 18n
Vasari, Giorgio 138, 140
Villemarqué, Hérsart de la 156, 174

Walker, Graham 16n
Welch, Robert 11n, 53n
West, Thomas 87
White, Hayden 162
Whyte, Nicholas 13n, 160n
Wilde, William 23, 174
William iv 77
Williams, Raymond 97
Williams, Richard D'Alton 128
Wilson, John (Christopher North) 57–8
Wiseman, Nicholas 142, 152
Wittgenstein 131
Wood, I.S. 16n
Woolff, Janet 14n
Wordsworth, William 87–8

Yeats, W.B. 10, 27, 106, 179, 183, 186
Young, Arthur 87, 89–90
Young Ireland 27, 109, 110, 117, 124, 127–9, 182, 184